Death or Deliverance

Studies in Canadian Military History
Series editor: Dean F. Oliver, Canadian War Museum

The Canadian War Museum, Canada's national museum of military history, has a threefold mandate: to remember, to preserve, and to educate. Studies in Canadian Military History, published by UBC Press in association with the Museum, extends this mandate by presenting the best of contemporary scholarship to provide new insights into all aspects of Canadian military history, from earliest times to recent events. The work of a new generation of scholars is especially encouraged, and the books employ a variety of approaches – cultural, social, intellectual, economic, political, and comparative – to investigate gaps in the existing historiography. The books in the series feed immediately into future exhibitions, programs, and outreach efforts by the Canadian War Museum. A list of the titles in the series appears at the end of the book.

Death or Deliverance
Canadian Courts Martial in the Great War

Teresa Iacobelli

UBCPress · Vancouver · Toronto

© UBC Press 2013

All rights reserved. No part of this publication may be reproduced, stored in a retrieval system, or transmitted, in any form or by any means, without prior written permission of the publisher, or, in Canada, in the case of photocopying or other reprographic copying, a licence from Access Copyright, www.accesscopyright.ca.

21 20 19 18 17 16 15 14 13   5 4 3 2 1

Printed in Canada on FSC-certified ancient-forest-free paper
(100% post-consumer recycled) that is processed chlorine- and acid-free.

Library and Archives Canada Cataloguing in Publication

Iacobelli, Teresa, 1977-, author
    Death or deliverance : Canadian courts martial in the Great War / Teresa Iacobelli.

(Studies in Canadian military history)
Includes bibliographical references and index.
Issued in print and electronic formats.
ISBN 978-0-7748-2567-2 (bound). – ISBN 978-0-7748-2568-9 (pbk.).
ISBN 978-0-7748-2569-6 (pdf). – ISBN 978-0-7748-2570-2 (epub).

    1. World War, 1914-1918 – Desertions – Canada. 2. Military deserters – Canada – History. 3. Capital punishment – Canada – History. 4. Executions and executioners – Canada – History. 5. Military offenses – Canada – History. I. Title. II. Series: Studies in Canadian military history

| KE7197.I23 2013 | 343.71'0143 | C2013-903265-7 |
| KF7618.D3I23 2013 | | C2013-903266-5 |

Canadä

UBC Press gratefully acknowledges the financial support for our publishing program of the Government of Canada (through the Canada Book Fund), the Canada Council for the Arts, and the British Columbia Arts Council.

This book has been published with the help of a grant from the Canadian Federation for the Humanities and Social Sciences, through the Awards to Scholarly Publications Program, using funds provided by the Social Sciences and Humanities Research Council of Canada.

Publication of this book has been financially supported by the Canadian War Museum.

UBC Press
The University of British Columbia
2029 West Mall
Vancouver, BC V6T 1Z2
www.ubcpress.ca

For Mom and Dad

We ask much of our men. We cannot ask more than a man lay down his life for an order. Surely then it is for us to do all we can to foster the good will of our men and gain their affection. To do less is a direct neglect of duty.

– Canadian Corps, Officers' School of Instruction,
"Notes on Leadership for Company Officers"

Contents

Acknowledgments / ix

Introduction / 1

1 Competing Ideologies / 11

2 Military Law: An Overview / 23

3 The Crimes / 37

4 The Court Martial Process / 65

5 The Confirmation Process / 83

6 Pardon Campaigns / 111

Conclusion / 129

Notes / 143

Bibliography / 165

Index / 173

Acknowledgments

SEEING THIS PROJECT THROUGH from original inception to book has involved several years, many edits, and much support along the way.

First and foremost, this book could not have happened without Jonathan Vance. While I was doing the research, he proved to be an insightful and patient mentor who gave freely of his time and support, and he continues to provide friendship and guidance. I have tremendous respect for his opinions and owe him a debt of gratitude for helping me along the way.

I also wish to thank Robert Wardhaugh and Brock Millman, two outstanding academics at the University of Western Ontario. Both men challenged me and have helped to make me a better historian. I also wish to thank Allyson May, Keith Fleming, Nicholas Kuiper, and Paul Dickson. I credit their comments with helping to improve the final product.

A special thank you to Tim Cook at the Canadian War Museum. I had the privilege of working alongside Tim throughout 2007 while we created a website devoted to the Canadian experience in the First World War. During that year, I learned an immense amount about public history, and in the midst of his busy schedule, Tim also found the time to ask about the progress of my own research, to offer advice, and to answer questions. His comments never failed to broaden my perspective on my research.

Thank you also to Dean Oliver, formerly of the Canadian War Museum, for his support as the series editor of Studies in Canadian Military History. I would also like to thank the editors of *Canadian Military History* for allowing me to reproduce portions my article "Arbitrary Justice? A Comparative Analysis of Death Sentences Passed and Commuted during the First World War," *Canadian Military History* 16, 1 (2007): 23-36. I also extend my profound gratitude to Emily Andrew, Lesley Erickson, and Holly Keller at UBC Press for guiding my manuscript through to publication. There is no doubt that their efforts have made this a better book; that said, any remaining errors remain mine alone.

This book has benefited from financial support from several sources. The University of Western Ontario, the Social Sciences and Humanities Research Council, and the Ontario Graduate Scholarship all provided funds that aided my research.

Finally, I would like to thank my wonderful support system. Thank you to my family, especially my parents, Palmino and Martha Iacobelli, who loved me, provided for me, and instilled in me a strong work ethic. Thank you to Chad Furrow for the encouragement, laughter, and love during this entire process. Thank you to Ryan Shackleton for the constant support and the help in last-minute research queries. Thank you to Lauren Ouellette for being a great friend and for providing a place to stay as I shuttled between Ottawa and London during the research for this book. Thank you to Magda Khordoc, an unbelievable friend, full of wisdom, compassion, and encouragement. Finally, thanks to a wonderful group of friends scattered throughout Ottawa, London, Toronto, Boston, Chicago, and Brooklyn – you know who you are!

Death or Deliverance

Introduction

ON 27 MARCH 1917, a cold wind blew, and showers of sleet rained down on the small village of Mont St. Eloi, located in northern France.[1] On this bleak day, a young Canadian soldier, twenty-one-year-old Arthur Lemay, stood before a field general court martial, the army's highest wartime court. He had been there before. Having volunteered to serve his country less than a year before, Lemay had already been subjected to field punishment number 1, a common yet humiliating form of public punishment, for charges of absence, as well as a previous court martial and a reprieved death sentence for the crime of desertion. A mere four weeks after this last court martial, Lemay once again stood before his accusers on two more charges of desertion.[2]

The odds were stacked against Lemay. His commanders and his fellow soldiers might well have believed that he would be among those "shot at dawn." Lemay came from the 22nd Battalion, a group of men who later became notorious for their bad behaviour and for their unforgiving commander, Lieutenant Colonel Thomas-Louis Tremblay. A three-time deserter, Lemay was already under a suspended death sentence. He had failed to prove himself in battle. His constant desertions meant that he had seen no action other than a little time spent in quiet sectors. His own commanders failed to find anything positive to present at his trial, and all of his superiors recommended that he be led to the firing post.[3]

After hearing the evidence and deliberating on their own, the members of the court martial reconvened as Lemay stood before them. To the surprise of no one, a verdict of guilty accompanied by a sentence of death was swiftly passed down. All that remained was for the commander-in-chief, Sir Douglas Haig, to sign off on the sentence and for the execution to be carried out. For a habitual offender such as Lemay, the deed seemed all but done.

The hours that followed revealed otherwise. Haig ignored all recommendations and inexplicably, once again, commuted Lemay's sentence of death. Lemay was sentenced to five years of penal servitude, and within six months he was free to rejoin his unit.[4] His story runs contrary to popular opinion regarding military discipline in the First World War. The conventional view has been that military discipline during this era was both brutal and unforgiving. Was Arthur Lemay the exception, or was he the rule? What saved him, and what, if anything, set him apart from those Canadians who were shot at dawn? What can his case, and others like it, tell us about Canadian military justice during the First World War? This book attempts to answer these questions.

My pursuit of this topic has grown out of a long-time interest in the First World War that began with the war poetry and the soldiers' memoirs that were mostly published in the 1930s and in many ways still define the wartime experience.[5] It was the harrowing experiences of average soldiers that most drew me into these accounts. I was compelled by how ordinary men reacted under the most extraordinary circumstances. I was also interested in the idea of what kept men fighting and in the question of what drove some men to flee. This passion for the literature of the war flowed naturally for me into historical research on ordinary soldiers' experiences of war, notably into issues of morale and shell shock. I was interested in the myriad ways in which history and narrative conjoined, and I was curious about how reflective postwar literature was on the actual trench experience.

The intersection of literature and history also provided me with an introduction to military crimes; in particular, I became interested in desertion and cowardice and the military's response to them. These crimes are frequently cited in the postwar literature, and authors having written about them both sympathetically and non-sympathetically. In *All Quiet on the Western Front,* the popular German anti-war novel by Erich Maria Remarque, the character Detering deserts his unit in the hope of returning home to his farm to see the cherry blossoms in spring. The novel's main character, Paul Baumer, knows of the desertion but remains quiet in the hope that Detering might make it safely home. Detering is ultimately captured by the military police, and Baumer remarks pitifully of the incident that "anyone might have known that his flight was only homesickness and a momentary aberration. But what does a court-martial a hundred miles behind the front-line know about it?"[6]

Conversely, in Frederic Manning's *Her Privates We,* the main character, Bourne, exhibits a more complicated understanding of desertion and perhaps a more accurate representation of the typical soldier's view of the crime. When a soldier named Miller might face a firing squad for his desertion, Bourne notes that men of his unit were swift in their judgment of him. As Manning eloquently writes,

> The fact that he had deserted his commanding-officer, which would be the phrase used to describe his offence on the charge-sheet, was as nothing compared to the fact that he had deserted them. They were to go through it while he saved his skin ... The interval between the actual cowardice of Miller, and the suppressed fear

which even brave men felt before a battle, seemed rather a short one, at first sight; but after all, the others went into action; if they broke down under the test, at least they had tried, and one might have some sympathy for them.[7]

Postwar literature has done much to pique my curiosity of the history of military crimes and punishments during the First World War, but I am equally interested in the historical evidence that speaks to the reasons that soldiers committed crimes and the military's responses to their offences. From a Canadian perspective, the body of well-researched academic literature dealing with military crimes, courts martial, and executions in the First World War has been relatively small. The works that have been published are generally excellent, but many stones remain unturned. Some archival sources have not yet been consulted, and questions regarding the military's responses to crimes, and the reasons for these responses, remain unanswered.

Chris Madsen's *Another Kind of Justice: Canadian Military Law from Confederation to Somalia,* published in 1999, provides an excellent overview of Canadian military law.[8] Although Madsen's work is useful for its basic coverage of military law and for defining what distinguishes military law from civilian law, when it comes to military crimes in the First World War, Madsen reasserts the familiar view that the majority of desertions could be blamed on irrational decisions brought on by shell shock. Because of the scope of his work, Madsen, perhaps necessarily, ignores a vast trove of archival material that provides evidence to the contrary.

The first work to deal exclusively with Canadian executions in the First World War was Desmond Morton's 1972 article "The Supreme Penalty: Canadian Deaths by Firing Squad in the First World War."[9] Morton's article zeroes in on two important issues: what the executions said about Canada's relationship with the British military, and how news of the executions was received by Canadians at home. Morton effectively shows that Canadians were generally accepting of the death penalty in the military.

More than twenty-five years after this article, historian Andrew B. Godefroy picked up on many of the issues where Morton left off. Godefroy's 1998 monograph, *For Freedom and Honour? The Story of 25 Canadian Volunteers Executed in the First World War,* compiles the stories of the twenty-five Canadians executed during the Great War.[10] Within the parameters of these twenty-five cases, Godefroy manages to address some of the major issues involved in the courts martial, including ethnicity, shell shock, and the disciplinary value of execution. A great strength of his research is his ability to look at the files in the context of their own time and to do so on a case-by-case basis, thereby avoiding sweeping generalizations of the executed men. However, his short study does not move beyond the cases of the executed and therefore makes it impossible for him to examine broader issues of military law and discipline that can only be addressed by a greater breadth of evidence.

My interest in military crimes and discipline during the First World War was also fed by the ongoing campaigns in Canada and Great Britain to pardon those soldiers executed for desertion and cowardice during the war. From the early 1990s onward, campaigners for pardons continuously lobbied federal governments, gaining support and eventually succeeding in achieving pardons for all executed British and Commonwealth soldiers in 2006. I have long wondered why this campaign existed at all and what accounted for its success. Why did it matter to a small group of people that an even smaller group of convicted soldiers be pardoned for their military crimes ninety years after they were convicted and executed for them? Why was this issue suddenly relevant and pursued with such vigour when it had not been during the course of the war? How did this small group manage to convince their respective governments to look back in time and to offer expressions of sorrow and pardons for a military policy that, in truth, affected a tiny portion of a large civilian military? Given the timing and the rhetoric of the campaign, I suspected that it had much to do with social memory or, put differently, a narrative of the Great War that had been constructed through sixty years of literature and historical writings. The larger issue for me as a historian was how much of this narrative was based on fact and how much was rooted in fiction. What exactly was the dominant social memory of the First World War, and how was it used to support the campaign for pardons? The roots of the campaign and its reliance on the mythology of the war are explored in Chapter 6 of this book.

There were 361 military executions carried out in the armies of Great Britain and the British Empire during the First World War. A further 2,719 death sentences were passed but eventually commuted.[11] Within the Canadian Expeditionary Force (CEF) specifically, there were 25 executions and another 197 death sentences that were commuted. This number includes a death sentence for desertion by a member of the Royal Newfoundland Regiment as well as three death sentences passed after 11 November 1918 for the crimes of murder and mutiny.[12] There were no executions or death sentences passed in the Royal Canadian Navy, and the Royal Canadian Air Force had not yet been created and would come into permanent existence only in 1924 and therefore remains outside the parameters of this book.

By far, the greatest number of death sentences was for the crime of desertion. British statistics as a whole indicate that 2,004 death sentences were passed for the offence, with a total of 272 executions.[13] Canadian statistics show 203 death sentences for desertion, 22 of which resulted in execution. These statistics indicate that, even if found guilty of desertion, a convicted soldier could live and even return to the front lines in a few months. Aside from these statistics, no other published sources of information can be found concerning the commuted death sentences. These cases have long been neglected in the literature because they lack the immediate dramatic impact and the sense of tragedy inherent in the cases of execution. In the commuted cases, we lack the image of a young soldier being led, blindfolded, to a firing post at dawn. I would argue, however, that the commuted cases are no less important for what they can tell us about military authority and discipline during the First World War.

I thus intend to pick up where the scholarship has left off through a comparative study of executed and commuted death sentences of the First World War. Studies that have focused solely on the executions paint a harsh picture of Canadian and British discipline in the war. These studies include William Moore's *The Thin Yellow Line*.[14] Moore criticizes British disciplinary measures and executions and points an accusing finger at the failure of British politicians to speak out against the policies of the British military during the Great War.

In the same vein followed Julian Putkowski and Julian Sykes's *Shot at Dawn: Executions in World War One by Authority of the British Army Act*, first released in 1989.[15] *Shot at Dawn* was a popular history meant to arouse the sentiments of a wide audience rather than provide an objective and thoroughly researched accounting of the facts. The work was highly polemical and sought not only to tell the stories of the executed men of the British and dominion forces but also to call for their exoneration. This call helped to ignite the modern campaign for pardons. In the authors' statement preceding their work, Putkowski and Sykes call on the Ministry of Defence "to have the courage to admit these injustices, and to initiate procedures for exonerating all 351 men who were executed by the British Army during the First World War."[16] Putkowski and Sykes paint the executed men as "unfortunate helpless victims, least able to help themselves."[17] Throughout their work, they rely on emotional language to further their arguments. Although their book can fairly be criticized as one-sided and lacking in thorough analysis, it should also be credited with bringing the debate on military executions into the public domain.

Death or Deliverance, which lends equal focus to the commuted cases and greatly expands the base of evidence, attempts to provide a fairer representation of military justice than can be achieved by looking only at the cases of execution. The examination of a greater number of court martial cases helps to tease out the nuances of Canadian and British military discipline from 1914 to 1918 and to challenge previously accepted notions that military law was harsh and inflexible during the Great War. Although the stories of executed soldiers have obvious emotive impacts, I believe that the stories of the commuted death sentences are of equal importance in historical analysis. If we are to understand the use of capital punishment specifically, and military justice generally, then it is just as important to know why someone was not executed as it is to know why someone was. Furthermore, this book speaks to issues of desertion and cowardice, the offences on which it focuses.

I rely heavily on the files of those who received commuted death sentences during the First World War. The individual personnel files as well as the court martial records not only provide statistical evidence of military discipline and specific trends in discipline during the war but also serve to humanize the individual stories of the soldiers in this book. I use the term "discipline" throughout to describe both how soldiers behaved individually or as a group and the punishments received in cases of poor behaviour. Case files are an important tool in this type of historical inquiry; in the words of noted Canadian social historians Franca Iacovetta and Wendy Mitchinson, case file research has the power to "expose the words and actions of authorities and experts, and to recover the lives of the less powerful."[18] This book is no exception. The court martial files speak to the actions and motivations of the accused, but they also lend important insight into the power structure of the CEF during the First World War and the motivations behind the decisions of commanding officers. However, problems in the evidence must be acknowledged. The documents contained in court martial records are not uniform in each case. In the cases of executed men, many of the transcripts of courts martial and most of the letters of recommendation do not exist. These records were destroyed by the Directorate of History before they could be transferred to Library and Archives Canada.[19] Without further information, it is impossible to know exactly why these records were destroyed; it might have been an oversight, or it might have been because of the records' contentious nature. This would not have been unprecedented; for example, records from the conscription tribunals of the First World War were destroyed because they were seen as a threat to national unity. In addition, because courts martial were held in the field in a hurried manner, there was likely little documentation to begin with since record keeping was not a main priority in light of the circumstances. In this case, the lack of evidence can be just as telling when it comes to the quick and at times improvised nature of the court martial process. Information that I gathered came from various documents, including field service records, letters from officers to divisional headquarters, and in some cases personal letters from relatives of the deceased.

Among the commuted cases, court martial files are more complete, containing crucial documents such as schedules listing both charges and pleas, summaries of evidence (including witness testimony), and, most telling of all, court martial transcripts and statements of superior officers regarding the character of the accused, the state of discipline in the battalion, and the recommendations for punishment. Again, the files are not standardized; some contain more information, some less, but on the whole these records are much fuller than the records of the executed.

In addition to personnel and court martial records, I use other archival documentation, including war diaries and memoranda on the practice of execution written in the aftermath of the First World War. These records were created by various government departments, including the Department of Militia and Defence and the Department of Justice. Finally, in order to address the perspectives of ordinary soldiers and civilians, at times I use personal accounts of executions and military discipline derived from newspapers, letters, diaries, and memoirs of ordinary soldiers and other persons of interest.

I have also consulted a breadth of secondary sources, such as existing monographs and articles on martial executions and military discipline during the First World War and numerous studies related to issues of morale and shell shock. Among the most important for this book were the works of Gerard Oram. Oram stands out in the literature on the British experience of First World War discipline in that he moves his scholarship beyond the cases of execution to look at courts martial more generally. Furthermore, in *Military Executions during World War I,* he questions how colonial ideas of race and ethnicity might have impacted court martial decisions. He moves his analysis beyond the military in order to place his questions and his findings in the context of British society at large and its popular attitudes at the time. Oram was also the first researcher to collect, synthesize, and use the large amount of untapped information found in the commuted cases – that material has been invaluable to this book. Oram's *Death Sentences Passed by Military Courts of the British Army, 1914-1924* provides a definitive list of those soldiers of the British Empire who received a commuted death sentence or were executed by military authorities during the Great War. This list allowed me to easily identify the cases of Canadian soldiers that I would study and to more quickly locate their court martial files at Library and Archives Canada.

To form a better understanding of issues of morale and shell shock, I turned to some of the classic books on the issue, including the often cited *The Anatomy of Courage* by Lord Moran as well as more recent works by Canadian historians who have sought to understand Canadian soldiers' trench experiences.[20] Among the historians whom my work in this area is indebted to are Desmond Morton and Tim Cook. Although Morton's *When Your Number's Up: The Canadian Soldier in the First World War* is a general study of war, Morton writes extensively on issues of morale and ultimately echoes Moran's finding that courage in men is a finite resource. Morton goes on to argue that a soldier's courage or morale is drained faster when the soldier is faced with immobility or is unable to defend himself, and for this reason the stalemated trench warfare of the First World War was particularly damaging to morale.[21] Cook's recent double volume on the Canadian experience in the Great War contributes exponentially to Morton's work, and his second volume, *Shock Troops: Canadians Fighting in the Great War, 1917-1918*, offers several excellent chapters dealing with issues of combat motivation and military discipline.[22]

In order to provide a comparative perspective between military and civilian justice in the early twentieth century, I consulted several articles and texts on legal history, including the recently published *The Practice of Execution in Canada* by Ken Leyton-Brown.[23] Brown's study was useful in providing a historical account of the practice of execution in Canada. His study clearly lays out the process of executions and the roles played by the various actors, including the convicted, the judge, and the federal cabinet. This information was helpful in drawing comparisons between the civilian and military worlds of 1914-18, and it proved useful when thinking about the process that preceded a military execution.

Finally, in order to discuss aspects of social memory related to the First World War, I reviewed cultural histories of the war that address its legacy in Europe as well as Canada. The most important work in this genre for my book has been *Death So Noble: Memory, Meaning, and the First World War* by Jonathan F. Vance.[24] Published in 1997, *Death So Noble* remains the best source for exploring how Canadians set about remembering the war and how these acts of memorialization contributed to a still-emerging national identity.

A number of popular films and websites also added significantly to my understanding of social memory, and these sources perhaps more than any others reveal popular attitudes regarding the war. A number of films address the subject of martial executions in the First World War, including *Paths of Glory, A Very Long Engagement*, and, in the Canadian context, *Passchendaele*.[25] Popular attitudes regarding the war are also revealed in a number of British productions, including *Oh! What a Lovely War* and the satirical television series *Blackadder Goes Forth*.[26] Finally, while there are numerous websites devoted to various topics of the Great War, including tactics or general histories, the most important for my book was *Shot at Dawn*, a website maintained by advocates of pardons in the United Kingdom, Ireland, and Canada. Combining essays, statistics, biographies, and arguments in favour of pardons, this site contributed much to my understanding of the goals of campaigners for pardons and their understanding of the Great War.[27]

I address a number of themes throughout this book in order to provide the most complete picture possible of the First World War courts martial. I begin with a description of military law as it existed from 1914 to 1918. Although focused on military law, I also make ample reference to civilian law during this time in order to provide both context and a comparative perspective. I avoid making obvious comparisons between today's military judicial system and that of 1914. A more useful comparison is that of the civilian legal system with the military legal system during the same era. By understanding the application of the death penalty in civilian society, we can begin to understand why the military attributed such value to it as well.

The central question of this book is why some Canadian soldiers faced the firing squad during the First World War while others with similar crimes and disciplinary records had their sentences commuted. I attempt to answer this question by looking at both the motivating factors behind the crimes of desertion and cowardice and by asking which factors were crucial in leading to confirmation of the ultimate punishment. Commanding officers had a number of disciplinary options at their disposal, and they regularly took advantage of them. I argue that military discipline during the First World War, rather than being meted out by unyielding and callous generals who feature so prominently in movies and popular media, was surprisingly flexible and capable of showing great concern and even sympathy for the individual soldier.

The final major theme that I address in this book is the campaign for pardons and its link to the social memory of the First World War. The campaign emerged in the 1980s in Great Britain, Canada, and New Zealand and reached its conclusion in 2006. I contend that the campaign emerged because of an existing social memory of the First World War as a war of tragic futility. This memory has been encouraged in the media, through novels, films, and television documentaries, and was readily incorporated into the campaign for pardons and accounted for its groundswell of support.

Finally, a word on terminology. Throughout this book, I apply the term "justice" to the discussion of courts martial and military law. However, I use the word with some reservation. It is clear that courts martial were not conducted for the purpose of delivering justice as much as they were for group discipline. As stated in the *Manual of Military Law*, the definitive legal guidebook for the British and dominion forces from 1914 to 1918, "the object of military law is to maintain discipline among the troops and other persons forming part of or following an army."[28] However, even while keeping this in mind, I am forced to adopt the term "justice" because so many modern critics of the military legal system have done so. It would be impossible for me to critique their assumptions, or to provide my own revisionism, without using the term. Therefore, there are instances when I use the term while analyzing how the individual soldier fared against the military legal system; I cannot avoid the term, but I admit that it is a misnomer in the context of this book. However, while accepting the use of this term, I also hope to move my analysis away from modern notions of justice and shift it back to military law as it existed in 1914. I seek to assess military law as it was in the context of the times and not in the context of what we wish it was. This, I believe, is the only way to do justice to "military justice."

1
Competing Ideologies

MILITARY EXECUTIONS HAVE dominated the subject of discipline and punishment in the First World War. This has been especially true in the case of the British and Commonwealth experience, which has the largest body of literature on the topic by far. The execution of 361 British and dominion soldiers in an army of over 5 million men has garnered an inordinate amount of attention in the history. However, while the body of literature on martial executions might be substantial, it is also problematic. Most of the writings that exist on military executions are emotionally charged and polemical. For the most part, the scholarship on discipline during the Great War centres on the debate over the relative justice or injustice of military executions. In this debate, two opposing viewpoints have been overrepresented. On the one side, there are those who believe that the executions of the First World War were a necessary and measured response to rogue elements in the army. The adherents of this argument tend to portray the executed as cowardly ne'er-do-wells who thoughtlessly endangered the lives of their fellow soldiers.[1] On the other side, there are those who view the executions as direct results of the ruthless and heavy-handed military leadership that was characteristic of the First World War. They argue that the court martial system was riddled with injustice and, in some cases, class bias. Among this group, the image of the young, shell-shocked soldier dominates.[2] However, often missing from this debate are the facts, the context, and a middle ground.

In order to address new evidence and to arrive at a more thorough understanding of discipline and punishment in the First World War, it is first necessary to detail what has come before. I must begin by casting a wide net. No discussion of discipline can be undertaken without examining the issue of morale. A comprehensive reading of sources related to military morale turns up only one certainty among authors – that morale is an abstract concept and, consequently, difficult to define. One of the first important modern studies to deal with the topic was *The Anatomy of Courage,* by Lord Moran, published in 1945.[3] Moran based his study on diaries that he kept while serving in the trenches with the First Battalion of the Royal Fusiliers from 1914 to 1917. For him, morale is something akin to courage. It is personal, internal, and cannot simply be imposed by discipline. This courage, Moran believed, is a finite resource in each man;

once used up, it cannot be replaced. Although many works on morale have been published since Moran's study, his argument still maintains its legitimacy among modern military historians.

What any thorough study of morale brings more clearly into focus is the question of combat motivation. What is it that makes men fight, and, conversely and just as important to this book, what makes them stop? There must be inducements for average men to continue fighting through the worst of conditions, as the British and empire forces did, almost without fail, from 1914 to 1918. Although these forces did experience some collective disturbances, they managed to stave off the major mutinies that plagued the armies of France and Germany.[4] As historian John Keegan points out, "while war may be rational, combat is not. It defies one of the strongest of all human instincts, that of self-preservation."[5] What is it that helps men to defy this most basic instinct?

Since the First World War, military historians have identified a number of key factors responsible for both maintaining morale and inducing combat motivation. Based on a case study of the Second Scottish Rifles and their actions at Neuve Chapelle from 9 to 15 March 1915, when the unit showed extremely high morale in the face of battle, John Baynes identified a number of key factors contributing to morale, including regimental loyalty, a sound relationship among officers and other ranks, strong discipline to foster obedience, a sense of duty, and a sound administration to ensure that all of a soldier's requirements are met.[6] Historians have also found that some of the most important inducements in the First World War included creature comforts such as cigarettes and alcohol. In *Firing Line,* Richard Holmes credits these comforts with making the intolerable tolerable as well as easing the stress of battle and assisting in the process of group bonding.[7] Tim Cook echoes these findings. He confirms that in the Canadian case creature comforts affected the individual soldier far more than grand operational plans. In the case of rum specifically, Cook notes that it raised morale and was used as both medicine and reward, all the while helping to reinforce ideas of hierarchy and masculinity.[8]

In many respects, the institutions of civilian life motivated men to continue fighting throughout the Great War. J.G. Fuller makes a case for leisure activities and entertainment in helping to motivate soldiers and sustain British and dominion morale throughout the Great War. Fuller's *Troop Morale and Popular Culture in the British and Dominion Armies, 1914-1918,* published in 1990, looks at the importance of sports, entertainment, and other aspects of civilian life in maintaining morale during the weariest years.[9] By studying newspapers produced by front-line units, as well as the details of the daily lives of soldiers, Fuller demonstrates that trench entertainment paralleled what existed at home, thereby humanizing the war and helping the average soldier to adjust to the extreme circumstances. Entertainment was especially important during periods away from the front lines, when the risk of indiscipline was the greatest. Furthermore, sports proved useful in affirming a sense of community and in mitigating class antagonisms within the military.

In addition to activities that mirrored civilian life, the promise of home was among the most important factors in sustaining morale. In his essay "Discipline and Morale in the British Army, 1917-1918," David Englander states that both British and French army censors cite leave as the primary topic in correspondence, and he goes on to credit leave with being the most important factor in morale, "more than just a respite for war weary troops; it was also a chance to reaffirm their humanity, to express their identities as members of families and coherent communities."[10]

When leave or other combat motivations could no longer support the soldier, and when morale did collapse, battle exhaustion – more commonly termed shell shock, neurasthenia, or hysteria in the era of the First World War – remained a potential threat to the individual soldier and to the military organization as a whole. Some historians have argued that the prevalence of shell shock among soldiers of the First World War can be directly linked to the peculiarly technological nature of the war and that neurosis was the natural result of the soldier's experience with the new modes of destruction.[11] It is true that the First World War was more mechanized than any war that had come before and that this mechanization helped to remove the soldier from the traumas of hand-to-hand combat, but it also took from the soldier the ability to defend himself from the increasingly modernized weapons and forms of warfare. A sense of powerlessness and fear was often the result for the ordinary soldier.

While the shock of modern warfare might have played its part in leading to the large number of breakdowns, other factors have been cited as well. Asking why the British Army in the Second World War did not produce the epidemic of mental disorders that the First World War did, Ben Shephard, author of *A War of Nerves: Soldiers and Psychiatrists, 1914-1994*, identifies a number of probable reasons. Shephard notes that, while the First World War was characterized by static trench warfare, the Second World War was a war of movement, allowing soldiers the opportunity to respond when attacked. Furthermore, Shephard argues that soldiers of the Second World War had access to better leadership and training and that they entered the war with fewer illusions about the romance of war than did their predecessors. Finally, doctors were simply better equipped to deal with neurosis in the Second World War, and those vulnerable to mental breakdown were rooted out much earlier.[12] Although the poor quality of leadership in the First World War has been overstated by the "lions led by donkeys" thesis, which purports that valiant infantry soldiers were led by inept and indifferent generals, Shephard's points regarding the improvements in medical care are important ones to consider, for doctors were better equipped to identify mental health issues both during the recruitment process and in the field during the Second World War.[13]

Throughout the First World War, it was common for shell shock to be viewed by military authorities as a threat akin to malingering or the more serious crimes of desertion and cowardice. During the course of the war, there was concern that some soldiers faked psychosis in order to escape from military commitments. Since the war, perceptions have changed, and it has become a common belief that shell-shocked soldiers were often misunderstood as cowards and dealt with too severely. For example, those soldiers of the First World War who stood before firing squads have been portrayed as shell-shocked boys who had run out of the courage to withstand the trying circumstances. But was this really the case? Was military justice unnecessarily severe, and can we typify those soldiers who deserted? In recent years, this topic has been tackled by more than one British and Commonwealth historian through the narrow scope of military executions.

Within the subject of these executions, there have been considerable shifts in opinion regarding the severity of military discipline as well as the portrayal of those who ultimately faced firing squads. The first work to deal exclusively with the issue of executions in the First World War was Ernest Thurtle's political pamphlet *Shootings at Dawn: The Army Death Penalty at Work*, published in the 1920s.[14] A member of Parliament for the Labour Party and a veteran of the war, Thurtle led a contemporary campaign to abolish the military death penalty. The campaign proved to be quite effective since by 1930 the death penalty was abolished for most crimes in the British Army, excluding treason and mutiny. That year the death penalty was also abolished in the Canadian military for the crimes of desertion and cowardice, though the penalty remained for other offences, including murder, treason, and mutiny.[15] *Shootings at Dawn* compiled the stories of executions that had taken place during the war, and it was meant both to inform the British public and to influence public policy. Thurtle's work was never intended to be an objective account of the use of the death penalty in the Great War. At the time of his writing, official documents regarding the executions were not yet open, and consequently *Shootings at Dawn* relies heavily on eyewitness accounts and hearsay. What results is a highly emotive and at times factually incorrect account with little analysis.[16] Despite these problems, Thurtle's account was influential in setting the tone for future works on military executions of the First World War.

Following his account, the topic of military executions received little attention until a resurgence of interest in the 1970s and 1980s. The first book of this era was William Moore's *The Thin Yellow Line,* published in 1975. Moore's work is a criticism of British disciplinary practices and the British politicians who supported them.[17] His work was followed by what are still two of the most popular works in this field, Anthony Babington's *For the Sake of Example: Capital Courts-Martial, 1914-1920,* published in 1983,[18] and Julian Putkowski and Julian Sykes's *Shot at Dawn,* first released in 1989. All of these works can be considered popular histories, meant to arouse the sentiments of a wide audience rather than provide an objective and thoroughly researched account of the facts.

Babington, a judge, looks at the executions from a legal standpoint and concludes that they were acts of mass injustice. His work is one sided in that it neglects to touch on opposing arguments, yet it is important for two reasons. First, Babington had an advantage over previous authors in that he was the first researcher to gain access to official court martial files. This was accomplished by an agreement with the British government in which he promised not to cite the names of the executed. Second, as a judge, Babington was able to examine knowledgeably issues such as legal representation and sentencing procedures and thus raise interesting questions regarding the legal process of military courts martial.

Since this first wave of books have come a number of more recent publications on the executions of the First World War that, while not necessarily defending the military's actions during the war, have at least sought to understand them better by providing more context for the executions. These works step away from the emotive accounts of individuals standing before firing squads and focus more on the nature of the crimes that led condemned individuals there and how these crimes might have affected the morale of a battalion overall. These later works also attempt to seriously question the disciplinary and morale-building values of the executions as well as to provide more balanced – and usually gentler – portraits of military leaders. Among these works are John Peaty's 1999 article "Capital Courts-Martial during the Great War"; Cathryn Corns and John Hughes-Wilson's *Blindfold and Alone,* published in 2001; and Gerard Oram's *Military Executions during World War I,* published in 2003.

Peaty deals with three main subjects. First, he discusses the executions themselves, using existing studies of the court martial records but adding little new research. Second, he discusses *Shot at Dawn,* its purpose, problems, and impact. Third, he critically analyzes Britain's campaign for pardons. His article is a major revision of all that has come before. Peaty challenges assumptions that shell shock and youth typified the cases of the executed, describing British disciplinary measures as "not too soft, not too harsh," but "about right," especially in light of the disciplinary collapse experienced among the other major powers.[19] The article is strongest when addressing the issue of pardons. Peaty presents convincing arguments against both blanket and selective pardons. He believes that the convicted were judged according to the standards of their times and that it is not for historians or governments to revisit such judgments out of context: "History is history. What happened, happened. We may not like our history, but we rewrite it at our peril."[20]

The work of Corns and Hughes-Wilson,[21] like that of Peaty, is a reaction against earlier accounts that were extremely sympathetic to the executed. Although their points are well argued, this is a popular work whose foremost concern is not objectivity but revision. They argue that their study approaches the use of the death penalty within the context of its own times rather than in hindsight. Their conclusions thus prove to be more forgiving of both the military system itself and commanders such as Douglas Haig who were responsible for sealing the fates of condemned men. Also like Peaty, Corns and Hughes-Wilson add no new research to the court martial debate; rather, they revisit existing material from a different angle.

It is in this regard that Oram's work stands out. Rather than simply revisiting old arguments, *Military Executions during World War I* is an impeccably researched academic work that reframes the entire debate. Looking beyond the right or wrong of the British military's use of executions, Oram attempts to determine why the British were so inclined to use the punishment. He notes that the death penalty was usually used in order to assert or re-establish authority at the divisional level and that it was often timed with critical offensives. But his book is also significant for going beyond the military history and moving the research toward British society and culture, which he describes as "every bit as important in defining the respective armies' approach to the death penalty."[22] Oram sees the military death penalty as an extension of typical British values regarding discipline and punishment. Because Britain counted on the death penalty in civilian life as a form of deterrence, it was applied more widely in the British military for the same reason.[23]

All of the works mentioned deal with the issue of military courts martial of the First World War by focusing on the cases of execution. Scholarship dealing with courts martial in general, or with death sentences passed but commuted, is much less extensive. In *Worthless Men: Race, Eugenics, and the Death Penalty in the British Army during the First World War*, published in 1998, Oram looks at the role of race, ethnicity, and eugenics in the maintenance of discipline and the application of the death penalty in the First World War, his central question being "what was so special about a relatively small group of men that they were picked out to be executed?"[24] To answer this question, Oram moves beyond the cases of executed men and looks at the cases of those whose death sentences were commuted. His conclusion is that the death penalty was used more readily against the Irish, colonial troops, labourers, and those whom the army deemed to be degenerate or of an inferior quality.

From both an international and a comparative perspective, much work remains to be done on the topic of discipline and punishment in the First World War. At this point, only a few works exist. Among them is Christopher Pugsley's 1991 *On the Fringe of Hell: New Zealanders and Military Discipline in the First World War*, which seeks to provide a comparative analysis of those New Zealanders who had their death sentences commuted and those who faced firing squads. Although New Zealand's numbers are much smaller, with only five executed soldiers and twenty-three commuted death sentences, Pugsley's approach provides an important framework for the Canadian cases.[25]

Keeping within the Commonwealth experience, there is much room for research in the Australian example. Australia's decision not to execute soldiers speaks volumes about the country's relationship with Great Britain throughout 1914-18, and it provides an opportunity to make informative comparisons with the Canadian and New Zealand experiences.

Outside the British literature, probably the most attention given to discipline during the First World War has been in French scholarship. Since 1967, when Guy Pedroncini published the first account based on archival sources and records of military justice, the mutinies of 1917 have dominated the historiography of French discipline in the Great War. Pedroncini was interested in determining the root causes of the 1917 mutinies. His research reveals that a lack of confidence in the decisions of the high command that led to repeated losing offensives was a chief factor in mutiny. The ordinary French soldier did not want to quit fighting, but he did want new strategies and leaders. In this regard, the mutinies were effective in moving the French Army toward a policy of defence rather than offence.[26] More recently at the forefront of French scholarship has been the work of Leonard V. Smith. His seminal 1994 work, *Between Mutiny and Obedience: The Case of the French Fifth Infantry Division during World War I*,[27] contends that the 1917 confrontations between French soldiers and their commanders shifted the balance of power in the French military. Smith argues that the French soldiers were political beings who negotiated how they would fight. In this respect, the mutinies of 1917 had a strong political component and were not simply outbursts of bad behaviour. Smith convincingly shows that the typical French soldier was willing to fight aggressively as long as the demands made of him were proportional to the advantage expected to be achieved. Soldiers refused to follow orders blindly, thus fundamentally changing traditional relationships of authority and consent in the French military.

Outside the French and Commonwealth experiences, little has been written on the topics of martial execution and general discipline in the Great War. Most scholarship comes from articles scattered among various sources. There is little depth when it comes to comparative analyses, and in some cases a lack of evidence has not even allowed for an accounting of the facts. For example, Italian records are incomplete, though it is believed that approximately 750 Italian soldiers were executed, making Italian justice among the most severe in the First World War.[28] In the American Army, ten soldiers, all of them black men, were executed in France for the non-military crimes of rape and murder. In addition, thirteen black men were executed at Fort Sam Houston in Texas in 1917 following an alleged mutiny.[29] The institutionalized racism suggested by these statistics is obviously a topic worthy of further investigation. Among the Central Powers, the numbers of executed are often inaccurate, though it is clear that disciplinary problems were a concern. Within the Austro-Hungarian Army, insubordination became particularly problematic in the rear areas. According to historian Mark Cornwall in his 1997 article, "Morale and Patriotism in the Austro-Hungarian Army, 1914-1918," "in one incident in Galicia, 550 soldiers deserted from a train heading towards the southwest theatre. By the end of the war there was said to be a quarter of a million deserters roaming around the interior and sheltered by the local population, but the AOK *[Armee-Oberkommando]* always lacked the manpower to tackle the problem."[30] For the Austro-Hungarians, poor morale could be directly attributed to meagre resources. By 1918, visiting staff officers were commenting on the lack of food and boots and in some cases soldiers without shirts or trousers. As a staff officer inspecting the 20th Corps commented in September 1918, "morale is indeed being damaged by material hardships."[31]

Given the experiences of other nations, Germany's wartime record of discipline is surprising. Considering Germany's reputation as an intensely militaristic society, its numbers of executions remained low throughout the war, with only forty-eight executions being documented in official records.[32] Historians agree that this number does not take into account the strong possibility that summary executions might have occurred regularly on the German lines; however, with the destruction of many official records during the Second World War, any more detailed information on possible executions is unavailable.[33] The reality was that from 1914 to 1918 German soldiers actually had more rights than their other European counterparts, and convictions for desertion were harder to obtain in the German Army than in the British Army.[34] This, it seems, was to the great disdain of Germany's General Erich Ludendorff, who wrote that "the Entente no doubt achieved more than we did with their considerably more severe punishments. This historic fact is well established."[35] In reality, "this historic fact" is not "well established." Allied victory and Allied morale cannot simply be attributed to severe punishments. Ludendorff's statement fails to account for Allied strategy, materiel, or home-front support. Furthermore, as indicated by numerous authors cited in this chapter, morale was more dependent on the provision of material comforts than on the threat of severe punishments.

As we near the centennial of the outbreak of the First World War, it is interesting that the issue of military executions has remained on the radar not simply as history but also in contemporary political debates. The emergence of the campaign for pardons in Great Britain, Canada, New Zealand, and France in the 1980s ensured that the issue of martial executions did not simply fade into history. Specifically discussing Great Britain and France, author Nicolas Offenstadt relates the campaign to these nations' collective memory of the Great War, essentially a memory of tragic futility.[36] Undoubtedly, the campaign has found success largely because of this social memory of the First World War that remains relatively fixed despite any recent scholarly works that might dispute it. Since the 1960s, a collective memory of this war has steadily developed and paints the conflict as a futile one characterized by ruthless and inept leaders and young, shell-shocked soldiers. Popular literature and film have both been influenced by and reinforced these ideas. In Great Britain, the 1963 stage play (and later film) *Oh! What a Lovely War* and the 1989 television series *Blackadder Goes Forth* satirized the conflict and in particular the British leadership.[37] In a particularly relevant episode of *Blackadder Goes Forth*, titled "Corporal Punishment," Captain Blackadder faces a court martial for eating a messenger pigeon. Charges are subsequently brought against him by General Melchett. Blackadder arrives at his court martial only to find that the same Melchett who brought the charges against him is also the judge, to which Blackadder ironically remarks, "I love a fair trial." Referred to as the "Flanders Pigeon Murderer" by Melchett during the trial, Blackadder is quickly sentenced to death and stands before a firing squad before he is given a last-minute reprieve.[38]

The ruthlessness of French discipline has been depicted in director Stanley Kubrick's 1957 classic *Paths of Glory* and more recently in 2004 in *A Very Long Engagement*.[39] *Paths of Glory* tells the story of a group of French soldiers who fail to carry out an attack that they know to be futile. The attack, ordered by the power-hungry and promotion-seeking General Mireau, is an inevitable failure. In response, Mireau orders junior officers to choose three soldiers to be executed. The trials afforded to the soldiers are simply for show, for the three men are ultimately shot by a firing squad. The movie is based on the novel by Humphrey Cobb, the son of American parents who lived abroad in various locations before enlisting in the CEF in Montreal in 1916. He served for three years, including at the Battle of Amiens. Cobb notes in his afterword that, while the characters and places in his novel are fictitious, the book is based on real events involving four French corporals of the 136th Infantry Regiment who were executed in March 1915 following a failed assault at Souain.[40]

Similar to *Paths of Glory*, *A Very Long Engagement*, adapted from the popular French novel of the same title by Sébastien Japrisot, tells the story of unsympathetic French military justice. Five soldiers, some falsely accused and some attempting to escape from the horrors of the war, are convicted of self-mutilation and ruthlessly thrown unarmed into no man's land, the shattered landscape between the two armies. Susceptible to machine gun fire, the men are left to be caught in the crossfire and to face almost certain death.[41] This story is said to have been based on a real-life incident in which twenty-five self-mutilators sentenced to be shot by firing squad were instead thrown into no man's land overnight on General Pétain's orders.[42]

Similar works exist in Canadian literature and film as well. Although no one Canadian film deals with the issue of Canadian discipline in the First World War, *Passchendaele,* released in 2008, does touch on the subject.[43] Appearing before a medical board to determine whether he is fit to return to war, the film's main character, Sergeant Michael Dunne, is revealed to have gone absent without leave before he was medically evacuated with neurasthenia. Unwilling to explain his actions to the authorities, Dunne is warned that if he is deemed fit to return to the front he will be charged with desertion and "more than likely ... executed." Like their French and British counterparts, Canadian works tend to paint the war as a tragic experience and the executed as unfortunate innocents.

This perception of the war is introduced to Canadians from their first contact with the subject. For example, *And in the Morning* (2003), by John Wilson, is a work of teen fiction that introduces young readers to generally accepted notions of the First World War as well as to the topic of martial executions. Using real letters, diaries, and histories of the Highland Light Infantry Battalions, Wilson constructs a story of the war from the perspective of a fictional underage British soldier named Jim Hay. Hay begins the war filled with a sense of purpose and adventure, but he quickly learns to hate the war and how it is transforming him. His opinions on the war, notably on military discipline, experience a drastic shift as the war progresses. Confronted with the case of the soon-to-be-executed deserter James Crozier, Hay initially remarks that "execution may seem harsh, but army discipline must be maintained, and a firing squad is at least a quick and clean way to die. One man who doesn't do his duty can put many of his comrades at risk."[44] However, after witnessing Crozier's execution, Hay drastically alters his attitude. Crozier's drunken and botched execution causes Hay to realize that a firing squad is far from a clean way to die and that executions are not always warranted. In the book's final irony, Hay himself becomes the victim of a military court martial and execution following a conviction for desertion. Wilson uses the character of Hay to emphasize the extraordinary pressures that the war put on young men and how the executed soldiers of the war were undeserving of their fate.

Similar themes are found in Colin McDougall's 1958 novel *Execution*.[45] Although it is set in Italy during the Second World War, the novel reinforces popular attitudes toward military executions and suggests that these opinions transcend any particular conflict. Based on the real-life execution of Canadian Harold Pringle, *Execution* in part tells the tale of the dim-witted Jones who is to be executed for his role in the murder of an American soldier. Jones is innocent of the crime, yet his execution proceeds because of American pressure and an unstoppable bureaucratic process. Throughout the book, McDougall shows military discipline to have been a matter of politics rather than justice. His work was popular in Canada and went on to win the 1958 Governor General's Literary Award for English-language fiction. The novel also helped to contribute to an image of abusive military power.

In 2002, the real-life story of Harold Pringle's execution was published. Using his skills as a journalist, author Andrew Clark weaves together the story of the Italian campaign with that of Pringle's crime and subsequent execution. As a work of non-fiction, Clark's book is certainly more nuanced than McDougall's, but again the result is a sympathetic portrayal of Pringle, focusing on the injustices of war that led to the execution of a Canadian volunteer on trumped-up murder charges. Although not an overtly political work, Clark's story does end with a plea: "Harold Pringle deserves some vindication. An official recognition that he was not a cold-blooded killer but rather a young, rebellious, shell-shocked rifleman would help heal his family, who were never free to publicly mourn their son, even though he lies in a military cemetery."[46]

This stream of films and books shows that, while the number of executed soldiers in the First World War might have been relatively small, interest in them has not been. Yet, in addition to these works of fiction and popular histories, the body of academic literature that deals with the issue of courts martial and executions from a specifically Canadian perspective is limited. As mentioned in the introduction, the first work to deal exclusively with Canadian executions in the Great War was Desmond Morton's "The Supreme Penalty," in which Morton effectively shows that Canadians readily accepted the death penalty.[47] This article was followed by Andrew Godefroy's *For Freedom and Honour?*, which provides descriptions of the cases of the twenty-five executed Canadians.[48]

Dealing specifically with the executions of French Canadians in the First World War, Jean-Pierre Gagnon's 1986 study *Le 22ᵉ Bataillon (canadien-français), 1914-1919* is worthy of mention.[49] Although his account is a history of the

22nd Battalion and not specifically related to discipline and punishment, it does include a very credible section on discipline and leadership in the battalion. The 22nd, the only entirely French-speaking Canadian battalion, experienced five executions, more than any other Canadian battalion. With thorough primary research, Gagnon provides some definitive answers regarding the relationship between French Canadian soldiers and military justice. He effectively dispels myths that French Canadians were victims of gross injustices. Instead, he shows that the extraordinary number of courts martial in the 22nd Battalion could be traced back to poor discipline and severe leadership.

Also focused on the experiences of French Canadians in the First World War is Patrick Bouvier's 2003 *Déserteurs et insoumis: Les Canadiens français et la justice militaire (1914-1918)*,[50] which examines the experiences of French Canadian deserters, including those men who deserted from the front and those who were conscripted but failed to present themselves for overseas service. Although Bouvier provides some useful statistical evidence in his quest to define the typical deserter, his work offers little else to the body of literature. Bouvier questions the conclusions of Gagnon, but he fails to offer alternative explanations. A large part of his work is focused on the existing historiography rather than new evidence.

As the story of death sentences of the First World War continues to develop within both a Canadian framework and an international framework, it becomes clear that this topic captures the popular imagination because it speaks not only to the collective memory but also to the collective conscience. Some of the more important issues have been tackled by historians of discipline and punishment in the First World War, but other areas remain to be explored. The historian must move beyond the executions and attempt to situate the topic within a broader international context and within the broader frameworks of military, legal, and social histories. To accomplish this, it is imperative to understand the rules and regulations as the soldiers and their commanders understood them and experienced them between 1914 and 1918. The following chapter describes military law and the options for punishment available to commanders during the First World War in order to provide the necessary background for understanding the military crimes discussed in this book and the circumstances under which commanders chose to initiate court martial proceedings.

2
Military Law: An Overview

IN 1917, *MILITARY LAW MADE EASY* by Lieutenant Colonel S.T. Banning of the British Army was published in its revised eleventh edition.[1] First published in 1900, and originally designed as a manual to assist officers in preparing for their military law exams, the fact that this manual was already in its eleventh edition by 1917 speaks to the rapidly evolving nature of military law. By 1914, the volume was in its seventh edition. Between 1914 and 1917, Banning's work was revised five times in four years, Banning noting each time the various amendments to the laws and regulations that had been made since the previous publication. Furthermore, the irony of the title of his work is evident. The vast majority of courts martial for desertion and cowardice in the CEF took place in 1917, with a total of 104 trials, 7 of which ended in executions. At a time when more and more British and imperial soldiers were breaking down under the strains of trench warfare and finding themselves at the mercy of courts martial, this handbook attempted to simplify the very complicated matter of military law. In 1917, this publication might have been more useful than ever to young officers who were rushed, out of necessity, through the ranks and lacked the formal training of their nineteenth-century counterparts, who had been expected to attend formal courses in military law and pass written examinations for each promotion in rank.[2] To the soldiers on trial during the First World War, there could have been no comfort in knowing that their cases were in the hands of men who were hardly more experienced than them yet given the right to pronounce judgment while armed only with the minimum knowledge of military law.

Past studies of military discipline in the First World War have gone astray in that their primary motivation was to argue the relative justice (or injustice) of military law. This approach ignored the reality that, unlike civilian law, military law in Western society is concerned with the application of discipline more than the application of justice. Military law is deliberately a different system, intended to deal with issues of morale, discipline, and efficiency that are irrelevant to the civilian legal system. Discipline, obedience, and order constitute the backbone of the military system. This is especially true in wartime, when these three factors are essential to the maintenance of morale and successful operations. Upon the breakdown of discipline, commanders require a course of action.

During the First World War, members of the Canadian Corps were subject to the British code of military law as laid down in the Army Act of 1881. This act was an amalgamation of various orders in council, acts, royal warrants, and amendments that required annual approval by Parliament, which in part helped to keep the act current.[3] The death penalty was the most severe punishment enshrined in the act, and it has been the most documented in the literature on military discipline during the Great War. In 1914, the death penalty was applicable to a number of crimes, including offences such as casting away arms in the presence of the enemy, giving intelligence to the enemy, or misbehaving or inducing others to do so in a manner that showed cowardice. These crimes, many of which aided the enemy and could be construed as treason, were considered so severe by the military that they were deemed to be punishable by death under any circumstances. In addition to these offences, included in the Army Act were crimes that were punished more severely in wartime than during times of peace. They included offences such as sleeping or drinking at post, leaving a patrol or post without orders from a superior officer, and desertion.[4]

I am primarily concerned here with application of the death penalty to the crimes of desertion and cowardice, though death sentences were passed for a number of other offences in the CEF. Among its executed men, Alexander Butler and Benjamin De Fehr were both executed for murder. Butler shot a fellow soldier to death without warning in June 1916, while De Fehr shot a regimental sergeant major in the back in August 1916. Although De Fehr claimed during his defence to have been drunk, witnesses insisted that he had been sober at the time.[5] In addition to the 184 commuted death sentences for the crimes of desertion and cowardice, there were 11 death sentences passed and commuted for crimes against inhabitants (including burglary, robbery, and rape), disobedience, insubordination, quitting post without orders, and mutiny.[6]

As defined by the *Manual of Military Law* of 1914, desertion "implies an intention on the part of the offender either not to return to His Majesty's service at all, or to escape some particular important service."[7] Therefore, *intention* is the most important feature, that which distinguishes desertion from the lesser charge of absence without leave, which was typically punished by confinement to barracks, docks in pay, or field punishment number 1 or 2. Although the length of absence or the distance from the unit was not sufficient in itself to prove desertion, it could be used as evidence. Irrefutable evidence of the intention not to return to one's unit or to evade a particular duty was also required. After an absence of twenty-one days, a commanding officer could choose to initiate the proceedings of a court of inquiry that would enter a charge of desertion on the record of a non-returning soldier, thus ensuring a trial for desertion if the absent soldier returned, whether by his own will or under arrest.[8]

Cowardice could be linked to disobedience or refusal to obey orders, but it differed from these lesser charges in that, according to a War Office memorandum, "the essence of the offence of cowardice is that it must occur 'before the enemy', that is to say actually in the presence of danger."[9] Cowardice was a much more subjective charge and therefore harder to prove. There was thus unwillingness or even inability to bring about this charge, and this is reflected in the statistics. From 1914 to 1918, 266 men from the British and dominion forces were executed for desertion on the western front, while only 18 were executed for cowardice. Most of these charges for cowardice came early in the war, when commanders were more inclined to prosecute the offence.[10]

The subjectivity of cowardice meant that there was also a fine line between it and desertion. The inability to differentiate one crime from another, and the leeway given to commanders to bring forth charges, at times led to confusion and questionable decisions. One need look no further than the cases of Dimitro Sinizki and John Jacques to prove this point.

John Jacques was a woodworking machinist from St. Thomas, Ontario, before enlisting for service in October 1914. While serving with the 18th Battalion, he was informed on the evening of 13 August 1917 that his unit would be proceeding to the trenches. Jacques was present at roll call and began the march with his fellow soldiers when, according to all witness accounts, before entering the village of Aix Noulette in northern France, he promptly fell out of line and sat on the side of the road, refusing to proceed any farther. When asked what the problem was by Sergeant W.K. Gray, Jacques only replied, "it's all right."[11] Court martial testimony later revealed that Jacques had reported sick to the medical officer, who had found him fit for duty. Jacques's actions in 1917 ultimately led to charges of desertion and failing to obey the command of a superior officer. Jacques was found guilty and sentenced to death; however, his sentence was commuted to ten years of penal servitude. He survived the war and was demobilized on 10 June 1919.[12]

In August 1917, Dimitro Sinizki found himself in strikingly similar circumstances to those of Jacques but with a very different outcome. Sinizki was a Russian immigrant who had left his job as a labourer to enlist in Winnipeg in 1915. Serving with the 52nd Battalion, he seems to have broken down when, according to records, he refused to continue up to the line with his battalion. He eventually continued on under escort, but the next day he continued his protest, sitting down and stating that he would rather be shot than return to the trenches. His commanding officer decided to charge him with the crime of cowardice rather than desertion. Sinizki was found guilty and, though it was his first offence, executed for the crime in October 1917. He was the only Canadian shot for cowardice during the First World War.[13]

The reasons for his charge and subsequent sentence remain unclear, and the evidence simply does not exist to arrive at a firm conclusion. One can speculate that Sinizki was charged with cowardice because he never actually deserted his unit, but given that the crime did not occur in the presence of the enemy, as a charge of cowardice demands, it is unclear why he was not charged with failure to comply with an order, as in the case of Jacques. In a summary of Sinizki's case written by Major General J.H. MacBrien in 1922, he noted that "this was one of the worst cases occurring in the Canadian Corps."[14] MacBrien gave no reasoning for this statement, and without trial transcripts from the case it is impossible to form a full understanding of the statement. The available facts of the case and my own research suggest that there were many offences far worse than Sinizki's and many offenders who posed far greater disciplinary threats to their units. Both the timing and the circumstances of Jacques's and Sinizki's offences bear many similarities, but without complete records for Sinizki there is nothing but the personal decisions of the commanding officers to help explain the discrepancy in the charges.

Although a primary purpose of this study is to investigate the court martial process, a thorough review of soldiers' disciplinary records clearly indicates that court martial proceedings were not typically a first resort. Most soldiers experienced military discipline at the platoon, company, and battalion levels. In an interview conducted with the Canadian Broadcasting Corporation in the early 1960s, veteran M.A. Searle of the 18th Battalion recalled that, when he overstayed his leave by a few days during Christmas 1917, he was dealt with by his commanding officer rather than being charged with desertion and sent to a court martial. As Searle recalled, "well, I was up before the OC [officer commanding] and I got seven days in the clink and two days Royal Warrant, two days Royal Warrant, that's loss of pay."[15] When the lack of severity of the crime allowed for it, some company commanders and commanding officers preferred to deal with disciplinary issues on their own, in part because bypassing more official routes was simply easier. Furthermore, and perhaps most importantly, there was a sense of camaraderie in infantry units that characterized officer-soldier relations. Because of this, many officers preferred to show leniency and to keep offences within their own units especially when the offender was not a chronic disciplinary problem or the infraction was slight and presented no larger threat to unit discipline or morale. Private Deward Barnes recalled an incident on night watch when, "one night, all the men on the outpost next to us ran away and left their post, every man of them. Sergeant Scott was too good to report it. They got frightened."[16] Scott's empathetic response reveals a deep understanding of his troops' actions likely born of shared experience. His response no doubt saved the men from receiving serious stains on their records, or possible courts martial on charges of desertion, but likely it also helped to strengthen the sense of camaraderie and trust between him and his men.

A number of offences did not require commanders to refer to a superior authority in order to mete out punishment to their own troops on active duty. The list of crimes was extensive, ranging from striking a superior officer to absence without leave to ill treating a horse, to any action that could be considered harmful to good order and military discipline.[17] Disciplinary records show a variety of punishments, the most common being stoppages in pay, confinement to barracks, and field punishments. Of these, perhaps field punishment number 1 was the most controversial among soldiers. Nicknamed "crucifixion" among soldiers, it entailed labour duties as well as restraint by handcuffs or fetters to a fixed object such as a wheel or post.[18] The punishment could not take place for more than twenty-one days in total, and restraint could only occur for up to two hours a day and for no more than three consecutive days.[19] The punishment was meant to deter indiscipline by striking fear in soldiers, while for the convicted it was meant to cause physical discomfort and impose a sense of public shame. The punishment was a novelty to volunteers without prior military experience, leading many to describe the practice in their letters home. For William Antliff Shaw, a former commerce student who had enlisted for service with the No. 9 Canadian Field Ambulance in 1916, the extra work and the deprivations involved in the punishment were among its worst features: "The latter [field punishment number 1] consists of being tied to a wheel for a couple of hours each day, doing pack drill, breaking stone and mending roads all day, living on bully, hard tack and tea without milk or sugar, doing without tobacco and generally being bullied around by the military police in charge."[20] In addition to creating fear among soldiers, the punishment fostered resentment among some. As one British soldier wrote, it

> turned our minds against the British Army, as we had not enlisted for our own benefit, we were all civilians, who had never entertained the idea of being soldiers before the war started, and to see men strapped to the wheels for an hour was nothing more or less than cruelty, and to be on view of all passer by's was not pleasant.[21]

The effectiveness of field punishment number 1 remains unclear. Many in command remained steadfast in their support of it. Writing in 1919, Commander-in-Chief Douglas Haig himself stated that "I am quite certain that it would not have been possible to maintain the high standard of discipline in the British Army in France if Field Punishment No. 1 had been non-existent."[22] Certainly, some soldiers were deterred by the threat, or by the receipt of this punishment, but disciplinary records also tell another side of the story. Individual disciplinary records showing repeated instances of the receipt of this punishment provide proof that for many soldiers it barely figured in their decisions to commit offences.[23] For many, in a calculated decision, it was better to have their fun getting drunk in a local *estaminet* or absenting to surrounding villages or cities and to suffer the potential consequences later.

When the severity of a military crime forced it to become public outside the unit, as in the case of an arrest of a deserter by military police and a subsequent report to headquarters, or when a commanding officer felt compelled to initiate a court martial to set an example for the battalion, the battalion officer would apply through his brigade headquarters to initiate the proceedings. The process would involve forwarding all the necessary documentation summarizing the evidence of the case. A convening officer of the court would review this material and make a decision on whether to proceed.[24] If a court martial was deemed to be warranted, there were four types that an accused soldier could face: regimental, district, general, and field general. Regimental and district courts martial dealt with minor crimes, while general and field general courts martial (FGCMs) were reserved for serious offences and could result in a punishment of death. Given that my research deals with the crimes of desertion and cowardice by soldiers and non-commissioned officers on active service, I am commenting exclusively on FGCMs. Officers were subject to general courts martial with a stricter adherence to the rules of procedure as set out in the *Manual of Military Law*. FGCMs differed from general courts martial in that they were held in the field and, in the interest of expediency, simplified in both routine and requirements. Procedural rules were relaxed in order to deal effectively with conditions of war on the ground. Throughout the First World War, FGCMs were far more common than general courts martial.

The convening of an FGCM with full punishing powers required that no fewer than three officers be in attendance, unless this was determined to be impossible for operational reasons. These officers could come from any corps or unit of the CEF, including the accused's own unit, though the defendant's commanding officer was not eligible to sit on the court martial. The sitting officers were usually a major (or above), a captain, and a lieutenant. Chosen from among the officers' ranks, the individuals who sat in judgment held no extra training in military law. In fact, as the war dragged on, and as more officers were killed, experience in and knowledge of military law became even rarer among officers. There were few resources and little time to train new officers in the complexities of military law. It simply could not have been considered a priority.

In addition to their lack of knowledge of military law, the majority of men who sat on courts martial certainly were not trained in its civilian counterpart.

Officers chosen for this duty were ordinary volunteers and therefore representative of the spectrum of men who served in the CEF in that they came from a variety of occupational backgrounds, both blue and white collar. David William Agon was tried for desertion in 1917, and the members of his court martial offer a typical example of the officers who would have received orders for such a duty. Agon's court martial panel consisted of four members, including the president of the court martial, Major Ewan MacDougall, a trained architect. The other members were Captain Frank Lindsay Bradburn, who had identified himself as a businessman on his attestation papers; Lieutenant Robert England, a student training for the ministry; and Lieutenant Ernest Archibald McFall, who had been working as a salesman in Canada at the outbreak of war.[25]

Court martial trials proceeded in a manner that was somewhat similar to their civilian counterparts. Evidence was presented and recorded. Witnesses were brought forward and cross-examined. In addition to witnesses of the crime in question, character witnesses could be called, though it was noted that

> evidence of the accused's bad character cannot be given by the prosecution unless he has called evidence to show he has a good character, in which case the Prosecutor can call witnesses to rebut this evidence. On the other hand, evidence as to character is relevant for the defence, and an accused can always call witnesses to prove his good character, or he may call for the production of his Conduct Sheet.[26]

By 1915, all capital cases required a plea of "not guilty" by the defendant to ensure that evidence would be heard. This rule was instituted by the military following the execution of Joseph Byers of the 1st Royal Scots Fusiliers. Byers pleaded guilty to a charge of desertion at a British FGCM in 1915. Because of his plea, evidence was heard but went unchallenged, and Byers went undefended. He was found guilty, and all of his commanding officers recommended that the death sentence be carried out.[27] Byers was executed on 6 February 1915. However, in spite of the recommendations, some reservations were expressed in regard to the sentence. Voicing his concerns to the deputy judge advocate general, General Sir Horace Smith-Dorrien, commanding Second Army, wrote that

> I should have unhesitatingly have recommended that both Death Sentences be carried out, but I think it right to point out that no. 15576 Pte. J. Byers pleaded guilty and therefore no sworn evidence was taken and although this is legally correct it is just a question of whether when a death sentence is involved the Court should not make the man plead not guilty and take sworn evidence.[28]

Based on these concerns, instructions for courts martial were amended to make a not guilty plea mandatory in any case involving the possibility of a death sentence.[29]

The *Manual of Military Law* also included rules that helped to guarantee the accused the right to tell his version of the events in a case: "The accused is to be allowed great latitude in making his defence, and will not, within reasonable limits, be stopped by the court merely for making irrelevant observations."[30] The same section on court martial protocol also stipulated that "the accused is allowed to have a friend to assist him, who may be either a legal advisor or any other person."[31] This person was termed a "prisoner's friend" and, though chosen by the defendant, was often an officer with little or no knowledge of military law and procedure. In some cases, prisoners also chose to defend themselves.[32] However, criticisms of proper legal representation in the court martial system must be remembered within the context of the times. The era of the First World War preceded the establishment of legal aid in both Canada and Great Britain. That every soldier, regardless of rank, was offered a lawyer or a prisoner's friend to represent him at a court martial exhibited a level of fairness that in many ways was ahead of its time. In the early twentieth century, an ordinary prisoner's defence in civilian matters was typically dependent on his or her wealth. It was not until 1930 with the amendment to the Poor Prisoner's Defence Act that British subjects were offered legal aid in all criminal proceedings. The original Poor Prisoner's Defence Act of 1903 applied only to a small number of specially chosen and serious cases.[33] In Canada, no official body mandated legal aid in the early twentieth century. A poor person charged with a crime was dependent solely on the charity of others. Religious groups and the Canadian Bar Association attempted to do what they could, and in cases of murder, in which the accused was subject to the death sentence, defendants were given priority for charitable legal counsel.[34] It was not until 1951 that the Law Society of Upper Canada established a voluntary system of legal aid, but still lawyers remained unpaid for their work. The passing of the Legal Aid Act in 1967 finally established in law the right to legal aid for all persons and created a system to pay lawyers for their efforts.[35]

In addition to issues of representation, prisoners had to contend with another reality of the FGCM: witnesses could be difficult to find because of confusion in the field brought on by the conditions of war. For example, during the trial of Edward Millar, from the 1st Canadian Machine Gun Battalion, charged with desertion in September 1918, no character witness could be produced from his own battery since all of his officers were either dead or wounded. Millar deserted on 30 August when he left the village of Chérisy while the rest of his unit assembled for an attack. He reported back to his company on 8 September. He stated at his trial that he had been knocked out by a shell and had stayed for two days at a dressing station. He had then left the dressing station and had stayed with other units until he had found his own. Millar was found guilty and sentenced to death, but his sentence was commuted to five years of penal servitude. His commutation was likely based on recommendations that cited his youth (twenty years old) as well as his previous twenty-six months of service, which had included engagements at the Somme, Vimy Ridge, and Amiens. Millar survived the war and was demobilized in May 1919.[36]

Following presentation of the case by both the prosecution and the defence, the accused, or the prisoner's friend, was invited to make a closing statement before the members of the court martial adjourned to consider the facts of the case and make their final decision. It was a requirement that the most junior officer sitting on the court martial be the first to give his judgment so as not to be influenced by or simply echo the opinions of more senior officers. In addition to being found guilty or innocent of the offence for which he was charged, a soldier could be found guilty of a lesser charge. For example, a soldier accused of desertion could be found guilty of absence without leave, a non-capital offence.

Following the decision and the reading of the verdict, the accused, if found guilty, was invited to make a statement in mitigation of punishment. This statement was typically a plea for mercy in which a soldier often apologized or detailed the extenuating circumstances of his case. In the cases that I examined, it was typical for soldiers to request mercy based on their youth, their length of service, or their participation in particularly notable engagements. Soldiers also made pleas for mercy based on their circumstances at home. For example, James Albert Burtch, a labourer from London, Ontario, convicted of desertion from the 38th Battalion in September 1917, was not unique in his plea for leniency: "My mother and father are entirely dependent upon me. I assign a portion of my pay to them."[37] John Wellman Campbell, a labourer from Cochrane, Ontario, absented from the 3rd Canadian Machine Gun Battalion on 25 September 1918 only to be arrested on a leave train one day later. In his statement of mitigation, Campbell noted his past service and extenuating circumstances to save his life: "I have been about fifteen months in France. I was wounded on the Somme in 1916 ... I received a letter from home saying that my mother was dead before I went away."[38] Campbell had sustained gunshot wounds to his left arm and right leg on 29 September 1916. He was found guilty of desertion, but, based on his short absence and extenuating circumstances, his death sentence was commuted to fifteen years of penal servitude. He survived the war and was demobilized on 20 September 1919.[39]

For convictions of desertion and cowardice, the death penalty was the harshest form of punishment. In passing a sentence of death, it was required that all members of the court martial be in agreement. Interestingly, many death sentences passed by FGCMs were accompanied by recommendations for mercy. Why the court would impose such a strong sentence only to recommend that it not be carried out is somewhat unclear, though it has been suggested that junior officers, uncertain of their role, thought it necessary to impose maximum penalties and that they depended on the commander-in-chief to reduce the penalty as he saw fit.[40]

Upon imposing a death sentence, confirmation was the next step in the judicial process. Before a death sentence could be confirmed in the CEF, three letters of recommendation had to be requested from superior officers, who included the accused's commanding officer, who would comment on the soldier's disciplinary and fighting record; a brigade commander, who would comment on the overall discipline of the battalion; and a divisional or corps commander, who would offer his opinion. These letters were not always consistent. At times, likely because of the conditions of war, some ranks were substituted in these letters of recommendation.[41] All of the commanders were to state their views on whether the sentence of death should be confirmed or commuted. These letters were then forwarded up the chain of command to the commander-in-chief.

Because the final decision in any death sentence rested on the commander-in-chief, these individuals have often been the focal point in the debate over military executions in the First World War. On the western front, where 90 percent of the death sentences were passed, John French was commander-in-chief from August 1914 to the end of 1915; thereafter, Field Marshal Douglas Haig occupied the position. That Haig confirmed the majority of the death sentences (253) has helped to fuel the popular representation of him as an uncaring and ruthless leader, the "Butcher of the Somme." Yet the fact that 90 percent of the death sentences passed were eventually commuted disputes this characterization.[42] Both French and Haig believed that executions were an effective punishment and that examples needed to be made. However, these views were not unique among contemporaries; they were suited to the context and beliefs of the time, products of the society from which they came. These men valued the death penalty in large measure because Great Britain valued it. Between 1900 and 1914, an average of twenty-seven death sentences were passed annually by the criminal courts of Great Britain, while an average of fifteen executions actually took place each year. In contrast, France had an average of five executions per year.[43] In Germany, by 1840, abolition of the death penalty was a topic of serious debate, and the punishment had ceased to be used for property crimes not involving homicide.[44]

In Canada, in 1914, the death penalty was accepted and practised in civilian society for the crimes of treason, rape, and murder. In the century before, the death penalty had undergone the significant transformation of moving from the public sphere to the private sphere through An Act Respecting Procedure in Criminal Cases, and Other Matters Relating to Criminal Law, 1869. This act mirrored a British law passed just one year before, and under it hangings disappeared from public squares and were moved inside prison walls, to be witnessed by a few select individuals, including a religious official of the condemned's choosing.[45] Still prior to 1961, all murder convictions resulted in an automatic sentence of death. However, the governor general of Canada, upon review and advice of the federal cabinet, had the power to practise the royal prerogative of mercy to commute any sentence of death to a term of life imprisonment.[46] Like the commander-in-chief, the governor general was not obliged to justify any decision to commute a death sentence. The process of issuing a royal prerogative of mercy closely resembled the process of confirmation in the CEF. Upon announcement of a death sentence, cabinet was called on to review all relevant information pertaining to the case and then to offer its recommendations to the governor general.[47]

As in the military, executions in civilian society were meant not only to punish but also to serve as an example severe enough to deter similar crimes and to maintain authority. Between 1914 and 1918, a total of forty-eight executions took place across Canada, almost double the number of executions that took place among members of the CEF on the western front during the same period. In addition to the forty-eight executions, there were sixty commuted death sentences.[48] Although these statistics clearly show that the chances of receiving a death sentence in civilian society might not have been as great as they were in the military during wartime, they also show that a civilian death sentence was less likely to be commuted.

A private member's bill to remove the death penalty from the Canadian Criminal Code was introduced in Parliament in 1914 by an MP for the riding of St. Lawrence, Quebec, Robert Bickerdike, but his attempt failed. He tried again in 1915, 1916, and 1917, yet he consistently met with little support. The death penalty would not be debated again in Parliament until 1924, when once again attempts at abolition failed after a free vote.[49] Bickerdike also voiced protest over use of the death penalty in the military. Writing on behalf of the National Prison Reform Association, he expressed his concerns in a 1918 letter to Sir Edward Kemp, minister of overseas military forces of Canada. He presented the association's concerns within the framework of Canadian autonomy, asserting that appeals for clemency should be decided by the government of Canada. Bickerdike was reassured by Kemp that, "although the death sentence is frequently imposed by courts-martial at the front, it is in rare instances carried into effect."[50] Undeterred, Bickerdike responded that "it is the old issue of

Canadian autonomy versus Whitehall government ... This Association is of [the] opinion that the people of Canada are justified in asking that their own Government shall have full jurisdiction over its subjects while engaged in warfare on foreign soil."[51] His arguments held little weight. An examination of parliamentary debates yields no evidence that there was any controversy over use of the death penalty in the military. Given that the Army Act had been voted into law by Parliament, and that it required annual approval, it is reasonable to suggest that the Canadian government was aware that the execution of volunteers was a distinct possibility. The lack of debate suggests that Canada's military and political leaders were comfortable with the laws as they were.[52]

Kemp's reassurance to Bickerdike that death sentences were rarely carried out is true. Ninety percent of death sentences were ultimately commuted to lesser punishments; however, though the rules for convening a court martial were clearly laid out in the *Manual of Military Law*, the requirements for sentencing were far more vague. As in the civilian legal system, guidelines for sentencing existed, but they directed only minimum and maximum punishments. Between these two poles lay much latitude for interpretation and leeway in sentencing. Furthermore, the *Manual of Military Law* directed that maximum punishments were to be used sparingly. As stated in Chapter 3 of the manual, "the punishments named in the Act for each particular offence are maximum punishments, and a maximum punishment is only intended to be imposed when the offence committed is the worst of its class, and is committed by an habitual offender, or is committed in circumstances which require an example to be made."[53] Although this maxim is clear, it fails to go any further in suggesting an appropriate system to determine lesser punishments. The 90 percent rate of commutation suggests that this guideline was widely applied by military authorities in the First World War, but there were exceptions to this rule. There were men who were not habitual offenders and whose crimes were not among the worst in their class but who nevertheless found themselves blindfolded and standing before a firing squad. The case of Frederick Stanley Arnold represents one such contradiction. Arnold, an American by birth, had seen previous service in the US Army before joining the First Brigade of the Canadian Field Artillery in 1914. He served at Festubert and Givenchy before being admitted to hospital for shell shock in January 1916. Upon discharge in June, Arnold went absent and was captured in plain clothes a few weeks later in Boulogne. He was found guilty of desertion and suffered death by shooting on 25 July. It was his first offence. His previously clean disciplinary record, and his desertion from hospital rather than a front-line position, leave many unanswered questions regarding confirmation of his death sentence. Although his civilian clothing was clear evidence of guilt, and the fact that Arnold deserted during the Battle of the Somme must be acknowledged, these two factors do not appear to be enough to override a clean disciplinary record and the other circumstances of the case, including a recent bout of confirmed shell shock.[54]

In the cases of commuted death sentences, standard punishments were inflicted, including hard labour, imprisonment (which could be served with or without hard labour), and penal servitude. According to the *Manual of Military Law,* a sentence of penal servitude required that the convicted be transferred to a special penal facility either in Great Britain or in a British colony, while a sentence of imprisonment could be served in military custody, in a detention barrack, in a public prison, or in a combination of these institutions.[55] While the options for punishment were consistent, its durations varied widely. In the cases of the commuted death sentences of Canadian soldiers, sentences ranged from two years of hard labour to fifteen years of penal servitude. Unlike civilian law, military law was not concerned with precedents. What took place at a court martial the previous year, last month, or the day before was of no relevance to the officers sitting in judgment. Members of the court martial were not obliged to consider precedents when determining guilt or innocence or handing down sentences. Furthermore, each court martial was different in its makeup, with different officers presiding over each trial. This factor made consistency in trials and punishments far more difficult to achieve.[56]

More often than not, sentences of penal servitude or imprisonment were further commuted in accordance with the *Field Service Regulations,* which stated that "officers confirming courts-martial should fully exercise their powers of commutation, so that the effective strength of the troops may be reduced as little as possible."[57] This power of commutation was further reinforced in 1915 with passage of the Suspension of Sentences Act. According to a 1918 report by the Ministry of Overseas Forces in Canada, the Suspension of Sentences Act was meant to "give men who had committed serious military offences, because of exhaustion, or their loss of courage or for other reasons, a chance to save their reputation and to win a remission of their sentences."[58] This act made it extremely unlikely for any soldier sentenced to a term of imprisonment or penal servitude to languish away in a military prison. Instead, a soldier's sentence was typically suspeded immediately after its announcement or within a few months. Upon suspension of a sentence, a soldier was reviewed every three months, at which time, if good conduct had not been maintained, a sentence could be reimposed. On the other hand, if a soldier showed good behaviour, or performed a deed of particular gallantry, his sentence could be reprieved. The Suspension of Sentences Act was more than an act of mercy toward soldiers; it also prevented the overcrowding of military prisons and managed to balance the military's two strongest needs – firm discipline and an ample supply of men for the front lines.

Thus, the topic to be pursued is not the relative justice or injustice of the court martial system. Court martial procedures were clearly laid out in the *Manual of Military Law*. However, while these principles were clear, their application was often confusing, and the outcomes of courts martial were not always clear. Which factors influenced the decision to carry out or to commute a death sentence? What made the authorities choose to sentence a man to two years of imprisonment with hard labour rather than ten years of penal servitude? These decisions, which often appear to have been arbitrary, show that the courts had little guidance on how to sentence a convicted soldier. Yet the irregularity in punishments also highlights the element of flexibility present in the military system of discipline. Although guidelines for military discipline might have seemed rigid, their application in fact proved that a range of punishments could be imposed by military authorities and that input on punishments was expected by the various levels of command.

Before one can begin to analyze the punishments handed down to Canadian soldiers during the First World War, and which factors might have distinguished a commuted from a confirmed death sentence, it is imperative to understand the crimes that these soldiers committed. Beyond the military's legal definitions of desertion and cowardice, it is helpful to understand the individual motivations behind these crimes. Why did Canadian soldiers risk their reputations and ultimately their lives in committing these capital offences? The vast majority of death sentences handed down in the Great War were for desertion. Only four Canadians received death sentences for the crime of cowardice, and of this number only one man, Dimitro Sinizki, was actually executed.[59] As stated in this chapter, the subjective nature of the crime of cowardice meant that officers were less inclined to seek charges for it. Yet every act of desertion carried with it the assumption of cowardice among military commanders, fellow soldiers, and even those on the home front.

3
The Crimes

IT IS A COMMON PERCEPTION that most deserters in the First World War left their units in the heat of battle – gripped by fear, a soldier panicked and refused to proceed over the top of the trench. This, however, was not the reality. Some soldiers deserted in these conditions, of course, but many others planned and carried out their escapes while their units were in rear areas and away from the intensity of shell fire, and yet others, without premeditation, simply seized opportunities for escape as they became available. During the First World War, a soldier's schedule revolved around periods of rest. The trench system was designed with four main areas: the front lines; the support trenches, 200 to 400 yards behind the front lines; the reserve trenches, another 800 to 1,000 yards back; and finally the rest billets. Soldiers spent four to six days in each section, proceeding from front to back, until completing and then beginning the cycle again.[1] In the case of commuted death sentences, there were only ten men whose records indicate that they deserted from front-line trenches; this number includes desertions during major engagements, such as Passchendaele.

Desertions were a more frequent occurrence behind the forward zones, with soldiers abandoning their units while in rear areas and rest billets. The records that I consulted indicate that it was most common for soldiers to disappear after being informed about duty, whether for a work party or for the front-line trenches. Soldiers either typically failed to present themselves for roll call or parade or seized opportunities to desert while their units were proceeding forward in the trenches. It was not uncommon for soldiers to claim in their defence that they did not know that orders had been given to proceed up the line.

Patrick Leo Doyle was a labourer from Belleville, Ontario, who enlisted for service in March 1916. Charged with desertion from the 2nd Battalion, he stated at his defence that he had received no order that his unit was proceeding to the trenches on 5 November 1917.[2] The battalion's war diary shows that orders were issued to proceed to the forward trenches at Wieltje, Belgium.[3] Instead of proceeding with his unit, Doyle made his way to a coffee stall, only to return to find that his unit had already left. He went on to say during his trial that he had attempted to find his unit but had eventually given up. He had been arrested at the transport lines without his equipment. Doyle was found guilty of desertion, and he received three recommendations in favour of commutation and one against. His death sentence was commuted to three years of penal servitude. Doyle survived the war and was demobilized on 24 April 1919.[4]

Like Doyle, Eugene Dubue claimed never to have received orders to proceed with a working party to the front. Dubue, a member of the 52nd Battalion, failed to join his unit at the Flanders front on 25 October 1917. He remained absent until he was apprehended by military police at Rouen, France, on 28 October. Although he was already serving a sentence of sixty days of field punishment number 1 at the time of his offence, and although all of his commanders agreed that his crime was committed deliberately, his death sentence was ultimately commuted to ten years of penal servitude. Dubue survived the war, and he was demobilized on 6 November 1919.[5] Why Doyle and Dubue failed to receive the same orders as the rest of their comrades was never made clear at their trials. In their defence, they gave no explanation for their alibis.

In addition to those soldiers who deserted while with their units, other men simply failed to return from leave. Soldiers on leave typically headed for London or Paris for much-needed rest and relaxation, but when their ten to fourteen days were up some made the decision not to board the train that would carry them back to the war. A diary entry from Corporal John Patrick Teahan of the First Hussars described London as being "overrun with Canadian soldiers (absent without leave) who are practically beggars." He went on to write that "some of them meet the trains begging for a few pence, even a copper is not despised and they have sold half their uniforms, it is not uncommon to see Canadians dressed in semi-military fashion with overalls, serge and bowler hat, or wearing a ragged smock instead of greatcoat."[6] In my research, a total of twelve men overstayed their leave passes only to be arrested, tried, and sentenced to death. The case of Arthur Anderson is typical. Anderson was a farmer from Parkside, Saskatchewan, before enlisting in the CEF in March 1916. He was granted leave to England on 30 November 1917 but failed to return to his unit on the specified date of 14 December. He was arrested by military police in Liverpool on 17 December when, dressed in plain clothes, he attempted to register at the Aliens Registration Office. Anderson faced a court martial in February 1918 and was handed a sentence of death for the crime of desertion. All of his superior officers recommended that his death sentence be commuted because of the high standard of discipline in the 46th Battalion and because, according to Lieutenant Colonel H.J. Dawson of the battalion, "owing to his employment as Batman, he had little or no opportunity of showing his worth in the frontline. For this reason I recommend that the award be commuted to such punishment as will afford this man an opportunity to retrieve himself."[7] The sentence was commuted to ten years of penal servitude. Anderson survived the war and was demobilized on 5 July 1919.[8]

Others who failed to return from leave were quick to blame alcohol for their behaviour. For example, Samuel Chapman of the 1st Canadian Divisional Train was granted leave in December 1915 but failed to report back to his unit and remained absent until his arrest in September 1916. At his court martial, Chapman cited both alcohol and fear of punishment as the reasons for his desertion: "While on leave I got drunk and did not mean to stay away, but when sober, and finding I had overstayed my leave, I was afraid to come back. I then took off my uniform and went to work at [illegible] in Scotland."[9] Chapman was found guilty of desertion, but despite the length of his absence his sentence was remitted to three years of penal servitude. He was demobilized on 10 July 1919.[10]

While soldiers such as Chapman expressed fear of military discipline, their actual knowledge of the military legal system and its possible punishments is difficult to measure. Although it was standard practice to read sections of the Army Act to soldiers on parade, they might have had conflicting views of military discipline depending on their own experiences of it and on the behaviours and subsequent responses that they witnessed in their own battalions. Every soldier likely knew someone who had disappeared for three days only to return to his battalion with tales of drunken revelry and another charge of absent without leave on his record. Yet soldiers might also have known of men who deserted for three days but failed to return immediately to their battalions. For these men, capture was followed by a period of detention in a cell as they waited to be brought up on charges of desertion at court martial. The accused soldier's mates would ultimately learn the fate of their comrade once he returned to his unit after being found innocent of his crime. Conversely, members of the battalion would learn the fate of the accused right along with him once he returned to his unit to await the news of a suspended sentence of death or, more chillingly, to hear his name called out during parade, informing the entire battalion of his impending execution for the crime of desertion. Experience did not necessarily indicate to soldiers how the crime of desertion would be handled. These inconsistencies might have further encouraged desertion. Armed with the knowledge that, if caught, they stood a good chance of being treated leniently, some soldiers might have found additional motivation to flee their duties.

This lack of consistency in sentencing not only affected front-line soldiers but also annoyed their commanders. Weak sentences that sent mixed signals to soldiers appear as frequent complaints in the recommendation letters of commanding officers. Commanders worried that, for many soldiers, the prospect of jail time was preferable to front-line service. Writing on the case of Alexander Daley, who was absent for one week in August 1917 before giving himself up at Camp Boulogne, Lieutenant Colonel G.F. McFarland of the 4th Canadian Mounted Rifles complained that "there have been numerous cases of absence without leave in this battalion, amounting to some cases of desertion, largely due, I believe, to the fact that sentences on former offenders have invariably been commuted or reduced."[11] Despite McFarland's complaint, and his description of Daley as "erratic and undependable," Daley's death sentence was commuted to fifteen years of penal servitude.[12] Daley survived the war and was demobilized on 29 April 1919.[13]

Whether real or feigned, this unawareness of possible consequences ultimately helped some soldiers to evade the firing squad. One only need consider the case of William Holmes of the 44th Battalion. He was found in a rear-area dugout when he was supposed to be at the front lines at Lievin on 24 August 1917. During his trial, Holmes told the court martial panel that, when given the order to proceed, he had no rifle, so he went to look for one. When he eventually began making his way to the front, Holmes stated, the shelling commenced, and he subsequently lost his nerve. He was eventually found in a dugout and arrested on 26 August.[14] Holmes was convicted of desertion and sentenced to death, but in recommending commutation Lieutenant Colonel R.D. Davies of the 44th Canadian Infantry Battalion wrote that "Pte Holmes is a young soldier and his action for which he was tried by FGCM is put down to lack of realization of the seriousness of the consequences and I do not consider the crime was deliberately committed."[15] As a result of such recommendations, his sentence was reduced to two years of hard labour and subsequently suspended.[16]

The case of William Holmes becomes more interesting in that it shows that, even with a full awareness of the consequences of their actions, some soldiers chose to continue to disobey military orders on the chance that they would receive lenient treatment. Following his initial suspended death sentence for desertion in August 1917, Holmes deserted his unit again just two months later. This time there could be no doubt that he knew the consequences of his actions. Holmes, along with Private Stephen Fowles, deserted the 44th Battalion on 23 October. Lieutenant Colonel R.D. Davies had reached his capacity for sympathy for Holmes by this time and for the crime of desertion. On 16 December, Davies wrote to Military Headquarters:

> The situation in the Battalion [44th], in regard to this particular crime [desertion], is very bad and in my opinion this condition is directly due to the fact that men are aware that the usual punishment for desertion amounts to nothing except several weeks under close arrest awaiting Court Martial ... Desertions have increased considerably in this Unit for the reasons above mentioned, and I would say, as Battalion Commander, that it is most disheartening, after making every effort to bring men to realize the necessity for good discipline, to have cases such

as the one in point, where a man is able to openly defy authority, feeling secure against punishment. The exemplary power of one single Death sentence carried out would, in my opinion, absolutely stop desertion, but I submit, with due respect, that the continuance of the present methods of dealing with this crime will, without doubt result not, perhaps, in desertion becoming very much more frequent but that in every case where a man becomes nervous in the line desertion will be the outcome.[17]

Despite Davies's strong recommendation for execution, Holmes's death sentence was once again reduced to a sentence of fifteen years of penal servitude. Holmes survived the war and was demobilized on 3 October 1919.[18]

Cases such as that of Holmes prove that, while many soldiers might have been ignorant of the consequences of absenting their units, many others were fully aware of the potential risks yet calculated their odds and thought that desertion was a risk worth taking. While assigned to work as a provost, John Patrick Teahan wrote in his diary that

yesterday I was Provost again and had 16 prisoners handed over to me. Most of them were up for absence without leave. The interesting ones were the old soldiers who had as many as four or five charges against them at one time. Their line of conversation was good. Real good. Some of them frankly stated that they intended to cut up capers until the RCDs [Royal Canadian Dragoons] got so sick of them that [they] would be given their papers – or as one fellow put it, an eight dollar suit and a ticket to Toronto![19]

In an interesting side note, historian Jonathan Vance has argued that, for a particular group of men in the CEF, desertion might not even have been considered a crime. His research has shown that forestry units in the CEF experienced high rates of desertion. However, according to the code of behaviour for this particular group of men, they might not have viewed leaving one's unit as desertion so much as seeking better job opportunities. The men who served in forestry units were those who worked as loggers in civilian life. They were accustomed to a transient existence in which jobs were easily taken up and left based on better offers and better pay. Deserters from the forestry corps likely did not see themselves as cowards or deserters. While they might have been accused of betraying the ideals of patriotism, they had enlisted for economic reasons, and they viewed their jobs in the CEF just like any other job in a logging camp or sawmill.[20] Despite the high rates of desertion, no man from a forestry unit was ever handed a death sentence for this crime during the First

World War. These men were likely treated more leniently than front-line soldiers simply because in their roles it was less imperative that the strong example of an execution be set.

While the men of the forestry units might have had specific reasons for their high rates of desertion, the motivations of the majority of other soldiers in the CEF for the crime of desertion were both internal and external. Internal motivations included individual responses to war, whether they were psychological or physical, and other circumstances that affected a soldier and might have caused him to shirk his responsibilities. External motivations included issues that might have affected more than the individual. Even though desertion was ultimately an individual act, the problem to which a soldier was responding might have affected the entire battalion, such as failures in leadership or the breakdown of esprit de corps.

The reasons for desertion were undoubtedly varied and often complex. It is insufficient to sum up these men in general terms such as "shirkers," a common term during the Great War for men who neglected to fulfill their duties. The majority of men who received a death sentence for either desertion or cowardice in the war were early enlisters. A total of 135 of these men had enlisted by 1915.[21] No conscripted man ever received a death sentence for a military crime. Furthermore, these men enlisted prior to the lowering of standards for physical and mental abilities. Early in the war, the CEF was in a position to demand that its men pass a stringent medical exam, which included looking for healthy teeth, good eyesight, and arched feet. Men were required to be between the ages of eighteen and forty-five and to stand at least five foot three inches tall with a chest measurement of thirty-three and a half inches. Healthy men, and those with previous military service, were the first to be recruited.[22]

By 1916, affected by growing casualty lists and a diminishing pool of recruits, enlistment lagged. In order to combat the problem and to meet manpower needs, the army significantly lowered its standards and readily accepted men who had no chance of meeting the physical or mental requirements of 1914. The result was that by 1916 Canada was sending men overseas who were more prone to physical and mental breakdowns, and potential disciplinary problems, including at least an estimated 700 men who were released from prison in order to join the CEF.[23]

Although most of the men whom I studied enlisted early in the war, both Melville Franklin Orr and Arthur Thorne offer good contrasts as men who were accepted into the ranks in 1916 even though their ailments might have prevented them from joining earlier. Orr, a plumber from Cornwall, Ontario, was found guilty of desertion from the 2nd Battalion in October 1917 after leaving the trenches near Lens. Six days later he gave himself up to authorities at a billet located four miles from the front-line trenches. During his defence, Orr claimed not to have remembered where he was going when he left the trenches, but he also claimed that he had suffered from these bouts of memory loss, as well as hearing loss, prior to his enlistment. His medical history contained in his personnel file backs up this claim. Records indicate that "[Orr] had measles, whooping cough, scarlet fever. Has had trouble with throat, nose and ears since birth and underwent four operations for these troubles."[24] Given this medical history, it is unlikely that Orr would have been accepted into the ranks prior to 1916.[25]

Likewise, in spite of substandard eyesight and lateral curvature of the spine from a prior injury, Arthur Thorne, a cook from Winnipeg, was able to enlist in the 101st Battalion in 1916. Afflicted with back pain during service, Thorne, at some point during the war, discovered that opium eased the pain. He developed an addiction that might have contributed to his desertion in November 1917 when he, now serving with the 16th Battalion, left the Gravenstafel area near Passchendaele after his unit was ordered to relieve the 42nd Battalion. Thorne was later arrested by military police near St. Pol on 16 December. He was found guilty of desertion; however, in recommending commutation of his death sentence, Brigadier General G.S. Tuxford of the Third Canadian Infantry Brigade wrote that "I do not consider that his action has been of deliberate desertion, but from the evidence of the Medical Officer, may have been influenced by the use of opium."[26] Based on Tuxford's reasoning, as well as on the high standard of discipline in the 16th Battalion, Thorne's death sentence was commuted to seven years of penal servitude. Thorne returned to service but was killed in action on 1 October 1918 in an attack on Cuvillers.[27]

Because the majority of court martialled men came from the early pool of recruits, yet their crimes were committed in 1917, it can be convincingly argued that desertions had far more to do with prolonged periods of military service than with inherent flaws in the characters of the men. Although some men were simply prone to bad behaviour, most had more likely simply reached their limits of withstanding the rigours of warfare. As famously stated by Lord Moran in *The Anatomy of Courage,* courage is available in limited stocks. In 1945, Lord Moran, a medical officer in the First World War and later Winston Churchill's personal physician, wrote that

> courage is will-power, whereof no man has an unlimited stock; and when in war it is used up, he is finished. A man's courage is his capital and he is always spending. The call on the bank may be only the daily drain of the front line or it may be a sudden draft which threatens to close the account. His will is perhaps almost destroyed by intensive shelling, by heavy bombing, or by a bloody battle, or it is

gradually used up by the monotony, by exposure, by the loss of support of stauncher spirits on whom he has come to depend, by physical exhaustion, by a wrong attitude to danger, to casualties, to war, to death itself.[28]

Most deserters whom I studied had seen over a year of service and had been engaged in some of the war's most bitter battles. Their own statements of defence give clear signs of exhaustion. William John Fletcher was one example of a good soldier who had simply burned out. Before his enlistment in 1915, he was an electrician in Kelowna, British Columbia. His clean disciplinary record shows that he dutifully served in the 29th Battalion until he was accused of desertion while on duty with a carrying party on 7 May 1917. The battalion's war diary for the period indicates that the unit underwent a period of sustained shelling, including the day on which Fletcher fled. Only one day earlier the unit's diarist had recorded "the men beginning to show strain of continual bombardment."[29] Fletcher surrendered himself to the authorities on 8 September 1917. Before this crime, he was regarded as a good soldier. He had enlisted when only seventeen years old and had served at the Somme and the Battle of Vimy Ridge. Fletcher seems to have struggled with exhaustion and nerves for some time before he finally deserted. A fellow soldier described him as having nerves that were "all wrong," going on to say that "he would sometimes cry when out on sentry."[30] Captain G.J. Caldwell noted at the trial that, "when he [Fletcher] first came to us he was quite an efficient soldier. After a few trips I noticed quite a change. He became very nervous and his nerves seemed to have gone to pieces. He was the same in and out of the line. He gave up going out with the other boys."[31] In an attempt to explain his actions, Fletcher stated that "at the Somme I was buried by shells three times ... On the night of the 7th of May I was feeling very nervous before I went up. Every shell that came near us made me feel sick. I tried to stick it out."[32] Clearly, Fletcher was not a bad soldier or one who tried to rebel against military authority; he was simply a mentally exhausted young man who had reached his personal limit. He was found guilty of desertion and sentenced to death, receiving two recommendations for execution and two against it, based in part on his youth and previous good character. His death sentence was commuted to five years of penal servitude. Fletcher survived the war without physical injury and was demobilized on 30 July 1919.[33]

Like Fletcher, many soldiers suffered from the extreme psychological hardships of warfare. These mental strains were manifested in myriad ways, and some men chose extreme measures in order to escape from their circumstances. Self-inflicted wounds were one example of desperate behaviour. During the First World War, 729 Canadians, including three men discussed in this book, inflicted damage on their own bodies in order to escape from active service.[34]

This number likely represents only a minority of the attempts. Many more cases were probably not recorded at all or were recorded as legitimate injuries. Desertion was a more common response to the strains of warfare. In the entire British Expeditionary Force, there were 7,371 courts martial for the crime of desertion in the field, with a total of 2,004 death sentences and 272 executions.[35] In the CEF specifically, there were 203 death sentences passed for desertion, including the twenty-two that were actually carried out. Among the executed men, the medical records of only one man, Frederick Stanley Arnold, indicate treatment for shell shock, while the records of Leopold Delisle and Stephen Fowles give evidence of possible symptoms, specifically convulsions and mutism.[36] In the commuted cases, twenty-seven men claimed that shell shock had been the motivating factor in their decisions to desert, but of this number the medical records of only six men indicate neurasthenia, shell shock, or symptoms associated with the condition. Of course, simply because medical records fail to record shell shock is no proof that the condition did not exist. The term "shell shock" was both misunderstood and ill used by doctors and patients, and many men might not have been properly diagnosed. It is also likely that a number of men failed to report their symptoms to authorities because they did not recognize the seriousness of the problem or for any number of other reasons, including shame. Beginning in 1917, in an effort to deal with the mounting cases before them and the potential consequences for military success, medical officers in the field were instructed by the British Army in France to label any probable case of shell shock as "NYD" or "not yet diagnosed" until the soldier could be assessed by a specialist in the field of neurology or psychiatry. The term "shell shock" was no longer to be used by ordinary medical officers.

Just as a medical record that fails to indicate shell shock cannot be taken as absolute, so too the same reasoning holds for one that does. It is important to distinguish between an actual case of shell shock and what should be more properly understood as the natural inclination toward self-preservation that might have prompted men to absent themselves or desert. It is estimated that nine thousand officers and men of the CEF were diagnosed with shell shock during the First World War.[37] Knowledge of shell shock, or what is now referred to as battle exhaustion or combat stress reaction, grew dramatically during the Great War.

The term first became part of the lexicon in 1915. In that year, Charles S. Myers of the Royal Army Medical Corps (RAMC) published an article in *The Lancet* describing the condition as he witnessed it in three soldiers:

> They appear to constitute a definite class among others arising from the effects [of] shell-shock. The shells in question appear to have burst with considerable

noise, scattering much dust, but this was not attended by the production of odour. It is therefore difficult to understand why hearing should be (practically) unaffected, and the disassociated "complex" be confined to the senses of sight, smell and taste (and to memory). The close relation of these cases to those of "hysteria" appears fairly certain.[38]

During this early period, the condition was believed to be brought on by the actual explosions of shells. It was thought that artillery fire and proximity to bursting shells traumatically affected the nervous system and debilitated the senses. Doctors speculated about the exact cause, some hypothesizing that tiny particles from exploding shells injured the brain, while others blamed the explosive gases contained within the shells. By 1916, as more cases of shell shock were observed, it was frequently reported that the condition was occurring in soldiers who had not experienced direct contact with shell fire. These cases became the centre of interest to both military officers and doctors forced to determine whether their accounts amounted to malingering or a new type of mental illness produced by prolonged warfare rather than a purely physical shock to the body.

As Tom Brown notes in his article "Shell Shock in the Canadian Expeditionary Force, 1914-1918: Canadian Psychiatry in the Great War," as the war carried on, it became more obvious that most cases of shell shock had not been caused by physical proximity to shell explosions but could be likened more to a diagnosis of hysteria or neurasthenia, which had become more common in civilian life in the early twentieth century. While for civilians these conditions could be linked to any number of stresses, for soldiers the conditions seemed to be brought on by the constant threat of death and the increasingly mechanized nature of warfare that often left individuals without the opportunity to respond to attacks.[39] Artillery fire, one of the biggest killers of the war, simply had to be endured while in the trenches or during a march. There were few means of defence against its high-pitched sounds and random landings designed to obliterate men. Artillery fire kept assailants from view and erased the opportunity to defend oneself by hand-to-hand combat or by firing a rifle at a visible enemy. Exhausted men, forced to deal with the sights and sounds of combat, a steady stream of death, constant fear, tension, and uncertainty, simply reached their limits and responded with the various symptoms known collectively as shell shock. These symptoms included, but were not limited to, extreme anxiety, facial tics or uncontrollable shaking of the body, nightmares, and mutism.

By 1918, in response to greater awareness of the condition, the term "shell shock" was replaced by the more accurate term "war neurosis" by psychiatrists and others in the medical community. Acceptance of the condition did not come as quickly for many in the military, including some front-line doctors.

For these men, dealing with every imaginable consequence of war, it was difficult at times to accept that a wound could be inflicted without physical injury to the body. For military officers, shell shock was as much a disciplinary issue as it was a health issue. Many officers believed that shell shock was simply an acceptable term for cowardice, and they feared that, if legitimized, the excuse might spread through entire battalions.

This conflict between discipline and health had serious implications for soldiers in the field. Following the 1917 decision to put the label of "shell shock" into the hands of specialists in the field of neurology or psychiatry, soldiers diagnosed as shell shocked underwent further classification using a "W" or an "S." A soldier who exhibited symptoms of shell shock in the immediate aftermath of battle or from proximity to shell explosions received a "W" for "shell shock (wounded)" on his medical report, a designation that granted him a wound stripe. Soldiers who exhibited their symptoms later, away from the immediate impacts of shell explosions, were designated an "S" for "shell shock (sickness)" and were not entitled to wear wound stripes on their arms.

The military attempted to treat shell shock with several methods. For the lucky ones, typically officers of a higher social class, a rest-cure at a country estate allowed them ample rest and a return to nature as a means to restore their sanity. For privates, treatment was more hurried and designed to encourage a speedy return to the front lines. Popular treatments included hypnosis and electroshock therapy. While hypnosis coerced soldiers back to health through suggestive persuasion, electroshock therapy forced them to overcome symptoms such as mutism or body tics through the application of pain.[40]

By 1916, just as the true meaning of shell shock was falling out of favour among the medical community, the term itself was becoming widely known and used among the men of the CEF. With a proper name, fear not only became more acceptable but also more common. As a consequence, claims of shell shock not only became pervasive in the medical tents but also at courts martial. Although some claims were obviously legitimate, others were not.

For example, at his 1916 trial for desertion, Peter Bodnarchuk of the 1st Battalion explained his four-day desertion from Courcelette by stating that "after the shell broke near my dugout I felt shell-shocked and didn't know what I was doing nor where I was going. I did not ask permission to leave the trench."[41] The next day Bodnarchuk reported sick, and his records indicate that he was feeling better by the next morning. He was found guilty of desertion in October 1916, but his death sentence was commuted to five years of penal servitude.[42] Bodnarchuk might not have fully understood the condition of shell shock, but by 1916 he was familiar enough with the term to use it in his own defence. He certainly might have suffered a brief physical shock, yet his condition did not resemble the sustained symptoms associated with shell shock. Bodnarchuk returned to service and eventually died of gunshot wounds to his legs, arms, and head sustained near the trenches near Loos on 29 July 1917.[43]

Contrast his case with that of Robert Campbell of the 1st Canadian Field Artillery and we can understand the distinction between these two conditions. Campbell, a steamfitter from Kingston, Ontario, was first diagnosed with shell shock after serving at Ypres in April 1915. Although described as "nervous" in his medical record, he was returned to duty. While serving at Courcelette in 1916, he was buried three times by shell explosions within two weeks. Under the circumstances, he simply cracked. The term "shell shock" is clearly written across his medical record, and his noted symptoms included general weakness and nervousness, hand tremors, insomnia, and memory loss. In June 1917, a medical board stated about Campbell that "after twenty two months in firing line and with his age [thirty-seven] this man has just worn out."[44] He was eventually discharged as medically unfit.[45]

As for the medical evidence given at a court martial, according to *The King's Regulations and Orders for the Army*, an accused soldier was to be assessed by a medical officer on each day of his court martial.[46] However, by all accounts, this does not appear to have been the protocol followed. Available evidence indicates that medical reviews were called for only when shell shock was used as a defence or testimony indicated that it was a contributing factor to the offence. Even in some cases in which these factors were present, it does not appear that medical exams were ordered. In the cases in which medical officers were present, they were called on to deliver expert opinion on the state of the accused's psychological health or to provide confirmation of physical illness used as a defence. Medical officers had an extremely important role in the military judicial system, but they were in a precarious position because they were mandated to look after the needs of the patient while also considering the need of the military for manpower. Among the commuted cases in my research, twenty-seven men claimed to have been suffering from the effects of shell shock when they deserted their units, while twenty-eight men claimed to have been ill. There is evidence in eighteen cases showing that medical officers were present at the trials.[47] That they were not present at each court martial is a fact that should be assessed in context. Medical officers on the western front were already overstretched in dealing with what the army considered to be the more pressing needs of the physically wounded. In many cases, members of the medical corps simply did not have the time to attend courts martial or examine the mental state of a soldier accused of deserting his comrades. Describing the exhausting pace of his work, William Boyd of the RAMC wrote in his journal in March 1915, following the fighting at Neuve Chapelle,

> I have spent the greater part of the day at a dressing-station attending to the wounded who were being brought in straight from the trenches. The fighting at Neuve Chapelle has, of course, been desperate in the extreme, and during the last three days an incessant stream of wounded has been pouring through this dressing-station. Several of our officers have, therefore, been detailed to assist the ambulance people who were ready to drop in their places from utter exhaustion, and we started on our duties this morning ... The dressing-station was formerly a school, and every room was so packed with wounded, lying on stretchers on the floor, that it was with the greatest difficulty that we could move about. It was literally almost impossible to put your foot down without treading on a wounded man.[48]

Three years later the pace of work had not slowed down. Commenting on the opening days of the Battle of Amiens in August 1918, A.E. Snell of the Canadian Army Medical Corps (CAMC) wrote that "during the 8th and 9th [of August] the entire personnel worked at top speed, but in spite of all efforts a great congestion of wounded occurred."[49] In total, from 8 to 20 August, 7,763 wounded Canadians were evacuated from the front to casualty clearing stations.[50]

Given these circumstances, it is hardly surprising that at times medical exams were left out of the judicial process. Such exams were time-consuming for a system of justice meant to deal with crimes quickly and in the field, and it was a lot to ask of already overburdened doctors. The fact that a medical exam was not given for every soldier who faced a court martial does not indicate a gross miscarriage of justice. More problematic is that medical exams were not given consistently in cases in which shell shock was a probable factor. The reasons for these inconsistencies are unknown and likely vary. One possible reason was that in the First World War shell shock was not understood by medical or military authorities in the same way that it is today. To fault members of courts martial for this would be to displace our own knowledge onto the past. The lack of medical exams when required might also have been due to the individual wills of officers of the courts martial, wishing to hurry the process along. This deliberate disregard for relevant evidence is far more problematic, and it is what leaves the military judicial system open to modern criticisms and accusations of injustice. However, when faced with the choice of delaying a court martial to wait for the testimony of a medical officer, or proceeding while all other witnesses were in place, commanding officers might have chosen the latter option, believing it to be in the best interests of everyone involved, including the accused. In cases in which claims of shell shock or illness were supported by nothing more than the testimony of the accused, the importance of having a medical officer present at trial was negated.

Any lack of concern for issues of mental health in relation to military crimes might be better understood when given more context. Although the civilian criminal justice system might have been somewhat more advanced when it came to understanding the relationship between mental health and crime, popular opinion still lagged in the early twentieth century. By the 1880s, the opinions of physicians with expertise in issues of mental competence were a regular part of capital cases in the criminal justice system. However, the testimony of these experts was not always accepted by juries. Legal historian Carolyn Strange has stated that "Canadian juries were generally reluctant to accept the defence of insanity, even after the popularization of psychoanalysis in the 1950s and '60s."[51] With this bias in mind, the federal cabinet had made it a common procedure by the 1920s to consult the opinions of psychiatrists when determining confirmation or commutation of a death sentence; this was especially true in cases in which prior defences of insanity had failed to convince juries.[52]

In addition to mental fatigue, the body wore down under the strains of trench life and war. At times, illness was feigned. Malingerers, soldiers who concocted illnesses in order to get out of their duties, were a real problem during the war. B.J. Murdoch, a chaplain in the CEF, recalled in his memoirs that

> the soldiers called them "lead swingers." The ingenuity of some of these men was really extraordinary. I have seen a case come through three or four different posts, diagnosed as measles, until finally the doctor in the stationary hospital saw that the man had used a preparation of some oil to bring out the rash, and had raised his temperature with cordite.[53]

Yet, despite the malingerers, illness was a legitimate reality of trench life as well as an expression of free agency among soldiers. Illness could be a show of decision making in a world where men experienced little control over their day-to-day lives. Men determined when they were ill and decided on their own to fall out of a march or visit a medical tent. For example, Malcolm Selig, a soldier with the 13th Battalion, stated that he was feeling sick and asked permission to fall out of line while proceeding with a work party up to the front in January 1916. His request was refused, but he chose to fall out anyway. As a consequence, he found himself charged with desertion. Selig was found guilty and received a death sentence, subsequently commuted to ten years of penal servitude. He later served at the Somme, where he sustained a gunshot wound to the hip.[54] A total of twenty-eight men among the commuted cases cited physical illness as the reason for leaving their units. In some cases, the defence was wholly legitimate and corroborated by medical authorities at the trials; in other cases, the excuses were dismissed as just that – excuses.

At times, medical authorities could seem harsh in their diagnoses since they were forced to walk a fine line between looking after the health of men and keeping a steady supply returning to the front lines. Frederick de Bentley Corry of the 2nd Canadian Tunnelling Company was absent from roll call when his unit was ordered to proceed to the trenches on 12 July 1916. He was eventually found in a doctor's waiting room and ordered under arrest. At the trial for desertion later that month, Captain W.W. Turner of the RAMC confirmed that Corry had been "suffering from eruption of skin on the genitals" and "nervousness," yet he went on to state that there was no reason why Corry was not fit for duty.[55] Corry disputed this judgment, and stated in his defence, "I would not risk the chance of losing money and getting punishment for the sake of evading twelve hours work, if I could have walked up."[56] He was found guilty of desertion and sentenced to death. His sentence was commuted to ten years of penal servitude, and he was eventually discharged in February 1918 as medically unfit because of neurasthenia.[57] Corry's diagnoses might seem harsh now, but in the words of Sir Andrew MacPhail, author of the official history of the medical services in the First World War, "the medical officer was bewildered in his attempt to hold the balance between injustice to the individual and disregard for the needs of the service."[58]

Aside from issues of mental and physical health, a number of other personal reasons caused men to desert. A death in the family or any comparable misfortune at home caused many men to reach their breaking points and prompted some to leave without proper permission, which would have likely been denied in any case. Joseph Ellison of the 18th Battalion failed to return from leave after making the decision to remain in England, where he had found his brother, who had been discharged from the Canadian Convalescent Hospital at Uxbridge as incurable. Ellison decided to stay with his brother while he died and to suffer the potential consequences brought on by a charge of desertion. He surrendered to authorities on 4 June 1916. Although he was court martialled and found guilty of desertion, his death sentence was subsequently commuted to five years of penal servitude. Ellison returned to service and was eventually demobilized on 12 July 1919.[59]

Sad was the case of Alexander Daley, who left his unit because he simply felt unwanted. Explaining his desertion, he stated in his defence that

> the reason I left the battalion was because I was not getting a fair deal from the rest of the boys. They kept telling me that I should have been out of the battalion long ago. They told me that I should have stayed at home and would have been better out of the battalion all together. I am twenty-two years of age and all alone in the world and have no near relative. I never knew when my parents died. I

never really knew my father. I never went to school except for one month. I came to England with the 154th Battalion and have been in France ten months. I have always tried to be a soldier and keep out of trouble.[60]

Daley refused to call character witnesses at his trial, so without more information it is impossible to know why he was viewed as such an outsider among his fellow soldiers. Was there something inherently unlikeable about him? Did his own actions make him untrustworthy among his fellow soldiers? Research indicates that Daley had a difficult upbringing, which might have made it difficult for him to fit in with other soldiers. His discharge papers list his intended residence as St. George's House in Ottawa, Ontario, a Catholic institution run by the Sisters of Charity, who were charged with the care of orphaned children. It appears that Daley was raised in this institution. The only other information that can be gathered regarding him comes from the recommendation letters of his commanders, which were consistently unflattering. For example, Major General Louis Lipsett of the 3rd Canadian Division described Daley as "a man of low mind development."[61] His own disciplinary record also reveals very little information, showing only that before his charge of desertion Daley had one charge of absence without leave and losing equipment by neglect, a crime that cost him fourteen days of field punishment number 1.[62] In light of the information, it is impossible to know whether Daley deserved his poor reputation among his unit or whether his inability to fit in made him a vulnerable and easy target when an example needed to be made in a poorly disciplined unit.

Finally, for some soldiers, desertion was apparently not motivated by much more than bad behaviour. John O'Brien of the 4th Battalion freely admitted at his court martial that "it was not that I did not want to go into the trenches that I went absent, but I wanted to have a good time."[63] Despite his record, which included four previous charges of absence without leave and drunkenness, his death sentence was commuted to ten years of penal servitude on 24 March 1916. O'Brien returned to service and went on to receive a gunshot wound to his face while at Courcelette in October 1916. He survived the injury and was demobilized on 4 April 1919.[64]

The case of John Hannan of the 13th Battalion is interesting in that at his court martial for desertion in January 1918 he claimed that he had not been given his rightful leave and had thus deserted. Hannan had not received leave during his three years in the CEF and linked his desertion to what he thought was unjust treatment by military authorities. At his trial, a member of the RAMC stated of Hannan that "he is nursing what he believes to be a grievance, in that though he is one of the original members of the Battalion and has been nearly three years in France, he has not yet had leave. He recognizes however that his leave has been fairly stopped owing to his crimes."[65] Prior to this particular court martial in January 1918, Hannan had an extensive disciplinary record that included seven charges of absence, three of which had brought him before a field general court martial. Although Hannan attempted to use his defence to protest against his unfair treatment by army authorities, in light of his previous record his point carried little weight. His desertion had been precipitated by his desire to run from duty rather than a desire to register his complaints against the military system. Hannan was sentenced to death on 21 January, but in spite of his record his death sentence was commuted to ten years of penal servitude. He was eventually killed in action on 8 August 1918 during the Amiens offensive at Hangard Wood.[66]

Although many crimes were internally motivated, the crime of desertion was just as often motivated by external factors. Desertion could be an expression of dissatisfaction with the army system or the running of the war. Functioning of the army was dependent on an unwritten social contract between soldiers and their commanders. From soldiers, officers expected obedience, diligence, respect, and ultimately a willingness to give their lives if need be. Soldiers enlisted with the expectation that the army would take care of their personal and material well-being. This included the provision of necessary food rations and arms as well as creature comforts such as cigarettes, rum, the regular delivery of letters from the home front, and the promise of leave. Furthermore, entertainments such as *estaminets,* organized sports, and trench newspapers were also crucial in maintaining morale among soldiers during their downtime. These expectations were especially true of the citizen armies of the First World War. Volunteers during the war came from all segments of society, not only the poor or marginalized, and therefore on the whole soldiers had greater political awareness coupled with higher expectations. No longer was regimental loyalty sufficient in sustaining morale. Commanders of the Great War well understood this new reality and the positive relationship between high morale and discipline. Writing in June 1916, Brigadier General Reginald John Kentish of the BEF noted that morale, and thus discipline, would suffer if

1 The men, when resting from the trenches, are overstrained and overworked. This is a very common practice today, and is in my opinion, the chief destroyer of moral[e].
2 When men are not paid regularly.
3 When the men do not receive their bath and clean change of clothes regularly.

4   When the officers do not see that their amusements are not well catered for.
5   When the Commanding Officer fails to address and lecture weekly to his Battalion as a whole, and his Officers and N.C.O.s separately on every subject, confronting them and us today.
6   When the men are neglected.[67]

Thus, every commanding officer had a responsibility to the soldiers under his charge. Paternalism dominated officer-man relations in the First World War, and this quality helped to sustain morale in the British forces throughout the war. Commanding officers were directed to achieve "discipline that is born of mutual confidence between Officers and men" more than through a fear of punishment.[68]

But expectations from soldiers extended much further. They wanted leadership from their officers; they fully expected their leaders to show bravery in the face of danger and to lift their spirits and inspire them to action in dire circumstances. They also desired respect and expected that their lives would not be foolishly wasted. Officers in the Canadian Corps were instructed in their training that "leadership must be courageous, not reckless ... Don't foolishly throw your lives away, and don't foolishly throw your men's lives away."[69] Although every soldier understood that there was always a risk of death in war, they also expected that the risk would be fully calculated and that their lives would not be wasted on foolhardy schemes. When this unwritten contract fell apart, so did discipline. This theory was shown most convincingly by Leonard V. Smith in *Between Mutiny and Obedience*. Using the example of the Fifth Infantry Division of the French Army, Smith showed that the French mutinies of 1917 were rooted in the concept of proportionality. He contended that these mutinies were not simply outbursts of bad behaviour but political demonstrations by soldiers unwilling to participate in futile battles. They wanted their sacrifices to be proportional to the gains. The French were willing to keep fighting – but under reformed circumstances.[70] Although there were no major mutinies in the CEF during wartime, the same sentiments were expressed at times through individual acts of desertion.

Thus, good discipline arose out of good leadership, and an officer who could neither enforce nor inspire discipline risked the loss of legitimacy among his men. Good leadership is what sustained men in the tense weeks leading up to a major engagement and in the periods of reorganization and emotional strain following major losses in battle. There might be no better example than the contrast between Lieutenant Colonel Thomas-Louis Tremblay and Major Arthur-Édouard Dubuc. In September 1916, the 5th Brigade played a major role at the Battle of Courcelette on the Somme. Although the village of Courcelette was captured, the victory came at the cost of thousands of casualties, including the temporary loss of the 22nd Battalion's revered commander, Tremblay, who was forced to return to England for medical treatment. He was a highly respected soldier both among his superiors and among those whom he commanded. During his leadership, he earned the confidence and love of his men. Reminiscing on his qualities, W.R. Lindsay, formerly of the 22nd Battalion, said of Tremblay, "he was a wonderful man. If we had a bombardment we would see Tremblay in the front line, every time ... Oh yes, Tremblay was a wonderful man. He knew what to say to the boys. He was cool, he was calm, he never was frightened."[71]

Assigned to replace Tremblay was Major Arthur-Édouard Dubuc, who lacked Tremblay's superior leadership qualities. Dubuc failed to win the hearts of his men, and in the weeks following Courcelette he allowed the morale of the unit to fall apart and indiscipline to prevail. Dubuc failed to rein in deserters, and, upon his return to the unit in February 1917, Tremblay felt compelled to crack down on the problem by demanding a rash of executions to serve as a deterrent and to resuscitate morale.[72] In total, the 22nd Battalion received twenty-one death sentences for desertion, and five men were executed. Although in the past it was suggested that these executions were the result of bias against French Canadians, the evidence shows that they happened largely because of the advocacy of Tremblay, himself a French Canadian.

Just as damaging as poor leadership was the lack of steady leadership. The commonly held assumption that officers in the First World War stayed far behind the lines holed up in French chateaus is simply false. Describing the duties of an officer, historian Desmond Morton writes that

> they gave leadership, took responsibility, and set an example, if necessary, by dying. Officers were middle managers, transmitting the often inscrutable and sometimes absurd orders of their superiors; investing them with their own personalities; and convincing soldiers to obey, even at the near-certain cost of their own lives. Implicit was the assumption that the officer would be the first to die in battle. Officers were the first out of the trench in an assault or a night patrol, and the last out in a retreat.[73]

This reality is clearly reflected in the statistics. A total of 21,616 officers served in the CEF, of whom 2,989 died, a death rate of 13.8 percent compared with a rate of 9.5 percent among other ranks in the CEF during the war.[74] The deaths of commanders caused an instability that weighed heavily on soldiers. The resulting inconsistencies in leadership, and the replacement of experienced officers with younger men rushed through the ranks, undoubtedly lowered morale and fostered indiscipline. Commanders were fully aware of this effect, but given the conditions of war they had few available means to stop it. Commenting on the desertion of Pliny John Fetterley in June 1917, Brigadier General James MacBrien of the 12th Canadian Infantry Brigade wrote that "the discipline in the 38th Battalion during the past few months has not been good and has been caused, it is thought, by heavy casualties, particularly in experienced officers. Eight cases of desertion have occurred in this battalion during the past 2½ months."[75] In spite of his admission that external factors might have led to Fetterley's desertion from the trenches during the spring of 1917, MacBrien was unyielding in recommending that Fetterley be shot as an example to his fellow soldiers. It was a weak solution to the problem of desertion and failed to address a root cause of the issue over which MacBrien had no control. Despite his recommendation, Fetterley's sentence of death was commuted to fifteen years of penal servitude. Fetterley returned to active service but suffered a gunshot wound to his arm on 5 September 1918. He was eventually discharged as medically unfit.[76]

Just as casualties among officers impacted rates of desertion, so too did heavy losses among the ranks. Major losses inevitably led to indiscipline since reinforcements folded into existing battalions were often unfamiliar with the unit's standards of discipline. As the war dragged on, new reinforcements lacked the quality of training of their predecessors. Commenting on the desertion in October 1917 of Alexander Sokol, who had fled following an order to move to the support trenches, Lieutenant Colonel R.D. Davies of the 44th Canadian Infantry Battalion wrote that, "in the past three months, heavy drafts have been received from England and the morale of the men received is much lower than obtained amongst our original men. Where these drafts arrive shortly before the unit goes into action there is little time to impress on new men the serious aspect of shirking duty in the line."[77] In his defence, Sokol claimed that he had not been aware that his battalion was moving up the line and had not known what the term "forward area" meant. In spite of these claims, he was found guilty of desertion and received two recommendations that the death penalty be carried out. Mercy was shown, though, and his death sentence was commuted to ten years of penal servitude. Sokol survived the war and was demobilized on 23 July 1919.[78]

The problems that Lieutenant Colonel Davies experienced with reinforcements in the 44th Battalion were not unique. Similar frustrations were experienced among a number of battalions. Lieutenant Colonel Arthur Murray Jarvis, the assistant provost marshal of the 2nd Canadian Division, expressed concerns about the quality of reinforcements being received in 1917.[79] Dismayed by the wilful disregard for authority shown by some members of the 22nd Battalion, Jarvis recorded in his war diary on 7 March that

> the man Lemay of the 22nd Bn. who was returned to his unit yesterday under suspended sentence left the trenches and reported back to the guard room saying that he did not like the trenches and wanted to be locked up. Two more of this same unit also did the same thing and offered the same excuse. All these men were returned to the trenches ... The excellent discipline shown by this Battalion while in Belgium has been considerably marred by the advent of new reinforcements, almost all having proved very unsatisfactory and unreliable.[80]

In addition to the problem of reinforcements, high casualty rates affected the discipline of surviving battalion members. Major losses meant that surviving soldiers were left to deal with the loss of their unit structure as well as the destruction of important ties of comradeship. The stress of the experience always carried with it the potential for behavioural problems, and this might help to explain why so many men among the early recruits were deserting their units by 1917. Furthermore, the breakdown of the original units meant that men were less likely to have the personal or community bonds that compelled them to remain in the line and keep fighting.

Desertions were also undoubtedly prompted by the conditions of war. Within the Canadian Corps, by far the most death sentences for desertion were handed down in 1917. During that year, there were a total of 117 commuted death sentences. In contrast, 1916, the year with the second highest number of commuted death sentences, lagged far behind, with a total of 36 commutations. There are numerous explanations for these statistics. Nineteen seventeen was the longest and toughest year for Canadian and other Allied forces. On the Austro-Italian front, the Italian Army suffered a staggering defeat at Caporetto in the autumn. The collapse of the Italian Army demanded that British and French troops be moved to the area to maintain the Allied position. In the east, Russian soldiers deserted en masse, propelled in part by Bolshevik propaganda and the events of the October Revolution. On the western front, morale reached new lows as stalemate settled in. Soldiers faced miserable weather, fewer material provisions, and little change in the war's status.

While the whole of 1917 was difficult, certain months stand out in the statistics. For example, August had the most death sentences passed for desertion. This is of interest because, while engagements at Hill 70 and Lens did occur during this time period, prior to these actions the Canadian Corps had not been involved in any significant actions since Vimy Ridge. May-July can be described as a quiet period. Those who deserted during these months might have done so simply because they saw the opportunity. Commutations of death sentences were common since there was no pressing need for examples while the army was in reserve. However, sixteen of the twenty men who deserted in August 1917 did so immediately prior to, during, or following the operations at Hill 70 and Lens from 15 to 25 August.[81] The operations at Hill 70 and Lens were offensives meant to gain strategic vantage points and to wear down German forces. Although the attack at Hill 70 was successful, it came at the cost of 9,198 Canadian casualties.[82] Men most likely deserted prior to and during the Battle of Hill 70 out of fear. As operational orders were repeatedly given and cancelled in the days leading up to a battle, fears heightened and tensions grew, causing some soldiers to make a hasty decision to flee. Faced with having to abandon their months in reserve, some simply could not handle the thought of returning to action. William Alexander, a platoon sergeant with the 10th Battalion, was ordered to lead an attack on Hill 70. When zero hour approached, he could not be found, and another man was forced to take his place. The attack was ultimately successful, but Alexander's absence undoubtedly caused major confusion. Alexander was captured two days later in a nearby village and ultimately shot for desertion on 18 October 1917. Prior to the incident, he was a well-regarded soldier with a spotless disciplinary record.[83]

October and November 1917 also saw a particularly high number of death sentences for desertion. This number was likely linked to the miserable conditions of the Battle of Passchendaele, the focus of the Canadian Expeditionary Force during these months. In attempting to force a breakthrough in Flanders, the BEF launched an attack on 31 July 1917, suffering a total of 310,000 casualties to secure five miles of land. Unable to admit failure, the British leadership allowed the battles to continue far into the autumn. For Canada's part, in two weeks of fighting from 26 October to 6 November, the CEF suffered 16,000 casualties for the eventual capture of the village of Passchendaele.[84] The infamous mud and drudgery of Passchendaele simply caused some men to reach their breaking points. As described by veteran Elmore Philpott in an interview with the CBC in the 1960s, "Passchendaele was the most ghastly and hopeless mess. It was worse than we had anticipated. It was really hell on earth."[85] The conditions of Passchendaele caused soldiers to flee, which in turn precipitated a crackdown by authorities. They brought forward more charges, and more death sentences were passed in an effort to reimpose discipline on a faltering army and to avoid larger disciplinary problems such as the mass desertions in the Russian Army or the mutinies that had plagued the French Army. Worn down in part by the Nivelle Offensive, the French Army fell prey to mutiny in 1917. Although the army managed to recover and fight on, the incident heightened the fears of collapse among British and dominion leaders, for they too were losing men in extraordinary numbers in offensives that often seemed futile. A total of thirteen death sentences were passed in October, while seventeen more were passed in November. Two Canadians, Dimitro Sinizki and Thomas Moles, were executed during the autumn of 1917. Whether their executions proved at all effective in maintaining morale is highly debatable. Likely, they were most useful among leaders in convincing themselves that they were doing all that could be done to maintain the fighting capabilities under the most wearing of conditions.

In addition to issues of health, leadership, and general conditions of war, other issues within the CEF, though minor, are nevertheless worth addressing as motivations behind desertions. In the era of the First World War, Canada's population was approximately 7.8 million, with the majority of citizens being of British origin.[86] Consequently, the CEF was also made up mostly of Anglo-Saxons, born in either Canada or Great Britain. For example, among the cases that I studied, ninety-three men were Canadian born, while sixty-three men were immigrants from Great Britain. However, among the cases of commuted death sentences for desertion in the CEF, one particular ethnic group repeatedly stands out: men of Russian descent. In total, twelve Russian immigrants who served in the CEF were sentenced to death in the Great War. Of this number, one man was executed, while eleven others had their sentences commuted.

The total number of Russians or Russian subjects who served in the CEF during the First World War is still unknown.[87] By 1914, there were thousands of Russian and Ukrainian immigrants in Canada as well as Russian and Ukrainian subjects working as temporary labour immigrants. Statistics from the 1911 census show that the population included 44,376 persons of Russian origin as well as 75,432 persons of Ukrainian origin.[88] When the war began in 1914, some of these Russian and Ukrainian men were able to return to their homes, but many others remained in Canada and joined the CEF. These men joined for the same reasons as their Canadian counterparts. Some enlisted out of loyalty to Canada or the Russian Empire, some to escape from the boredom of daily life, while others enlisted for the steady and relatively good pay offered by the CEF. In addition to their CEF salaries, men also received a separation allowance of twenty dollars per month that they could send back to their families who remained in Russia. At a time of economic depression in Canada's labour market, enlistment in the CEF provided many with a much-needed financial opportunity.[89]

Yet in the army these men were at a distinct disadvantage. As recent or temporary immigrants, most did not speak fluent English. Attestation papers are indicative of the problem. Of the twelve Russian immigrants whom I studied, five had signed their attestation papers with an X in lieu of their own signatures. An additional two men had signed their own names, though it was clear that the forms had been filled out by another person, for the written responses to the questions did not match the shaky penmanship of the signatory.[90] In spite of these obstacles, these men were readily accepted into the ranks, though no concessions were made to deal with the language barrier.

In some cases, this inability to communicate between soldiers and commanders led to cases of desertion in order to resolve a problem peculiar to Russian soldiers. There were numerous instances of soldiers' families at home in Russia failing to receive their promised separation allowances. Of the twelve Russian soldiers in my research, three deserted in an attempt to resolve this issue. Unable to communicate with their commanders, they instead chose to leave their units to seek redress. Some men left to seek the Russian Army in the hope of finding an individual to help communicate their needs. Given the distance of the Russian Army on the eastern front, and the chances of finding an English speaker among the soldiers, this idea must have sounded ridiculous to both military police and senior officers. Other Russian soldiers in the CEF tried their luck by attempting to reach the Russian Consulate in Paris for the same purpose. Men in these cases were not attempting to abandon the CEF permanently; rather, they were seeking individuals who could speak their own language and aid them in resolving the issue of military pay. These soldiers did not perceive their actions as disloyal or as desertion; they were simply attempting to get what was rightfully owed to them. The inability of their leaders to communicate with them in Russian, and their own inability to speak English, put them in a situation in which they believed there was no other option but to abandon the Canadian lines. While in the minds of the Russian soldiers their actions could be completely justified, in the eyes of military leaders they were deserters. Yet, once they were convicted of desertion by court martial, their commanders did extend sympathy. Speaking through a translator, whom a court transcript indicates was found for his trial for desertion in September 1917, Nazar Oleinik, a soldier from Podoski, Russia, who had enlisted at Toronto in 1916, stated that

> I was married before enlistment and on enlistment applied for separation allowance for my wife and also assigned $20 per month to her. Up to present date my wife has received none of this money. I tried several times to obtain redress through my various superior officers but without success. Finally, in July last I asked my platoon commander to leave me out of the line until the matter was cleared up. I was afraid that I might be killed and that there would be nothing for my wife and no one to look after her. After going into the line, I left it to go to the

Russian Army so that I might find someone there to straighten out this matter for me. My intention was to get things straightened out and return to the 38th Canadian Battalion.[91]

Writing on his behalf, Oleinik's superiors urged clemency in his case. Brigadier General James MacBrien of the 12th Canadian Infantry Brigade recommended a commuted death sentence

> for the reason that it is not considered the cause in this case is lack of discipline but more on account of the accused thinking he was not being fairly dealt with by the Canadian Government in the matter of separation allowance. Private Oleinik is a Russian and is not able to speak much English and possibly did not thoroughly understand the terms of service. It is understood there has been some trouble among the Russians in the Canadian Expeditionary Force, owing to the fact that their dependants in Russia have not been receiving any separation allowance.[92]

Agreeing with MacBrien's recommendation, Major R.F. Parkinson, of the 38th Canadian Infantry Battalion, wrote that Oleinik's actions were "prompted more by a desire to have a grievance adjusted than with the idea of avoiding service … With his very slight knowledge of the English language, it was difficult to convince him that everything possible was being done."[93] Based on the recommendations, his death sentence was commuted to five years of penal servitude. Oleinik survived the war and was demobilized on 19 August 1919.[94] By war's end, no Russian soldier had been executed by the CEF for desertion related to the issue of separation allowance.

The issue that Russians had with the separation allowance was indicative of the bigger problem of communication with minority groups in the CEF. As mentioned, certain segments of Canadian society were accepted into the ranks, but there was an inability to address their particular language needs. This problem was most notable among French Canadians outside the 22nd Battalion, Aboriginal Canadians, and Russian and Ukrainian soldiers. When confronted with orders that they did not understand, many of these soldiers found themselves facing disciplinary measures. Attempting to explain his desertion in 1918, Samuel Ukovitch, originally from Grodno, Russia, defended his actions by stating that he simply had not understood the instructions to proceed up the line. Testifying at the court martial, Sergeant R.A. Hobbs confirmed this defence: "I don't know whether he understood me when I told him that he was going up the line, but I did my best to explain it to him by movements. Apparently he did not understand any English."[95] Recommending that the death sentence be carried out, Major Ryan of the 102nd Infantry Battalion unsympathetically stated that "it seems to be a great pity he was ever enlisted, as he either did not or would not understand English."[96] Soldiers such as Ukovitch who failed to learn English quickly often were written off as unintelligent and alienated from their fellow soldiers. Ukovitch's own defence witness, Lieutenant R.J. Smith, noted that Ukovitch, prior to his desertion, had given him no trouble but still found it necessary to comment that his intelligence was "rather low" and that he was "considered as a joke by the men in the platoon."[97] Despite four recommendations for execution, Ukovitch's death sentence was commuted to ten years of penal servitude. Ukovitch survived the war and was demobilized on 2 August 1919.[98]

His situation was mirrored by that of John Lipowich. Like Ukovitch, Lipowich was a Russian immigrant and written off as unintelligent by commanders who lacked the patience, knowledge, and resources to deal with him. Lipowich, of the 8th Battalion, was charged with desertion following a brief absence from Passchendaele from 8 to 9 November 1917. He surrendered to the military police at Ypres of his own volition and reported to the authorities that there had been confusion in the lines and that he had become separated from his unit. Despite the validity of his alibi, and the acknowledgment by Brigadier General Frederick Loomis of the Second Brigade that "the hostile shelling at the time was the most severe experienced at any time by this Battalion," Loomis felt compelled to write that "he [Lipowich] is a very dull, unintelligent individual and did not associate with the other men of his platoon, probably on account of his lack of knowledge of the English language." Loomis went on to describe Lipowich as "a very inferior type of soldier."[99] Although Lipowich was found guilty of desertion, his death sentence was commuted to five years of penal servitude. He survived the war and was demobilized on 4 August 1919.[100]

Cases such as those of Ukovitch and Lipowich can tell us more about early-twentieth-century assumptions about ethnicity than anything else. How these assumptions affected military discipline in the CEF is a topic worthy of further exploration (see Chapter 5). As for the CEF's belief in the links between level of intelligence and crime, no relationship can be proven. Attestation papers provide no record of formal education received prior to enlistment, and recruiters or medical examiners offered no comment on one's perceived level of intelligence. There is no evidence to show that low intelligence or a lack of education made a soldier more prone to commit a crime, but the issue of intelligence was nevertheless a factor at court martial, a point that I revisit in the following chapter.

Although the acts of desertion and cowardice were undoubtedly brought on by common pressures, both internal and external, the court martial transcripts also reveal that each soldier had a unique story to tell. Standing before the authorities, some men fully accepted responsibility for their actions, some lied regarding the circumstances of their crimes, and others felt compelled to relieve themselves of burdens and share the experiences that had led them to their crimes. The responses of the authorities are the focus of the next two chapters. We have seen what existing trial transcripts reveal about the defendants, but what do they tell us about the authorities? How did ordinary soldiers experience power and authority in a court martial during the First World War? Which factors had the biggest influence on those who were given the responsibility of sitting in judgment? Do these factors reveal a clear pattern that helps to explain why some men died at the firing post while others lived to fight another day?

4
The Court Martial Process

In April 1916, Charles Douglas Richardson of the Princess Patricia's Canadian Light Infantry wrote of his experience working as a military prison guard:

> I shall be glad when we get out of here ... Steve and I were on guard yesterday and we had the experience, not pleasant at all, of seeing a man hang himself, at least so nearly so that I almost wish he had finished the job. I think he will die yet from the effects of it. He was a prisoner in one of the cells and used his puttee for a rope. He comes from Calgary and was awaiting trial for desertion.[1]

Accounts by Canadian prisoners during the First World War are few and far between, but this quotation from a prison guard provides a glimpse into one experience of detention in military barracks. There are a number of descriptions of the prison conditions faced by convicted men on the eve of their executions, but journal accounts of day-to-day prison life on the western front are limited, and I have found no accounts by soldiers in which they detail the days preceding their courts martial. For the historian, these moments, and the thoughts that soldiers might have experienced before their trials, remain unknown. History opens up again only when the trial begins.

Trials were recorded in longhand, and they give voice to the past not only by letting us hear statements of the defendants but also by giving us insights into the actual process of a court martial. That process is the focus of this chapter. Courts martial, in many ways, mirrored civilian trials; they were not as far removed from the civilian practice as one might think. In this chapter, I also use trial transcripts to deduce which factors were of primary interest to members of a court martial and which factors might have been most influential in their sentencing decisions. Although the available court martial records are not uniform in every case, for the most part they reveal a pattern followed in a typical trial.

Conducted in the field but far removed from any danger, courts martial gathered in locations that ranged from abandoned farmhouses and chateaus to taverns or *estaminets*. Each trial was organized and conducted individually rather than being delayed so that numerous trials could be held on one day and in one central location. This practice likely involved far more organization, time, and resources, but in the interest of expediency for each case it was retained for the course of the war. While ad hoc and hurried, these trials still retained a sense of formality by following a set of basic rules that legitimized the overall process. The rules of the military legal system were carefully laid out in the *Manual of Military Law,* a document that, while unique to the military, also reflected many of the rules and procedures of civil law characteristic of the period, including rules governing the admissibility of evidence and the right of appeal, which was non-existent in military courts martial and severely restricted in the civilian judicial system in the early twentieth century. The Criminal Court of Appeal was established in England only in 1907, and even with its establishment, the right to an appeal was not automatic: it had to be based on clear errors that might have occurred in procedure or evidence.[2] However, though the right to an appeal was technically non-existent in the military, I would argue that the confirmation process described in the next chapter acted as a type of automatic appeal. In making recommendations that a death sentence be commuted based on the extenuating circumstances of a case, or on an individual's service record, commanding officers were asking for a change to an official decision made by a military court martial, thus fulfilling the same role as a formal right of appeal.

Courts martial were called to order once three officers were in attendance. The officers were sworn in, and the accused entered the makeshift courtroom hatless and in restraints. With the presence of all relevant persons confirmed, the charges were read out, and the soldier was asked to enter a plea. As of 1915, all capital cases required a plea of not guilty to ensure that all evidence was heard and that a fair trial could be conducted.

The prosecution, often an adjutant who was a senior officer in charge of the administration and discipline of the accused's unit, began the trial by describing the crime and calling witnesses to substantiate the case. As in civilian court, the defendant could be called on to answer questions, and cross-examination of the prosecution's witnesses was allowed. Once the prosecution rested, the defence made its arguments. The defence case was presented by the defendant himself or by a "prisoner's friend" chosen by the defendant. In many instances, the prisoner's friend had no special legal training but was chosen for his likeability or close relationship to the accused. For example, in the case of John Edward Owen of the 27th Battalion, trial records indicate his prisoner's friend to have been Lieutenant Colin Douglas Mackenzie, also of the 27th Battalion. Furthermore, the trial transcript records specifically that Mackenzie was "not a qualified Barrister or Solicitor."[3] An examination of his attestation papers shows him to have been an electrician prior to enlistment.[4] Although Owen was found guilty of desertion in July 1918, his death sentence was ultimately commuted to ten years of penal servitude. In all likelihood, this commutation probably had more to do with his mental condition than with the case put forward by Mackenzie. The fact that Owen was found naked in a dugout, living off the scraps of food left in old trenches, was enough to convince the court to order a mental examination and for his commanding officers to recommend mercy.[5] His medical records indicate that he went on to suffer a nervous breakdown in the month following his trial. He was sent to England and demobilized in July 1919.[6]

To begin the defence, the accused made a statement on his behalf, addressing the specifics of the crime. The defence had the opportunity to call their own witnesses, including character witnesses, who could speak to the defendant's positive character traits and previous service even if they were not familiar with the crime. In some cases, credible witnesses were unavailable because they were fighting on the front line or had died or been injured by the time the trial was convened. During the trial of Harry Sekum, the witnesses were deemed crucial enough to actually delay the trial. Sekum absented himself from his unit when he was informed about duty in the trenches on 13 October 1916, and he was apprehended by his own sergeant on 18 November. His court martial was postponed until his battalion, the 4th Canadian Mounted Rifles, had returned from front-line action in the Écurie Sector and was back in divisional support. Sekum was eventually tried and found guilty of desertion on 23 January 1917. He was sentenced to death, but his sentence was commuted to five years of penal servitude. His treatment was unique in that military authorities were not typically willing to allow significant delays in a trial. Sekum returned to service but suffered gunshot wounds to his arm and back at Passchendaele on 29 October 1917 as well as a bout of Spanish influenza in 1918. He was discharged as medically unfit due to his wounds on 1 May 1919.[7]

In the case of Samuel Chandler, accused of desertion from the 42nd Battalion, records indicate that the trial was adjourned so that he could attempt to produce character witnesses from his battalion. Chandler was absent from a roll call to parade on 13 June 1916. He reported back to his unit three hours later and was charged with desertion. In preparation for his trial, wires were sent by his request to three possible witnesses. Two men were unwilling to come to the trial to testify. The first witness claimed that he did not have a significant recollection of Chandler's behaviour, while the second witness responded that he had not seen Chandler since 1915 but that he recalled his behaviour to be "indifferent."[8] The third witness wired back to the authorities, "regret cannot attend tomorrow at ten o'clock. Have been detained for Court Martial at Connaught lines at same hour."[9] The records do not show that there was any suggestion of further delaying the trial in order to accommodate this witness. Based on the evidence available to the court, Chandler was found guilty of desertion, but his sentence was commuted to ten years of penal servitude. He was killed in action at Passchendaele on 3 November 1917 during an operation to capture a German pillbox.[10]

After the evidence was heard and the witnesses were examined, the defendant was invited to make a closing statement on his behalf. When both sides were satisfied that their cases had been sufficiently stated, the officers of the court adjourned, and private deliberations followed. Court martial deliberations were secret and went unrecorded in official records, so it is impossible for us to know exactly how the proceedings were conducted or which factors of a case featured most prominently in the discussions among the officers. What we do know of these deliberations is that it was mandated that the junior officer in the room be the first to express his opinion. This rule was instituted to ensure that junior officers were not influenced in their decisions by more senior members of a court martial. In a world where rank was of no little importance, this rule helped to legitimize the military legal system.

Once the court martial panel eventually came to a decision, the accused was led back into the courtroom, where he was met with either a guilty or a not guilty verdict. It has been calculated that 89 percent of all courts martial in the BEF resulted in a guilty verdict.[11] In some cases, soldiers were convicted of lesser charges. For example, a soldier charged with desertion could instead be found guilty of absence without leave, a non-capital offence. After the decision was read, non-guilty soldiers were simply returned to their units. In the case of a guilty verdict, a convicted soldier was given the opportunity to make a statement to address extenuating circumstances or to offer a resumé of past service that might help to sway the court martial when settling on a final punishment. Research on commuted death sentences suggests that these statements had little effect and that a recommended punishment was likely already in place before a soldier made his plea.

Although one might see this high rate of guilty verdicts as a reason to discredit the entire military legal system, one should also consider that likely only the most extreme cases, or the ones for which overwhelming evidence existed, were brought to trial. The time and the manpower required for a court martial likely dissuaded officers from convening a trial for petty crimes or offences that could be handled within the battalion. Good leadership required that commanders knew when to make the distinction between the need for official disciplinary procedure and a sympathetic ear coupled with a warning. These types of decisions were a regular part of life on the western front. In fact, during the course of the war, some in authority, such as Brigadier General Reginald John Kentish of the 3rd Division of the BEF, lobbied in favour of officially giving commanding officers more authority to deal with crimes within their units in the hope of diminishing the need for so many courts martial. He believed that the unprecedented resources and manpower required in this war demanded change and that the disciplinary methods in use were "old-fashioned." According to him, too many commanding officers rushed to courts martial in cases in which the seriousness of the crimes did not actually necessitate it; this resulted in twenty to thirty courts martial being handed out daily and in "everybody's time being taken up with cases, which, if Divisional Commanders would only act, would never occur." As Kentish wrote in 1916,

> we must get rid of some of our old-fashioned methods to which I have referred and bring our system up to date and more in keeping with the situation confronting us today. We no longer rely on shrapnel for our 18 Pounders. We realize that the situation today demands High Explosive. Give Commanding Officers more High Explosive to use when dealing with their men.

In requesting high explosive, Kentish was asking for increased powers for commanding officers. He suggested that they be allowed to award up to three months of punishment rather than the standard twenty-eight days. He also advocated the removal of the right of convicted soldiers to decline the commanding officer's punishment in favour of a court martial.[12]

Many of the death sentences issued by courts martial during the First World War were accompanied by recommendations for mercy. These recommendations were influenced by a number of factors, including previous good service and good character. The age of the defendant was also a consideration. Among the thirty-eight recommendations for mercy issued following a sentence of death that I studied, twelve were based on the extreme youth of the defendant. In fact, the age of a convicted soldier was not to be included in the court martial papers that crossed the desk of the commander-in-chief, and age was not ultimately meant to be a consideration in sentencing. However, some soldiers convincingly pleaded their cases.[13] Vernon Treveleyn of the 38th Battalion was charged with desertion after his arrest in Paris in April 1917. He fled again and was recaptured in May. Treveleyn received a sentence of death but with a recommendation of mercy based on his extreme youth following an emotional plea during his defence statement in which he noted that he was eighteen years old and had enlisted in the CEF when only sixteen. His sentence was ultimately commuted to fifteen years of penal servitude. He survived the war and was demobilized in June 1919.[14]

The question that remains is whether these recommendations for mercy had any real effect during the confirmation process. References to these recommendations do not appear in the majority of supporting letters, but this does not mean that they did not have an effect. Many of the authors might have considered the recommendations for mercy yet simply did not make specific reference to them in their letters to the commander-in-chief. In the small number of cases in which references to recommendations for mercy do appear, the commanding officers did take the recommendations to heart. For example, in the case of Norman Henderson of the 78th Battalion, convicted of desertion in 1917, Brigadier General James MacBrien stated that "it is considered that the recommendation of the Court to mercy on account of youth be supported and that the sentence be commuted."[15] Henderson was sixteen years old when he enlisted in the CEF, and he was one week away from turning eighteen when he was sentenced to death in December 1917. He had absented from Château de la Haie on 17 August and had been apprehended by military police three months later, on 18 November, when he had been found hiding in a motorcycle shed. His death sentence was commuted, and he was instead given ten years of penal servitude. Henderson survived the war and was demobilized on 12 June 1919.[16] Possibly, in cases in which commanders were on the fence in deciding whether to commute or confirm a death sentence, these recommendations for mercy provided by the court might have been influential in the decision to ask for a commutation.

The reasoning behind the recommendations for mercy remains somewhat unclear. Why would a court martial sentence an individual to the harshest penalty allowed, only to attach a recommendation of mercy? Perhaps the members of the court martial thought that their decisions were being judged by their superiors and thus felt bound by the rules of military law as codified in the *Manual of Military Law*. In this position, officers might have felt obliged to hand down the strictest punishment at their disposal, if for no other reason than to prove how seriously they took their responsibility to impose discipline. They might also have handed down the strictest punishment because they simply did not realize that they had any other option. Relating his experience of sitting on his first court martial, Guy Chapman, who served with the Royal Fusiliers, recalls in his memoir *A Passionate Prodigality* that, following a verdict of guilty passed against a sergeant for drunkenness in the trenches, he, as the most junior officer on the court martial, was asked to give his opinion on sentencing first:

> I hurriedly turned the pages of the *Manual of Military Law*, and found to my horror that the punishment was death, tout court. So when Major the Hon. George Keppel turned to me as junior member of the court and demanded my sentence, I replied, "Oh, death, sir, I suppose." Major Keppel blenched and turned to my opposite number, Gwinnell. Gwinnell, who was as young and unlearned in expedience as myself, answered, as I had, "Death, I suppose." Our good president

looked at us from the top of his six feet and groaned: "But, my boys, my boys, you can't do it." "But, sir," we protested in unison, anxious to justify ourselves, "it says so here." It was only after a moving appeal by the president that we allowed ourselves to be overborne and to punish the old ruffian by reduction to the rank of corporal in the place of executing him; but we both felt that Major Keppel had somehow failed in his duty.[17]

Officers of the court martial might have left it up to (and even depended on) the more experienced commanders, who had a greater amount of authority and flexibility, to commute the harsh sentences that they had felt forced to impose. Anthony Babington, a British judge who examined British executions and published *For the Sake of Example* in 1983, argues that the 10 percent rate of confirmation might have been a reflection that the military command was fully aware of the inexperience and lack of knowledge present in the court martial process. Armed with this knowledge, commanders were comfortable in regularly reducing punishments so as to balance justice with mercy.[18] Historian Gerard Oram suggests an even larger policy at work. Oram notes that the 10 percent rate of confirmation was consistent among the English, Scottish, Welsh, Canadian, and South African units. Oram believes that the statistics help to show that the 10 percent rate of confirmation was a planned policy and a managed response to discipline that allowed the army to use executions in numbers that were balanced yet useful in terms of deterrence while also maintaining the consent of troops and politicians at home.[19]

Once the trial had ended and a death sentence had been decided by the members of the court martial, the process of confirmation began. A copy of the court martial proceedings was sent through the chain of army command so that each commander could register a recommendation for either the confirmation or the commutation of the sentence. The command structure in the Canadian Corps included a corps commander under whose supervision there were four Canadian divisions. Each division included three brigades and artillery, engineering, medical, and service units led by a brigadier. Under the command of the brigadier were four battalions, and each battalion had four companies made up of four platoons. Each battalion, consisting of one thousand men, was led by a lieutenant colonel. Soldiers typically developed a unique military identity at the battalion level; however, their closest bonds were probably formed within their own platoons.[20]

While in some cases there were discrepancies, typically the papers proceeded from the condemned soldier's commanding battalion officer, up to his brigade commander, then up to his divisional or corps commander, before finally reaching the commander-in-chief, who was charged with making the final decision in any sentence of death or penal servitude. This process was important, for it helped to ensure that those who knew the condemned soldier best had a say in his eventual fate by speaking to his past actions and behaviours. Furthermore, this step-by-step process, which moved up the chain of command, helped to prevent the abuse of authority by any one commanding officer or by the members of the court martial. British sources have cited this process as taking up to two weeks, during which time the condemned soldier continued to serve in the trenches while he awaited a decision on his fate. In the Canadian example, a sample of ten cases shows that the confirmation process took an average of 10.8 days to complete.[21] In one particular example, Alexander Dumesnil of the 22nd Battalion actually went absent in July 1917 while awaiting sentencing for a previous FGCM for desertion.[22]

Like every other facet of the war, information regarding courts martial was part of the constant flow of information made available to the army's commander-in-chief. On the western front, where 90 percent of the death sentences were passed, the power of Field Marshal John French and Field Marshal Douglas Haig to determine the life or death of a member of the British and dominion forces did differ from that of other armies; for example, in the French system, death sentences were ultimately under the discretion of the nation's highest civilian authority, President Raymond Poincaré.[23]

Although the commander-in-chief's authority was required for the final decision in any death sentence, it is naive to assume that this one individual personally reviewed every case in which a death sentence was passed. Considering that, for Haig, the first priority was running the war, he likely had assistance in reviewing the case files.[24] Among the assistants would have been members of the adjutant general's corps, who took on various roles, including administration and legal services. Captain N. Anderson, deputy assistant adjutant general in the First Army, shows up repeatedly throughout 1917 and 1918 in the Canadian court martial records as an important voice during the review process. Anderson commented on issues such as questionable evidence or trial practices and in some cases threw out charges or called for new trials. Following a review of the trial of Harry Owen Townsend, Anderson made sure to delay a final decision until a medical examination could be administered. During the trial against Townsend for desertion from the 1st Canadian Mounted Rifles at Courcelette on 27 September 1916, a suicide letter written by the accused was produced by the prosecution as evidence that he was unwilling to fight and had every intention to desert. In the unsent letter, addressed to his mother, Townsend stated that he did not want to carry on as a soldier and be shot at any longer. He went on to state that he was serious about wanting to kill himself.[25] Based on this letter, and on his own testimony on his memory loss and weakened mental state, Anderson determined that the court martial had erred in not ordering a medical board and that no judgment could be found until a proper medical examination for mental health was administered. In the end, the medical board did find Townsend responsible for his crimes: "In the opinion of the Board he is, although of low mentality, mentally responsible for carrying on with the ordinary duties of a private soldier."[26] Townsend was found guilty of desertion, but he received three letters of recommendation in favour of commutation. His death sentence was commuted to five years of penal servitude. Townsend survived the war and was demobilized on 26 March 1919.[27]

The commander-in-chief received the same copy of the court proceedings that the commanding officers did as well as the letters of recommendation written along the way. These letters went beyond the mere facts of the crime, focusing instead on the accused's personal history and the state of his battalion. Commanding officers were expected to report on the accused's individual behaviour and service record; the state of the battalion and whether an example was required to enforce discipline; whether the crime in question had been deliberately committed; and, finally, any other reasons why the death penalty should be either carried out or commuted. Haig added little to nothing to the paperwork, usually just attaching the words *commuted* or *confirmed* to the proceedings.

Upon confirmation of a sentence by the commander-in-chief, it was finalized by members of the original court martial and publicly read to the convicted man and his entire unit while on parade. Involving the unit in the disciplinary process made the soldier in question an example, even if his death sentence was commuted. In addition to making an example of the soldier, reading out his sentence on parade reinforced his stigma, much like the function of field punishment number 1. The stigma of desertion and cowardice not only reflected badly on the convicted soldier but also, in tightly knit communities such as army battalions or platoons that reinforce a strong group identity, was taken on by the entire unit and became a problem for the unit to overcome. It became a matter of pride for the unit to prove its fighting value; conversely, it might have convinced the unit that the system of military justice was unfair.

In nine cases out of ten, the sentence of death was commuted. In the cases in which it was upheld, the convicted soldier was led away from his unit and held in confinement until his execution, which could take place as early as the following day. Recording the details leading up to the execution of Harold George Carter, who had deserted the 73rd Battalion just prior to the advance on Vimy Ridge while already serving under a suspended sentence for desertion,

Assistant Provost Marshal Lieutenant Colonel Jarvis noted in the 2nd Division's war diary on 19 April 1917, "Pte. Carter 73rd Can. Inf. Bn. under escort of MMP taken to the P of W cage [prisoner of war] ... Death sentence will be carried out at Dawn the 20th April. APM promulgated the sentence to the condemned man at 5:30 p.m."[28]

In the hours preceding an execution, the condemned soldier was provided with a chaplain of his own faith and with the facilities to write his last letters.[29] Chaplains helped to prepare the soldier to bravely accept the circumstances of his death, provided a final blessing, and performed the funeral rites following the execution. This duty was obviously rare among chaplains; however, for those who performed it, it was no doubt difficult. That said, most chaplains accepted the duty and understood the role of executions in maintaining discipline. Researching the accounts of chaplains who were asked to witness military executions in the First World War, author Michael F. Snape concludes that chaplains saw no reason to protest the executions and that "chaplains' attitudes towards capital courts-martial reflected the general attitudes of their Churches towards capital punishment *per se*."[30] During this period, church leadership among all of the major denominations supported the right of the state to inflict the death penalty, both in the army and in civilian society.[31]

Executions were always performed by a firing squad at dawn. In cases in which the death sentence was commuted, an alternative punishment was decided on, ranging anywhere from two to fifteen years of penal servitude or imprisonment with labour. No records exist to determine how these alternative sentences were arrived at, and no pattern can be discerned among the commuted cases.

The court martial process of the First World War has been the target of many accusations by historians and modern-day critics. In the era of the Great War, the subject of death sentences was raised among a few British parliamentarians and was of little concern to other segments of society, including the churches.[32] The topic of executions resurfaced in 1918 amid allegations that shell-shocked soldiers were being subjected to the death penalty. The debate was fuelled following the publication of an article in the journal *John Bull* that called for an inquiry into the court martial system. Published by known agitator Horatio Bottomley, the article achieved its goal of reigniting the issue in the British Parliament. However, by the spring of 1918, as the tide of war began to change, the issue once again fell off the public's radar.[33] In Canada, there was even less discussion directed toward the issue. As evidenced by the lack of debate on the subject in both the government and the media, these trials were deemed perfectly acceptable and even reflective of the civilian judicial system as it existed in Great Britain and most parts of the British Empire.[34] That said, there have been legitimate concerns about the process that might have affected the punishments handed down, and these concerns should be addressed in any study seeking to shed light on the military legal system.

The first concern, especially among critics of the military judicial system of the First World War, relates to the lack of legal training among court martial members. There was no requirement for legal training to serve on a court martial panel, and the lawyers and law students serving in the CEF were certainly not used to their fullest advantage. This was especially true in the early years of the war. In a random sample of 25 percent of my researched courts martial, I found that 10 percent of the panelists identified themselves as barristers on their attestation papers, while a further 10 percent had been engaged in law enforcement as police officers prior to the war, though police officers at this time, especially those who came from rural areas, did not necessarily have any significant amount of training in law. The great majority of other panelists had been employed in what could be described as white-collar professions, ranging from bank clerks to university professors, while 8 percent were described as students, and 10 percent had come from blue-collar professions, including labourers and lumbermen.[35] However, the lack of legal training on court martial panels should be weighed against the fact that the same held true for civilian juries. Members of a civilian jury in the early twentieth century (just like today) were not expected to have any legal training and were actually disallowed from jury duty if they did. In decrying the lack of legal training, modern-day critics of the First World War court martial process have held military justice to standards higher than its civilian counterpart, a misrepresentation that proved influential in the later campaign for pardons.

Most officers who sat on courts martial learned the rules and procedures as they went along. However, while the *Manual of Military Law* was always present in the courtroom, constantly referencing its contents could significantly slow down a trial. As the war dragged on, change was initiated. In 1916, the court martial officer was introduced into the British and empire forces. Court martial officers were most commonly persons who had received legal training in their civilian lives. The army took advantage of their presence in the military by applying their already acquired legal knowledge to the court martial system. It was the task of the court martial officer to ensure that all matters ran smoothly, efficiently, and according to rules of procedure. As it was laid out in a March 1916 memorandum by General Haig's staff, "the duty of the Court Martial Officer is to keep the Court straight on matters of law and procedure ... For instance, it is particularly necessary for him to check the tendency of many Presidents to ask irregular questions which lead to inadmissible replies, and therefore cause proceedings to be quashed."[36] Just how influential the role of court martial officers was is debatable. Although some historians have argued that these officers were an influential presence from 1916 onward, others, such as Gerard Oram, note that there was only one such officer per corps, so most cases were tried without the presence of a legally trained officer.[37]

Although the trial transcripts of CEF soldiers fail to indicate whether a court martial officer was present at trial, there is evidence among the Canadian cases to reinforce Oram's belief that the influence of this officer was negligible. For example, in September 1917, a retrial was ordered in the case of Herbert John Turner of the 28th Battalion. Turner was originally charged with desertion following an absence that he himself blamed on shock. After he was found guilty and sentenced to death, his sentence was called into question by Captain N. Anderson, deputy assistant adjutant general. Anderson believed that Turner's conviction was invalid due to "the wrongful admission of evidence of a previous offence in rebuttal."[38] Turner's previous offences included drunkenness, two charges of absence without leave, and an FGCM for failing to comply with an order given by a superior officer.[39] Anderson went on to clarify that "verbal evidence of bad character is not admissible. The conduct sheet alone can be produced ... The admission of evidence of a previous offence renders the conviction for desertion bad, because it may have influenced the court on the question of intention."[40] That Turner's trial proceeded despite the wrongful admission of evidence, and that no objection was made by any member of the court martial panel or the defence, suggest a trial that was conducted without the expertise of a court martial officer. It is reasonable to suggest that, if one was present, objections would have been raised and evidence disallowed. Instead, in the absence of a court martial officer, the trial proceeded, and errors were found only at the time of judicial review. The original trial was deemed to be useless, and ultimately a lesser charge of absence without leave was laid against Turner. His sentence was not confirmed, though, and he returned to service. Turner survived the war and was demobilized on 15 July 1919.[41] Yet, no matter how often a court martial officer was present at a trial or how influential his role when there, the army's attempt to address the problems of unfair trials and invalid evidence suggests that the military was making concerted efforts to introduce a more professional military legal system during the course of the war. It obviously had some distance to go before achieving full success, but reform was slowly creeping in to an old and insular institution.

Another major criticism of courts martial of the First World War has been the speed with which they were conducted. Yet this criticism must be tempered with the fact that speed was the express purpose of a field general court martial. Although trial transcripts do not list a start or finish time, given the amount of information contained in an average transcript, trials were likely conducted over several hours, but it is hard to imagine that they ever extended beyond half a day. The purpose of the FGCM was to provide a shortened version of the regular general court martial. An FGCM was meant to serve as an instrument of discipline that would not interfere with running the war. The FGCM needed to suit the context of the situation and operate successfully in wartime circumstances. Given these realities, any criticisms regarding the speed of FGCMs seem to be entirely displaced. Furthermore, it is wrong to assume that a slower trial would have been any more just. The more time passed, the more witnesses might be killed or wounded. Perhaps in no other situation does the old adage "justice delayed is justice denied" hold more true. On the western front, where hundreds of men died daily, this proverb had a practical significance. British sources indicate that, if averaged out, four hundred British soldiers died every day over four years of fighting.[42] Under such circumstances, if one were really concerned with justice, then it made the most sense to hold the trial as quickly as possible.

There is a distinction between a speedy trial and a poorly run trial. While one can safely argue that wartime trials were quick, it is more difficult to find evidence that they were improperly conducted. Accounts show that these trials followed the procedural rules as laid out in the *Manual of Military Law*. Court transcripts follow a familiar pattern from one case to the next, with a clear order of presenting evidence and conducting questioning. The transcripts also indicate that the defendant clearly had a voice at his trial. He was given multiple opportunities to tell his side of the story both during the trial and during his statement of mitigation. Quick justice was not synonymous with rough justice.

Yet, while trials were typically speedy, given the wartime circumstances there were sometimes delays because of operations or problems locating witnesses in the field. In addition, there were occasionally delays because of legal procedures, in some cases leading to retrials. In the case of John Fraser of the 1st Battalion, a wrongful admission of evidence during his trial in October 1916 brought on a month of delays and ultimately a second trial on a lesser charge. Fraser was charged with desertion following multiple arrests and escapes between December 1915 and October 1916. After being granted nine days of leave in December 1915, he failed to return and was arrested in London in January 1916; he was returned to the 36th Reserve Battalion, from which he eventually escaped, and was again arrested on 26 May. He was charged with desertion, escaped again, only to be arrested on 4 June. Fraser escaped from the hospital on 12 June and was again arrested on 25 September. He escaped from the guard room of the 36th Reserve Battalion on 4 October and was finally arrested for good on 6 October. He was initially convicted of desertion and sentenced to death, but N. Anderson, the deputy assistant adjutant general reviewing the case eight days after the initial trial, determined that the conviction could not stand "owing to the various irregularities committed and the wrongful admission of documentary evidence."[43] An unsigned letter from within Canadian Corps Headquarters agreed, noting that "a number of documents have been produced before the Court and attached as Exhibits which should not have been admitted, i.e. The letter of 8th of October from the Canadian Training Division, Shornecliffe, and the three charge sheets. Their wrongful admission is bound to have acted prejudicially to the accused."[44] Based on the evidence available to the court, a new trial was ordered, and Fraser was retried for the lesser, non-capital offence of absence without leave. He was given two years of imprisonment with hard labour for the offence. Fraser survived the war and was demobilized on 17 August 1919.[45] The fact that a retrial was ordered for a habitual offender such as Fraser based on the findings and the advice of the deputy assistant adjutant general shows that caution was taken before confirmation of the death sentence and that authorities cared for procedure and the rule of law. In a lesser system, the Fraser case would have been rushed through the review process with far less attention or care.

The final critique of the military legal system was its very fairness. How exactly was it decided whose death sentence would be commuted and whose confirmed? Given the limitations of the sources, this question remains clouded in mystery. One would assume that, with only a 10 percent rate of confirmation, the death penalty would be reserved for only the most serious crimes or the most delinquent soldiers. However, as will be explored further, this was not always the case. In some instances, habitual offenders did meet their deaths by firing squads, yet so did some first-time offenders as well as those who had previously given outstanding service to their nation. Thus, any criticism that the military judicial system could be unfair or arbitrary certainly carries some weight for those who would define a fair system as one in which punishments for crimes are clearly laid out and followed according to a set standard every time.

To determine just how valid the accusations of arbitrary justice are, we need to form an understanding of factors that might have weighed heavily on the minds of a court martial panel, as well as commanding officers, when determining the life or death of an errant soldier. The best way, and the only credible way, to form any conclusion in this regard is to examine the individual cases and the statements made at trial as well as those found in letters of recommendation written during the confirmation process. I will begin with the most important factors that arose at trial before proceeding to the process of confirmation.

The most important factor in any case of desertion is intention. Without proof of intention to desert, or knowledge by the soldier that he was abandoning a specific duty, a charge could merely amount to the non-capital offence of absence without leave. Because of this factor, during a trial it became the prosecutor's role to prove to the court martial panel through witness statements that an order to move forward, or to engage in a special duty, was issued prior to a soldier deserting. Equally common at trial was the accused claiming that he heard no such order, thereby absolving himself of intention.

George Marineau of the 22nd Battalion likely escaped from a confirmed sentence of death partly because of the inability to prove his intention to desert. In April 1917, he was marching with his battalion when he fell back with pains in his feet. He sat down, pulled off his boots, and rested, only to find that he could not put his boots back on due to severe swelling in his feet. Marineau struggled to keep up with his battalion but was forced to fall out again and ultimately found a dugout to rest in. After resting for three days, he intended to find his battalion, but upon receiving word that they would be passing by once more he decided to remain in the dugout and wait for them. More time passed, and Marineau was eventually found in the dugout and arrested by military police in August 1917. Speaking in his own defence, he stated that he did not know that his actions would make him a deserter or that his battalion would be engaging in any attack. In his statement of mitigation, he pleaded, "I have always been willing to do my duty and it was only illness that made me stay away from the battalion. I ask for the clemency of the court. I had no intention to desert."[46] Despite the length of his absence, his claims seem to have been supported. It certainly helped that Marineau remained in the dugout and never actually left the forward zone. Following the trial, Major General J.M. Thorpe of the Canadian Corps noted that the recommendation from the corps commander had not yet been asked for. As he stated in a letter to the deputy assistant adjutant general, "there is some doubt as to whether the charge of desertion is substantiated by the evidence. The weight of evidence seems directed to proving 'Absence without Leave' and with the exception of the duration of the absence there seems little evidence of the intention to desert."[47] Despite this communication, the case proceeded, and the corps commander's recommendation was eventually solicited. In the face of four recommendations for confirmation of the death sentence, and despite Lieutenant Colonel Dubuc's view that the crime had been deliberately committed with the intention of avoiding duty in the trenches, Marineau's death sentence was commuted to ten years of penal servitude. Marineau went on to receive a gunshot wound to his left foot on 31 March 1918. He was discharged as medically unfit in January 1919.[48]

A number of other factors were repeatedly introduced at courts martial as proof, or lack thereof, of intention to desert. Discarded equipment or a missing uniform, argued numerous prosecutors, was surely evidence of one's intention to evade duty. Although not enough to convict a man, being apprehended in plain clothes was considered to be circumstantial evidence of some importance. Soldiers were well aware of this fact and often brought it up at their trials to sway the court martial panels. Oswald Castonguay deserted from the 22nd Battalion in March 1917 after leaving his billets at Bois des Alleux and failing to return by the time his battalion had left for the front-line trenches. As stated by Castonguay during his defence,

> I left my company billets on 18th March last, after breakfast ... I went to the village close by to purchase some cigarettes with the intention of returning the next morning ... When I arrived there I found that the battalion had gone and I was told by a soldier there that it had gone to the trenches. Seeing the battalion was in the trenches I decided to wait until they came out so I returned to the village and not having money I decided to get some and for that purpose went to work on a farm. I worked there for four days. I then decided to see if the battalion was back but put it off from day to day as I was afraid of being punished.[49]

Rather than turning himself in, Castonguay was arrested by the French gendarmerie on 5 May 1917. He was quick to point out in his defence that "when I was arrested I was properly dressed."[50] Given his length of absence, and the fact that he had made no effort to return to his unit, the presence of a uniform was the only factor that Castonguay could offer in his defence. Outweighed by the other evidence, it helped little. Castonguay was convicted of desertion and sentenced to death. That he had been arrested in uniform was not referred to in any of the letters of recommendation, which all suggested that he be shot for his crime. Instead, his death sentence was commuted to fifteen years of penal servitude. Castonguay returned to service and eventually died of wounds sustained on 29 August 1918 after attacking enemy positions east of Chérisy.[51]

Just as a missing uniform could be contributing evidence of an intention to desert, so too defendants often used drunkenness to prove a lack of intention. Six men who received commuted death sentences used drunkenness as their sole defence during trial. Drunkenness was not a condition that the authorities simply dismissed; records show it to have been a legitimate excuse for poor behaviour, one that was not only thoughtfully considered by members of a court martial but also referred to in commanders' letters when making requests for commutation. Napoleon Barré of the 4th Battalion argued that his desertion had been precipitated by his inebriated condition. Accused of deserting his unit on 11 September 1917 after orders were given to proceed to the front-line trenches, Barré could only state that he had missed the orders because he had spent the afternoon of 11 September getting drunk at a local *estaminet*. After consuming more than a few beers, Barré had fallen asleep in a nearby field, only to wake up at 10:30 p.m., long after his unit had already left. This loss of control helped to prove Barré's lack of intention to desert and helped to reduce his death sentence to five years of penal servitude.[52] Barré went on to suffer a gunshot wound to his hand in February 1918 while fighting at Hill 70, and he was demobilized as medically unfit in August 1919.[53]

Without having access to the private deliberations of a court martial panel, it is difficult to have insight into which factors influenced their decisions. For example, it is impossible to know just how important it was that a deserter surrendered on his own to authorities rather than being arrested by military police. The issue came up at trials only as a simple fact of a case or when some individuals, such as James Gallagher of the 13th Battalion, made a point of mentioning his surrender during his defence statement. Gallagher was charged with desertion following a five-day absence in January 1916. There had been a warning to proceed to the trenches that Gallagher claimed not to have heard, and he had eventually returned to his unit on his own. The facts that Gallagher was found guilty and that no recommendation of mercy was attached to his sentence suggest that his surrender did little or nothing to affect the minds of the officers on the court martial. His death sentence was nonetheless commuted to ten years of penal servitude. He was discharged as medically unfit on 31 July 1918. His medical records note that, following his conviction for desertion, Gallagher went on to suffer a gunshot wound to his cheek, a diagnosis of tuberculosis, and a head wound caused by shrapnel.[54]

A court martial finding was far from the end of the story for an accused soldier. What mattered most in the entire process were the recommendations given by an accused soldier's superior officers. All evidence shows that these letters had the most impact on the final decision of the commander-in-chief. These letters also addressed major issues such as the overall behaviour of the battalion and the disciplinary record of the accused – factors that were not to be reviewed by the court martial itself but that undoubtedly influenced the decision to execute or commute. These letters, which give us the most insight into military discipline during the First World War, are the focus of the following chapter.

5
The Confirmation Process

ON 21 OCTOBER 1917, George Raymond Reed of the 1st Canadian Mounted Rifles absented himself in the vicinity of Vlamertinge, Belgium, while his unit was moving to the forward area at Ypres. Reed remained missing until he was apprehended by military police in January 1918. Once captured, he offered little to explain his absence, stating only that he had become separated from his battalion while enemy bombs were dropping and, unable to find them, opted to spend a night at the YMCA and wait for his battalion to come out of the line. He failed to offer an explanation for the length of his absence. For this crime, Reed was awarded a sentence of death by a military court martial in February 1918.[1] In spite of this clear case of desertion, Reed's commanding officer, Lieutenant Colonel R.C. Andros of the 1st Canadian Mounted Rifles, wrote passionately in Reed's defence:

> I would recommend that the sentence of FGCM of Death passed upon the said soldier, be commuted. My reasons for so doing are that, this man is only 19 ½ years of age and previous to this date he had always conducted himself, both in the line, and out in a soldierly manner. He has been continuously with this Battalion since June, 1916, and has been through the different engagements taken part in by this Battalion since then, and I have no complaints of his conduct. I consider that this crime was committed while under the influence of drink and that the accused on finding that he had been left behind became panicky, owing to his youthfulness and the bad advice given him by persons that he happened to be with at the time.[2]

Based on the letters of Andros and two more commanding officers, Reed's death sentence was commuted to five years of penal servitude. Reed survived the war and was demobilized on 28 March 1919.[3] In pleading on behalf of an errant soldier, Andros was not unique among his contemporaries. Letters of recommendation were a guilty soldier's best chance of avoiding confirmation of the death penalty. These letters from the corps, division, and battalion leaders were an extremely important factor in the confirmation or commutation of a death sentence. Fortunately for convicted soldiers, in the majority of cases, these letters lobbied for commuting death sentences and affording soldiers a second chance at honourable duty.

This chapter explores the themes that run through these letters of recommendation. They provide invaluable insight into the reasons why some death sentences were commuted while others were confirmed during the First World War. Letters of recommendation reveal which issues weighed most heavily on the minds of army commanders, and they speak to the amount of control that commanding officers had at this particular stage of the disciplinary process. Letters of recommendation indicate the importance attached to medical evidence, previous individual conduct, and battalion behaviour. In total, my research includes 352 letters of recommendation, the majority of which come from the levels of battalion, brigade, and division commanders. A significant number of letters also come from the corps commander, while two letters were written by company commanders and five by General Henry Horne, commander of the First Army, a BEF formation that included some British divisions as well as the Canadian Corps through a portion of 1917-18. Not every case file contains the standard three letters of recommendation; some cases are devoid of any letters, and some letters are simply illegible. In spite of these obstacles, we are fortunate in that court martial transcripts and letters do exist in the cases of commuted CEF death sentences. This is not the case in Britain, where the files of commuted death sentences have not survived, having been either lost or destroyed.[4]

Following a court martial, the trial transcript and any other relevant information pertaining to the crime were sent to each commanding officer, who was asked to contribute a recommendation. These papers moved up the chain of command, with the lowest level of authority being the first to express an opinion on the crime and a recommendation for punishment. Papers moved from battalion commanders, to brigade, division, and corps commanders, before being reviewed by the deputy judge advocate general and ultimately sent to the commander-in-chief. The importance attached to the trial transcript and the actual facts of the case by those responsible for writing letters of recommendation remains debatable. Commanding officers were more likely to comment on extenuating circumstances and on the personal qualities of the soldier rather than on the actual crime. According to instructions, commanding officers were asked to comment specifically on

(1) The character (from a fighting point of view as well as behaviour) of the soldier, his previous behaviour in action and the period of service abroad. This should be furnished by the soldier's C.O.
(2) The state of discipline of the unit concerned.

(3) The reasons why the confirming and reviewing authorities recommend that the sentence should or should not be carried out.
(4) In addition where the crime is that of desertion with intention of avoiding a particular duty ... the opinion of the C.O. based on his personal knowledge or that of his Officers, of the soldier's characteristics, as to whether the crime was deliberately committed with a view to avoiding the duty.[5]

Although most of the main points listed above were relatively straightforward, they were also vague enough to allow commanding officers great latitude in explaining the reasoning behind their decisions. For example, though not obliged to, many commanding officers brought up a soldier's weakened medical state. Although conditions such as shell shock were to be determined and dealt with at the court martial level, this was not always the reality. As stated in Chapter 3, according to the *King's Regulations and Orders for the Army*, any accused soldier was to be assessed by a medical officer on each day of his court martial.[6] In practice, however, this was not the norm. Typically, medical boards were called only when evidence indicated that shell shock might have been a motivating factor in a crime, and even in these cases there are many discrepancies and instances in which the court martial failed to consider medical evidence. In such cases, it was typical for battalion commanders to seize the opportunity to state that, despite court martial findings, mental incapacity was indeed a factor motivating desertion.

In the case of Charles Dionne of the 15th Battalion, the court martial did not see enough evidence to find him not guilty or even to recommend mercy or a medical inquiry. However, all three of his commanding officers recommended commutation of his death sentence based on his previous history of shell shock, for which he had been admitted to hospital exactly one year prior to his desertion. Dionne was cleared for duty by a medical board on 7 March 1917. He subsequently fled his unit on 8 September following an order to proceed with a work party. He remained absent until he was apprehended by military police at Amiens on 13 September. In pleading for Dionne's life, Major General Archibald Cameron Macdonell of the First Canadian Division referred to Dionne as being of "nervous disposition," and all three officers referred Haig to Dionne's troubled medical history, which, in addition to treatment for shell shock, included a gunshot wound to his thigh in 1915.[7] Macdonell's consideration of Dionne's condition was consistent with his concern for the men under his command. Ian McCulloch, author of "Batty Mac: Portrait of a Brigade Commander of the Great War, 1915-1917," described Macdonell as "one of the most eccentric, indomitable and beloved officers to have commanded troops in the First World War."[8] Given the supporting documentation that Dionne received from his commanders, his death sentence was commuted to five years of penal servitude. He returned to service, and his medical records indicate no further treatment for shell shock. He was demobilized on 20 April 1919.[9]

A soldier's mental condition even caused some commanders to admit their own errors in judgment. On 2 July 1918, Harry Sandelin abandoned the 4th Canadian Mounted Rifles while in the support line, and he remained absent until his capture on 9 July. Evidence emerged at his court martial that indicated a troubled history of shell shock. His comrade, Private H. Rumley, stated that in the days before his desertion "the accused was awfully nervous. He was scared of our own shells. He behaved in an extraordinary way. He ran and shook. He couldn't keep still."[10] Furthermore, a member of the Royal Army Medical Corps testified that he believed that Sandelin was unfit for duty and could not be held responsible for his actions.[11] In light of the testimony, the first witness, Lieutenant John Charles Wreyford, in charge of Sandelin's platoon at the time of his absence, admitted to the court that "I considered him fit to go into the line at that time. From what I have learned since I am [of the] opinion that the accused should not have gone in the line."[12] For inexplicable reasons, in spite of the clear evidence of shell shock, Sandelin was found guilty of desertion by the members of the court martial. However, his sentence was commuted based on three strong letters of recommendation. As stated by Lieutenant Colonel W.R. Patterson of the 4th Canadian Mounted Rifles, "from personal knowledge and from reports of his Company Officers, I do not feel that man is capable of carrying out his duties under fire. He is a cheerful, obedient worker out of the line, and I am certain that he makes every effort to overcome his weakness, and I do not believe his crime to be deliberate."[13] His sentence was commuted to five years of penal servitude. Sandelin survived the First World War and was demobilized on 27 August 1919.[14]

Of course, cases exist in which commanders did not display the same level of understanding as in the cases of Dionne and Sandelin. These former cases provide evidence of a much harsher disciplinary system that was insensitive to the strains of prolonged warfare. The case of Harry Jennings exemplifies the brutality that could at times be part of military discipline. On 29 December 1917, Jennings was on his first tour with the 58th Battalion after having spent the previous eighteen months in hospital recovering from a gunshot wound. Unable to withstand the fear of being back in the trenches, Jennings reported to Captain Orr of the CAMC that he was suffering from shell shock. At Jennings's trial for desertion, Orr conceded that the accused had indeed been frightened but went on to state to the tribunal that "I thought, if the accused had twenty-four hours in his dugout, he would pull himself together."[15] Jennings was found guilty of desertion on 14 January 1918 and sentenced to death. All of his commanders lobbied for the death penalty, showing little or no sympathy for his fear. Writing in favour of execution, Major General Louis Lipsett of the 3rd Division wrote that "I cannot see any reasonable excuse for this man's nerves being in bad condition on his first tour in the line after 18 months in hospital and England. In my opinion cowardice is the cause of his offence. I recommend that the sentence be carried out."[16] Despite the harsh tone of the recommendation, Lipsett was well respected among the men whom he commanded. He was especially well regarded among the soldiers of the 3rd Canadian Division for willingly sharing the same dangers that they endured. On 14 October 1918, Lipsett was shot in the face by a German sniper. He died as a result of his wounds.[17] In an interview conducted with the CBC in the 1960s, General George Pearkes of the 116th Battalion remembered of himself and his comrades that "we were tremendously proud of Lipsett, our divisional commander, and thought that he was the very best commander."[18] For unknown reasons, Haig ignored all of the recommendations of the commanding officers and chose to commute Jennings's sentence to ten years of penal servitude. Eight months later, in August 1918, Jennings was diagnosed with neurasthenia. He survived the war and was demobilized on 4 July 1919.[19]

Cases such as that of Jennings personalize the weaknesses of a disciplinary system that failed at times to understand the strain on the average soldier, and they serve as potent examples for those who seek to condemn the military judicial system of the First World War. Yet, for all of the criticisms, records show that cases such as that of Jennings were the exception rather than the rule. More often than not, commanding officers proved that they were keenly aware of the pressures that the ordinary soldier suffered. Military and medical authorities learned from the medical evidence gathered over four years of fighting, and they attempted to apply their knowledge in ways that balanced mercy with justice. This was not a callous system that sought to use men up until they simply had no more left to give.

ALTHOUGH COMMANDERS WERE not required to comment on a convicted soldier's perceived physical or mental health, they were asked to comment specifically on the fighting character of the soldier. It was at this point in the disciplinary process that one's record of service could prove to be a life-saving factor. A soldier who had proven himself in previous battles could typically count on the support of his battalion commander. For example, writing on the case of John Alexander Carleton in May 1917, Lieutenant Colonel Cameron Edwards of the 38th Battalion supported the commutation of Carleton's death sentence based on conduct prior to his desertion, including his actions at the Somme in November 1916, when Carleton "showed the greatest gallantry and devotion to duty."[20] Edwards explained Carleton's crime as an aberration, having more to do with nervous strain than any criminal intent. Carleton's death sentence was ultimately commuted to ten years of penal servitude. In September 1917, Carleton went on to suffer a nervous breakdown. On 26 March 1918, he was sent back to Canada and placed in an asylum in Kingston, Ontario, where he was diagnosed with confusional insanity. He was discharged from the CEF on 6 June 1918 as medically unfit.[21]

Edwards could be just as quick to identify soldiers who failed to prove themselves in action. In recommending that Frank Coulby be executed for his four-day desertion from the trenches on 11 September 1917, Edwards wrote that "the character of the marginally noted man from a fighting point of view is not good. He was in the attack at Vimy on April 9th, but there is no evidence of any nature as regards his action one way or another. His behaviour has been insolent and insubordinate."[22] Despite the recommendation that Coulby should serve as an example to the rest of the 38th Battalion, he was ultimately given a sentence of five years of penal servitude. He returned to service and was eventually demobilized on 16 June 1919.[23] In considering their recommendations, commanding officers such as Edwards were forced to separate the individual soldier from his record of service. Any personal sentimentality that a commanding officer might have harboured had to rank second to how a soldier had performed in battle and how that performance had affected the rest of his battalion.

While previous records of service were to be addressed in the letters of recommendation, disciplinary records were not. One would assume that, as in civilian law, an individual's disciplinary history would be one of the most important factors in sentencing and, therefore, one of the most accurate predictors of the final decision of the court martial.[24] This was not the case. During courts martial themselves, details of previous crimes were not admissible. Furthermore, and even more surprising, though previous crimes do appear to have been influential in some cases when it came to final sentencing, this happened because of a commanding officer's initiative and not because of any strict directive that required a disciplinary history to be considered during sentencing. No such directive existed. Thus, while some commanding officers chose independently to raise prior offences in their letters of recommendation, ultimately the commander-in-chief was entitled to ignore this information if he so chose. This is a clear difference between military and civilian law. That said, there were many cases of habitual offenders receiving the ultimate penalty. For example, Fortunat Auger of the 14th Battalion had three previous convictions for being absent without leave as well as a number of minor offences that preceded his execution for desertion in March 1916.[25] Similarly, James Wilson of the 4th Battalion had four convictions for being absent without leave on his record, and he had been the subject of numerous FGCMs before he was eventually shot for desertion.[26] Wilson absented himself on 25 February 1916 and then surrendered to authorities on 29 May. Instead of facing another court martial, he received an order to prepare for the trenches as a major German offensive was being launched at Mount Sorrel. Rather than returning to the trenches, Wilson fled again on 12 June, only to surrender four days later. In recommending his execution, Major General Arthur Currie of the First Canadian Division wrote that repeated sentences of field punishment had proven to be no deterrent to Wilson and that he had taken advantage of an opportunity during his release to desert during an emergency.[27]

As Currie rose in the ranks, his views on discipline remained consistent. A few weeks after being promoted to commander of the Canadian Corps, Currie was approached by Canon F.G. Scott, Protestant chaplain of the First Canadian Division, who pleaded for clemency on behalf of a soldier sentenced to be executed. Despite Currie's friendship with Scott and his respect for his mission, Currie upheld the court's decision. As his biographer, Daniel G. Dancocks, describes it, Currie's views on discipline were "uncomplicated ... He equated discipline with good behaviour, and as long as his men behaved themselves, he was satisfied."[28] His views earned him respect from subordinates and a reputation for fairness among ordinary soldiers.

Of the twenty-three soldiers of the CEF who were executed for desertion or cowardice, eighteen of them had previous criminal records that had included charges for desertion or absence without leave and in some cases both. Furthermore, seven of these individuals had been previously court martialled, including Charles Welsh, Stephen Fowles, and Wilson Norman Ling, but reprieved from death sentences.[29] Overall, ninety-one of the executed British, dominion, and colonial soldiers were serving under suspended sentences from previous courts martial, and forty of them had already received commuted death sentences.[30]

However, just as the cases of some habitual offenders conform to what might have been considered expected standards, so too a significant number of men seem to have been sentenced in contradiction to them. Four men with absolutely clean records were shot by order of court martial. Included in this group is William Alexander of the 10th Battalion, who had an exemplary disciplinary and service record prior to his crime and execution in September 1917.[31]

While men such as Alexander suffered because of inconsistencies in the court martial system, others benefited from them. Matthew Latto of the 13th Battalion was a long-time disciplinary problem for the Canadian Corps. Before his conviction for desertion in January 1916, he had seven disciplinary incidences, which included ten different charges, none of them a minor offence; among them were four charges of absence and four charges of disobeying the commands of senior officers.³² In recommending that Latto's death sentence be carried out, Major General Arthur Currie of the First Canadian Division wrote of Latto on 21 January 1916 that "this man has previously been tried and found guilty of a similar offence. He has further been guilty on several occasions of absence and also of insubordination. He has been sentenced to 18 months of I.H.L. (commuted to 6 mos.); to 2 years' I.H.L. and to 5 years' Penal Servitude without effect."³³ However, in spite of his record and another recommendation for death in addition to Currie's, Latto's sentence was commuted to fifteen years of penal servitude. Latto was ultimately discharged from the CEF for reasons of misconduct in October 1919.³⁴

His case does not stand alone. Forty-three men among the commuted cases had previous charges of absence without leave or desertion on their disciplinary records, while an additional twenty-four men could be classified as having very poor disciplinary records, which I have defined as having a previous FGCM conviction for desertion or absence or more than four convictions of absence without leave. However, while these cases might raise questions about the fairness of the court martial system during the First World War, there is nothing illegal about the decisions made. Disciplinary records were not admissible evidence at trial, so repeated offences were not required to be considered when deciding on a final sentence. While commanding officers were asked to comment on past behaviour, there was no requirement that confirmed charges on a soldier's disciplinary record be taken into consideration during sentencing.

Even an offender who had escaped from military custody could be granted mercy. From the sources, it can be determined that prison security was lax at times. Reasons likely included shortages in manpower to staff the prisons adequately. Among the cases that I studied were twelve instances of confined men escaping from custody, only to be arrested again later. Among the worst cases was that of Harold Edward James Lodge. He initially deserted from the 19th Battalion while at Passchendaele on 2 November 1917. He was eventually found over a month later in Boulogne, wearing a Red Cross uniform. Lodge escaped from his initial confinement on 21 December. He was found and arrested again on a ship on 7 January 1918. While proceeding to prison, Lodge escaped yet again by jumping off a train. On 14 January, he was found again in Boulogne. His repeated escapes helped to ensure that his death sentence was carried out. Lodge was shot by a firing squad on 13 March 1918.³⁵ While his case is no doubt extraordinary, many others managed to escape from military custody yet have their death sentences commuted. Chester Horace Elmer had been serving in France for twenty-six months when he initially deserted on 23 March 1918. He was arrested at Étaples, France, on 17 April, but he escaped from custody a short time later. In spite of this added infraction, when he was eventually brought to trial, his commanding officers recommended commutation of his sentence based on his previous good service and the generally good discipline among members of the 10th Canadian Field Artillery, to which Elmer belonged. He went on to suffer a nervous breakdown in November 1918 but ultimately survived the war.[36]

Given that commanding officers were asked to comment on fighting value and other personal characteristics of the soldiers under their charge, one would expect that these officers had a certain level of familiarity with them, but this was not always the case. It was extremely rare for any corps, division, or brigade commander to have intimate knowledge of the soldier for whom he was recommending that his life be spared or taken. More often than not, the letters of brigade commanders remained focused on the behaviour of the battalion as a whole. Recommendations were made with discipline in mind rather than personal character. In some instances, brigade and corps commanders simply referred back to the comments of battalion commanders when making their own recommendations, copying lines from battalion commanders verbatim into their own recommendations. At other times, higher authorities kept their recommendations simple, replying only with "I recommend the death sentence should be commuted" or "I recommend the death sentence should be confirmed." Over seventy such recommendations given by both corps and division commanders can be found among the letters of recommendation for convicted soldiers. In some cases, even battalion commanders admitted knowing very little about the soldiers for whom they had been asked to provide recommendations. In 1917, Major W.R. Patterson of the 4th Canadian Mounted Rifles wrote of convicted soldier Harry Sekum that it was difficult to express an opinion on whether his crime had been deliberate because he had very little knowledge of the man.[37] Even in cases in which battalion commanders did not explicitly state that they had no knowledge of a particular soldier, this was often likely the case. In a 1922 report, Major General J.H. MacBrien noted that, in compiling information for their letters of recommendation, it was common practice among commanding officers to seek the opinions of platoon commanders and platoon sergeants, who had the advantage of day-to-day interactions with soldiers and were thus in a much better position to speak of records of service and typical behaviours.[38]

Regardless of any limitations that battalion commanders might have faced when writing about soldiers, the most illuminating letters of recommendation found among the archival material still consistently come from this level of authority. Whether their opinions were based on their own experiences with convicted soldiers or on conversations with platoon and company commanders, generally these letters were the most revealing, for they addressed the personality and work ethic of a soldier in a way that higher levels of command simply could not. The insights offered in the letters of battalion commanders made them among the most influential when personal history was the major factor in deciding whether to commute or confirm a death sentence. Because of their proximity to the private soldier, or to those who knew him best, battalion commanders could prove to be extremely influential voices in the confirmation process. Their influence also helped to decentralize power from the army's highest ranks and proved the fluidity of the military disciplinary system on the whole. That the letters of battalion commanders were so highly regarded and so often referred to by division and corps commanders disputes myths of an authoritative and oppressive military regime in which power was concentrated solely at the top. Although the commander-in-chief was indeed the final arbiter in any death sentence, it was rare for him to act in contradiction to the recommendations of commanding officers. If the commander-in-chief did so, then it was often in the name of mercy. In total, twenty cases exist in which every level of commanding officer of a convicted soldier recommended that execution be carried out but the commander-in-chief chose instead to commute the sentence.

Because battalion commanders were more acquainted with young soldiers on a daily basis than their corps or division commanders, were they more likely to understand the hardships that the soldiers endured and therefore be more empathetic than high command and more lenient in their recommendations for punishment? Statistics indicate that this was not necessarily the case. Among the cases that I researched, the number of letters from battalion commanders recommending commutations and the number recommending confirmations are similar. There are fifty-two letters from battalion commanders urging commutation and forty letters pressing for application of the death penalty.[39] In cases without clear-cut evidence, battalion commanders were likely to give the soldier the benefit of the doubt and plead for commutation by referencing previous good behaviour or by insisting that the convicted soldier had not been fully aware of the consequences of his crime.

In the case of Thomas Albert Bishop, Captain A. Nation of the 7th Battalion admitted that he did not know why Bishop had fled, but he assumed that there must have been a good reason. As Nation wrote in his recommendation for commutation, "he [Bishop] had a clean sheet and was never in trouble in the company ... I should say that the man most certainly did not stay away to avoid duty but probably having overstayed his leave for some other reason, was afraid to come back for the fear of punishment."[40] Nation made this recommendation even though Bishop had "overstayed his leave" by five months before being arrested by military police. Bishop had left his unit for leave on 16 May 1916 and had failed to return by the assigned date of 25 May. He had not been arrested until October. During his trial, Bishop admitted that "while in England I was drinking heavily and had no intention of staying away the length of time I did. Part of the time I do not remember what I was doing."[41] In spite of his admission, he received two more letters in favour of commutation, and his death sentence was reduced to five years of penal servitude. Bishop returned to service and suffered a gunshot wound to his wrist in an attack on 2 September 1918. He was demobilized on 14 October 1919.[42]

Cases such as that of Bishop show that, when commanding officers thought it appropriate, they had no hesitation in interjecting personal feelings for soldiers into letters of recommendation if they thought that doing so would influence the commander-in-chief's final decision. In the case of Austin Edward Tobin, whose character witnesses at trial showed him to be a well-liked and well-regarded soldier of the 52nd Battalion, his commanding officer clearly outlined not only his support but also his sympathy for Tobin, accused of having deserted on 3 September 1917. At his trial, the second witness, Private G. Pritchard of the 52nd Battalion, recalled that he, along with Tobin and the rest of a Lewis Gun Section, were in a cellar before proceeding up to the line:

> In a cellar in which I was present with the accused, a shell exploded at the doorway, blowing candles out and tearing a curtain off the door. Accused was about a yard from the door at the time. We did not get much sleep that night. Accused showed signs of being badly shaken in his nerves the next day. The whole of the next day we were heavily shelled.[43]

Tobin testified that during this heavy shelling he had recognized that he was mentally unwell, so he had fled for the transport lines, believing that he could be of more use there than in the line. He had reported himself one day later to Regimental Sergeant Major Johnson of the 52nd Battalion, who stated at the trial that the accused had not seemed to realize that he had committed any offence.[44] Asked at his trial why he had not reported himself sick, Tobin replied, "I did not report sick because I had never reported sick in France and I thought I would be able to carry on by the time evening came." He went on to say, "I did not intend to desert and am sorry I acted as I did. I should like to carry on with my battalion again if given the opportunity."[45] Given that Tobin had no prior record of military crimes, his sentiments appear to have been sincere, and most importantly they were accepted by his commanding officer, Lieutenant Colonel W.W. Foster. Although Foster, in his letter of recommendation, acknowledged that a crime had been deliberately committed, he also threw his authority and his sympathy behind Tobin, writing that "the crime was deliberate, but undoubtedly this soldier was not in his usual frame of mind. There had been heavy shelling and he was obsessed with the idea that he would become a casualty during this particular tour in the line. Should clemency be exercised I would be glad to take him back on suspended sentence."[46] This letter of recommendation was important in that it clearly touched on factors that Foster was not obliged to discuss. In three short sentences, he managed to note extenuating circumstances such as the heavy shelling and Tobin's weakened mental state as well as his high regard for Tobin by stating that he would gladly welcome him back to his unit. Foster's influential recommendation was supported by Brigadier General F.W. Hill of the 9th Canadian Infantry Brigade as well as by Lieutenant General Arthur Currie of the Canadian Corps.[47] The death sentence was commuted to three years of penal servitude, and Tobin was quickly put back in the line. Unfortunately, he would die only months later, on 5 November 1917, of a gunshot wound to the head sustained at Passchendaele.[48]

Although Foster's letter proves that commanders were willing to comment on extenuating circumstances at the front, records show that they were not inclined to go beyond this. Soldiers used their statements of mitigation to comment on their lives at home, including factors such as being the sole support of a family, but these factors were left at the court martial and appear to have had no influence on the reports of commanding officers. No effort was made to plead the case of a soldier based on his home life in Canada. This was even true of soldiers who had wives and children back home. In total, 79.6 percent of CEF members were single.[49] In my research, there were only sixteen married men among both the commuted and the confirmed death sentences. Among these cases, only one letter, written on behalf of Tobin of the 52nd Battalion, briefly mentions that Tobin was married, and this fact might have been of some consideration when deciding whether or not to apply the death penalty.[50]

KNOWING WHOSE VOICES MATTERED is the first step in understanding the confirmation process; the second step is knowing what mattered to those who had voices. The state of discipline in a battalion was of major importance, and based on the evidence it was the one principle that overrode all others in the minds of commanders. In the words of Canadian historian Desmond Morton, "the avowed purpose of military law is not to do absolute justice to the individual but to maintain discipline."[51] It was a strongly held belief among the military hierarchy that the most disciplined army would go on to win the war. There are over 130 letters of recommendation that comment specifically on the state of discipline in the battalion and use this factor either to encourage or to discourage an execution. This is not surprising when one considers that a successful army unit is dependent on a strong group dynamic and the maintenance of morale. A single soldier's particular problems had to be considered secondary to the group's needs. Most commanders commented on whether there was a "need for an example to be made." The necessity of an execution was measured by its potential impact on the group more than its impact on the individual. Commanders were just as swayed by the needs of the battalion as they were by individual stories, often stating that it was urgent that an example be set to reimpose order and good behaviour.

In one interesting case, Colonel Arthur-Édouard Dubuc of the 22nd Battalion urged execution to reinforce already existing good behaviour. Alexander Dumesnil absented from the battalion on 8 July 1917 while his unit was in the trenches at Lens. When he was apprehended by authorities on 14 August, he gave an assumed name to his captors and lied that he himself was looking for a prisoner.[52] Following a verdict of guilty for desertion, all of Dumesnil's commanding officers, including Tremblay, now commanding the 5th Canadian Infantry Brigade, recommended that his death sentence be carried out. Writing as commander of the 22nd Battalion, Dubuc noted to headquarters in September that

> the state of discipline in the Battalion at present is very good. Absences without leave are very rare, probably because of the shooting of three men of this unit since the month of April. In my opinion the crime was deliberately committed, with the object of avoiding duty in the trenches ... I recommend the extreme penalty be carried out, in order that the men may understand that the crime of Desertion and Absence without Leave will not be dealt with leniently and in order to prevent the possible reoccurrence of cases of Desertion and Absence without Leave which existed before the shooting of the three men of this Unit.[53]

Despite recommendations to the contrary, Dumesnil's death sentence was commuted by the commander-in-chief to fifteen years of penal servitude. Dumesnil survived the war and was demobilized on 20 September 1919.[54]

Standards for what qualified as poor battalion behaviour obviously differed among commanding officers. Following a self-inflicted gunshot wound to his forearm on 1 April 1918, Francis Button returned to service with the 43rd Battalion. On 12 August, after being warned to go forward with his company during operations at Amiens, Button fled from his unit. He remained absent until he was apprehended at Boulogne on 23 August. Major General Loomis of the Third Canadian Division and Brigadier General D.M. Ormond of the 9th Canadian Infantry Brigade both recommended that Button be executed for his crime. General Henry Horne, commander of the First Army, stated that "the

Battalion reports three cases of desertion during the recent fighting ... I am of the opinion that an example is necessary and recommend the sentence be carried out."[55] His recommendation comes as little surprise. Although contemporaries noted that he ran an "essentially happy unit," he was also described as "impatient of indiscipline, of slackness, of eyewash."[56] However, while Lieutenant Colonel W.K. Chandler of the 43rd Battalion acknowledged the rash of desertions that Horne referred to, he also viewed them quite differently. Commenting on the case, Chandler stated that "instances of desertion have been limited to three cases all of which were men from desertion in the face of the enemy was to be anticipated, execution of the sentence of death would I submit be punitive only; the general state of discipline does not call for an example being made in this case."[57] Although one can only speculate on what accounted for the dramatically differing views of the state of discipline, for Chandler downplaying poor behaviour had its benefits. To place an inordinate amount of emphasis on poor battalion behaviour could call his own leadership into question. On the other hand, as a battalion commander, Chandler, with a more direct day-to-day relationship with his troops, was in a far better position than more senior officers to judge the battalion's overall level of discipline. Button's death sentence was ultimately commuted to fifteen years of penal servitude, but Button was eventually discharged from the army for misconduct in 1920.[58]

While officers fully understood that errant soldiers could hurt group dynamics and that executions could have a stabilizing effect, they also understood the need to choose who would be executed. Simply put, some soldiers served as good examples, while others were too well liked or popular for execution. The deaths of these men at the hands of Canadian authorities risked sparking dissent among surviving comrades. When recommending the commutation or confirmation of a death sentence, it was in a commander's favour to understand a soldier's standing among his fellow soldiers.

Following his execution, Henry Kerr was likely seen as no major loss to the 7th Battalion. Although the information concerning his desertion is sparse, from his personnel file it is clear that Kerr was a repeat offender, with five previous charges for the crime of absence without leave as well as charges of misconduct and breaking escort throughout 1915 and 1916.[59] These repeated charges clearly affected his reputation among his fellow soldiers. Canadian historian Andrew B. Godefroy writes of Kerr that "his conduct was so bad under shellfire that his platoon mates asked that he might be left behind in the future." Godefroy goes on to say that "Kerr is one of the few cases where fellow soldiers spoke out against one of their own."[60] When he was executed for the crime of desertion on 21 November 1916, there might have been little outrage felt among his comrades.[61]

The case of Kerr differed dramatically from that of Edward Millar, whose popularity among fellow soldiers helped to save him from the death penalty. Millar was convicted of desertion on 22 September 1918 after fleeing in August while the 1st Canadian Machine Gun Battalion was assembling for an artillery barrage at Hendecourt.⁶² Despite conceding that Millar's conduct sheet was not good, Lieutenant Colonel Watson of the 1st Battalion wrote to the deputy judge advocate general and Haig that "the boy is well known and popular, and gave a good account of himself during the operations at Amiens."⁶³ Major General Archibald Cameron MacDonell of the First Canadian Division concurred and went even further: "He is a well known and popular soldier in the Unit and if the death sentence were inflicted it would not be a good case for the purpose of example."⁶⁴ It seems that commanding officers were well aware of Millar's popularity and feared that his execution might increase ill feelings among the men of the battalion rather than put a halt to bad behaviour.⁶⁵

Although some commanders pushed for application of the death penalty more than others, there is no evidence to suggest real dissent or debate among commanders over the use or effectiveness of the death penalty. Sorting through the evidence today, it seems that camaraderie might have played a bigger role in deterring desertions than the threat of execution. Bonds among soldiers created unit cohesion built in part upon a sense of responsibility for, and obligation to, one's fellow soldiers – no soldier wanted to let the man beside him down. Where a lack of camaraderie existed, we are offered insights into possible contributing factors to desertion. In the case of the aforementioned soldier Alexander Daley, the social isolation from his unit and the absence of bonding help to explain his actions. Likewise, the same factor might help to explain the desertions of particular groups, including Russian and Ukrainian soldiers, who remained partially isolated from the units because of barriers in language and culture. Finally, the same reasoning helps to account for the impetus of soldiers to desert while on leave. Away from peer bonds, some men might have found it easier to walk away from their responsibilities, an action that some might not have undertaken had they been surrounded by a positive peer influence provided by the military unit.

In spite of this, it appears that in the early twentieth century most commanders believed in the deterrent impact of executions. The only evidence that I found questioning the policy of executions came from Brigadier General James MacBrien of the 12th Canadian Infantry Brigade, and his letter was much more an indictment of recruitment policies on the home front than the death penalty itself. In a letter regarding the death sentence of Vernon Treveleyn, charged with desertion from the 38th Battalion, MacBrien stopped short of questioning the death penalty outright but did question its use among volunteers when thousands of other men at home were failing even to enlist. Writing to the Fourth Canadian Division on 17 June 1917, MacBrien observed that

> it has been recommended that the marginally noted [Treveleyn], found guilty by Field General Court Martial of Desertion, be shot, as this is considered necessary in the interests of discipline. There is, however, another point of view which might be considered in connection with exacting the extreme penalty in the cases of Desertion by men who volunteered, and who have rendered service at the front for a certain length of time. There are thousands in Canada still, who have not volunteered and who have made no effort to come to the front, and the question arises, should a volunteer be shot for failing after attempting to do his duty. Once Conscription has been adopted then this question will not arise.[66]

MacBrien's letter came at the height of the conscription crisis in Canada and is as much a reflection of the military's frustration with the politics at home as it is with disciplinary policies at the front. By 1917, the number of soldiers volunteering for overseas service had significantly dropped. In response to the shortage of men, Prime Minister Robert Borden introduced a policy of conscription in May 1917 known as the Military Service Act. The proposal was met with strong opposition by several groups, including French Canadians and farmers, and it created divisions within Canadian society. Despite the protests, the Military Service Act was passed in August 1917, and conscription became law. The issue of conscription went on to define the 1917 federal election in Canada. To shore up support for his policy and his Unionist Party, Borden introduced the Military Voters Act, which gave the vote to soldiers and nurses serving overseas, a group largely in favour of conscription. The vote was also extended to female relatives of serving soldiers through the Wartime Elections Act. At the same time as these voting rights were extended, the vote was denied to anyone claiming the status of conscientious objector and to recent immigrants hailing from "enemy countries." Borden's electoral manoeuvres helped to secure his party's election win in December 1917.

Initial studies of the issue of conscription concluded that the policy had been introduced too late to have any significant impact on the Canadian war effort. More recent studies have suggested that the twenty-four thousand conscripts who arrived in France were enough to sustain the Canadian Corps for an additional six months, and, had the war dragged on any longer, more conscripts would have been absolutely essential to maintain the same level of Canadian participation.[67] No soldier conscripted into the CEF was ever executed during the First World War, and conscripted soldiers entered the war far too late to indicate any significant patterns showing that they were disciplined any differently from volunteers.

Even taking into account MacBrien's letter, it appears that all levels of command believed in the deterrent effect of executions. As Brigadier General F.P. Crozier of the BEF wrote in his memoirs following the war,

> the question of the ability to "stick it" or to do the right thing in the right way, in action, is largely one of morale; but the fact cannot be overlooked that fear of the consequences undoubtedly plays an important part in the reasoning powers of men distracted by fear, cold, hunger, thirst or complete loss of morale and staying power. I should be very sorry to command the finest army in the world without the power behind me which the fear of execution brings.[68]

Sir Douglas Haig's own faith in the death penalty was most demonstrable in his attitude toward Australian soldiers.[69] In the First World War, the Australian Imperial Force was the only army not to sanction use of the death penalty. There are two theories about why the Australians chose not to practise execution. The first theory attributes the decision to the "Breaker Morant" incident during the Boer War. In February 1902, Australians Harry Morant and Peter Handcock were shot by order of a British court martial for killing Boer prisoners. Popular opinion in Australia at the time was against the trial, believing that Morant and Handcock were being used as scapegoats for British Chief of Staff Lord Kitchener's own ill-fated order to shoot prisoners. Further fuelling Australian opposition was that British officers convicted of the same offence had received lesser punishments. Ultimately, the death sentences were carried out without the consent of the Australian government, thus setting the stage for its attitude toward the death penalty in the First World War.[70] The second theory argues that the Australian government refused to impose the death penalty because of its repeated attempts to pass conscription. Considering Australian public opinion about the death penalty, conscription was more difficult to achieve if the death penalty was allowed.[71]

According to the Australian Defence Act, a death sentence could be passed by a court martial against an Australian soldier, but the commander-in-chief of the British Army lacked the authority to confirm the sentence.[72] As a result of this policy, Haig thought that Australian soldiers were badly disciplined and smugly aware of their security when it came to court martial execution. Drawing comparisons with the Canadian Corps, Haig wrote to his wife in February 1918:

> I spent some time today with the Canadians. They are really fine disciplined soldiers now and so smart and clean. I am sorry to say that the Australians are

not nearly so efficient. I put this down to Birdwood, who, instead of facing the problem, has gone in for the easier way of saying everything is perfect and making himself as popular as possible. We have had to separate the Australians into Convalescent Camps of their own, because they were giving so much trouble when along with our men and put such revolutionary ideas into their heads.[73]

Furthermore, in March 1918, writing in his journal about the disproportionately high number of Australian soldiers in prison, Haig noted that "nearly one Australian in every hundred men is in prison. This is greatly due to the fact that the Australian[s] refused to allow capital punishment to be awarded to any Australian."[74]

Haig's comments were correct in that a high number of Australians served prison sentences, more than their British or dominion counterparts. However, though Haig saw this as indicative of the poor discipline of the Australian forces, perhaps Australian military leaders were simply more forceful with the disciplinary options open to them. According to historian Christopher Pugsley, prison sentences for Australian soldiers were, on average, lengthier than those for soldiers of other forces. For example, where a Canadian soldier might be given a sentence of fifteen years of penal servitude, an Australian soldier would be given a life sentence for the same offence. Furthermore, the sentence of an Australian soldier was far less likely to be suspended.[75] In addition, author John Peaty has even suggested that a form of vigilante justice existed among junior officers in the Australian forces: "In the field offenders were tried by officers from neighbouring units and executed by soldiers from their own units. In other words, they were judged and punished by their peers: men who had faced the same dangers and who had experienced the same hardships."[76]

Whether Australian discipline in the First World War was negatively affected by lack of the death penalty was debated at the time, and modern historians still do not agree on the answer. Although Haig obviously believed that lack of the death penalty hurt the Australian forces, others, such as British MP Ernest Thurtle, pointed to the Australians as an example that high performance could be obtained without the threat of the ultimate penalty. In a 1930 British parliamentary debate on a review of the Army Act, Thurtle, pushing to abolish use of the death penalty for the crime of desertion, stated that the Australians fought with as much "gallantry" and "courage" as other troops subject to the death sentence.[77] In a more recent analysis, Peaty referred to the record of Australian discipline in the First World War as "appalling," while Oram disagrees and states that "the Australians' immunity from execution does not appear to have reduced their fighting ability." Oram groups the Australians with the Canadian and New Zealand soldiers as "consistently the most effective soldiers in the British Army, playing major roles in the capture of Vimy Ridge and Passchendaele" as well as being of vital importance in the Battle of Amiens in August 1918.[78]

WHEN SPEAKING TO THE crime of desertion itself, commanders considered whether they thought that the crime had been intentionally committed to avoid duty in the trenches. Of all the major factors that commanders were asked to address in their letters of recommendation, this was the only one that related specifically to the particular crime that had led to the court martial. Unlike at trials, in which soldiers were apt to point to the presence of a uniform to convince a court martial that they had not intended to desert, this factor appears to have been of little relevance to commanders; only one letter in all of the research that I conducted refers to the presence, or absence, of a uniform, and this letter does so in a way that clearly negates the importance of this factor. As Brigadier General F.W. Hill of the 9th Canadian Infantry Brigade wrote of Percival John Young, who absented from the 58th Battalion on 7 October 1916 and was apprehended in uniform in an Amiens brothel on 27 February 1917, "non-concealment and absence of disguise, as in this case, do not, in my opinion, negative an intention to desert, which I think the length of absence establishes."[79] Despite Hill's view of the intent of the crime, Young's death sentence was reprieved, and Young was instead given a punishment of fifteen years of penal servitude. He was demobilized on 27 April 1919.[80]

More relevant than uniforms was where the soldier was eventually discovered when arrested. The farther away a soldier ran from the front lines, the less favour he would curry among his superior officers. In the case of Rueben Smith, not straying far from the forward area was a decisive factor in commutation of his sentence. Smith had enlisted in the CEF in September 1914, just weeks after the declaration of war. He served with the 2nd Battalion and was wounded at the Second Battle of Ypres. He returned to the western front in February 1916 but was once again wounded by a bullet to the leg. He returned to his unit in time for the Battle of Vimy Ridge but then deserted on 27 April 1917 while his unit was experiencing heavy bombardment in the Farbus Sector while attempting to capture the village of Arleux. Although Smith remained absent for two months, at no time did he actually leave the forward area or the war zone. He testified that he had gone without food for long periods of time, living on what he could find in abandoned trenches. At his court martial in July 1917, his prisoner's friend argued that his location indicated that Smith had not intended to desert.[81] In his own statement of mitigation, Smith echoed this sentiment: "I am prepared to admit I was absent without leave from my battalion from the night of April 27-28, 1917 until June 22nd, 1917, but during that time I was not out of what was then the forward area of the actual war zone." Smith went on to say, "I am anxious to go on in the service to be given an opportunity to redeem myself, to spare the 2nd Canadian Battalion from being discredited by any action of mine and to try and maintain its reputation of which I am proud and to fulfill the pledge I made when I enlisted."[82] The fact that Smith never left the forward area appears to have been as relevant as his record of service to his commanding officers writing on his behalf. Brigadier General William A. Griesbach, known as a "strict but fair disciplinarian" of the 1st Canadian Infantry Brigade, wrote that "the accused was arrested in the danger zone, therefore, it is apparent that he had no deliberate intention of entirely deserting from the service."[83] Major General Archibald Cameron MacDonell of the First Division agreed with Griesbach's assessment of Smith. Based on these recommendations, his death sentence was commuted to five years of penal servitude. Smith returned to service but absented once more in 1917. He was once again officially declared a deserter by a court of inquiry on 6 September 1917. In the absence of any further documentation, including demobilization papers, it appears that Smith was never apprehended, and his ultimate fate remains unknown.[84]

Finally, in speaking to intention, commanders questioned whether a soldier fully understood the nature of his crime and its repercussions. They pointed to factors such as age or perceived lack of intelligence that might have prevented a soldier from fully realizing the consequences of his actions. Sidney Payne of the 87th Battalion deserted while proceeding with his unit to relieve the 22nd Battalion near Passchendaele. Found guilty of desertion in November 1917, Payne was sentenced to death.[85] He had lied about his age, enlisting at sixteen years old, and was only eighteen years old at the time of his court martial. Commenting on his crime, the commander of the 87th Battalion, Lieutenant Colonel J.V.P. O'Donahoe, noted, "I believe his offence was deliberate," but "owing to his age perhaps he did not realize the seriousness of the crime he committed."[86] His death sentence was commuted to three years of penal servitude, and Payne was demobilized on 9 June 1919.[87]

The question of understanding the nature of one's crime frequently raised the issue of intelligence. There is no way of knowing the exact education or intelligence level of a soldier convicted by court martial (or of any other soldiers in the CEF), for attestation papers do not record levels of formal education, and standardized assessments of intelligence were not administered to Canadian recruits.[88] Of course, formal education was no indicator of fighting capability, nor did a lack of education make one unable to distinguish right from wrong or preclude one from understanding verbal orders. However, issues of intelligence persisted, creeping into court martial proceedings and letters of recommendation. In several cases, commanders argued that intention to desert was not a factor because the offender was simply not intelligent enough to plan the crime and fully understand its repercussions. The issue of intelligence does appear frequently in letters of recommendation. Interestingly, a lack of intelligence had as great a chance of saving a soldier as it did of condemning him. What many commanders referred to as "low mentality" provided an excuse not to execute a soldier who proved to be a detriment to his unit but to save him. One only needs to examine the case and recommendation letters of Walter Perkins of the 78th Battalion. On 23 August 1917, Perkins absented from a work party in support lines and remained absent until he was apprehended by military police at Bruay on 28 August. At his defence, Perkins claimed that while carrying shells he had become dizzy and rested. He had ultimately lost his way and attempted to find his billet the whole time he was missing.[89] Writing in favour of commutation, Lieutenant Colonel James Kirkcaldy wrote this of Perkins:

> While Pte. Perkins always evinced willingness, he was invariably dull and stupid. I am inclined to the opinion that he is somewhat mentally deficient ... While in my mind there is no question but that the crime with which Pte. Perkins was charged was committed deliberately, I am [in] accord with the opinion of his Company Commander that he did not fully realize the full significance of the act.[90]

His death sentence was ultimately commuted to ten years of penal servitude, and Perkins was demobilized on 12 June 1919.[91]

Private John Sewell also received a commuted death sentence based in part on his intelligence, though in his case the belief in his supposed lack of intelligence was rooted purely in his race rather than his record. Sewell, of the 87th Battalion, was the only Aboriginal soldier involved in my study. He was convicted of desertion in September 1917 after he fled a march to the trenches at Lens in August. His unit was being shelled at the time he ran. Sewell later testified that he had fled because of an attack of nerves.[92] In an attempt to explain his actions, Lieutenant Colonel J.W. Warden, commanding the 11th Canadian Infantry Brigade, wrote that Sewell was "a North American Indian. These people are of a low mentality and liable to commit any act under the stress of great excitement."[93] Despite this statement, Warden was actually in favour of commutation of the death sentence, arguing that Sewell should be granted a reprieve because his very nature, and low morale "due to hardships and arduous duties performed in the line," left him unable to endure the stress of warfare.[94] His death sentence was commuted to five years of penal servitude. On 20 May 1919, Sewell was discharged from the CEF as physically unfit. His discharge was likely due to conditions associated with shell shock; his medical records indicate that he suffered from nightmares involving gunfire and choking.[95]

In his seminal 1998 work *Worthless Men*, Oram argues that Irish soldiers and colonial labourers in the BEF faced a greater risk of receiving the death penalty because of their perceived racial and ethnic inferiority. It was believed that their racial and ethnic attributes made them lesser soldiers than their English counterparts and justified their executions. This stands in sharp contrast to the Sewell case, but with only one Aboriginal soldier in my study it is difficult to determine whether his treatment was an exception or the rule. Prevailing attitudes toward Aboriginal soldiers in the CEF were complex. Stereotypes of inferiority, as exhibited in Warden's letter, persisted throughout the war. However, in many cases, Aboriginal soldiers were also heralded as superior warriors, an image that has continued to this day. Evidence shows that this reputation was well earned. Historian Timothy C. Winegard effectively argues that traditional skills in hunting and trapping, part of the prewar lives of many Aboriginals, allowed Aboriginal soldiers to excel in particular assignments, such as sniping and scouting. Commanders recognized these skills and assigned the soldiers accordingly. Winegard cites the example of well-known figures such as the highly decorated Corporal Francis Pegahmagabow, who tallied the best sniper figure in CEF history, along with the case of thirty-five Ojibwa soldiers from Fort William, Ontario, who all went on to be assigned as snipers.[96] With only one Aboriginal soldier among the cases that I studied, it is impossible to draw conclusions about the treatment of Aboriginal soldiers in the military judicial system of the Great War; however, we can look at the treatment of particular minority groups in civilian society in order to assess how they were treated in the early twentieth century.

In a study of capital punishment in Canada, David Chandler shows that, historically, ethnicity and race were factors in decisions to execute criminals. He states that English Canadians (Canadian born, English speaking) convicted of murder were overrepresented among commuted death sentences in civilian society and underrepresented among the executed. English Canadians were less likely to be executed than their French Canadian and Aboriginal counterparts.[97] In addition to the prejudices experienced by Aboriginals and French Canadians, in the early twentieth century immigrants, especially those from Eastern and Southern Europe, were a particular target of both fear and discrimination. As mentioned in Chapter 3, Russian immigrants in the CEF stand out for their receipt of death sentences. Although their crimes can be linked in part to their inability to communicate with their leaders and to fully understand their commands, their high proportion of death sentences was also influenced by prevailing views of the "other" that were common in Canada at the time. In just one example of this early-twentieth-century xenophobia, white Anglo-Saxon men were more likely to be convicted of murder, but men of Eastern European descent stood a greater chance of facing the gallows.[98] This pattern can be linked directly to rising concerns over immigration, especially from parts of Southern and Eastern Europe. In a 1914 parliamentary debate arising from Robert Bickerdike's initial attempt to abolish capital punishment, Liberal MP Frank Carvell of Carleton, New Brunswick, stated that

> I cannot bring myself to agree with my hon. friend from Montreal [Bickerdike], that the time has come when we should abolish capital punishment ... In a young country like Canada we are bringing in hundreds of thousands of people from every corner of the habitable globe. You may say: Well, your immigration officers ought to keep out undesirable immigrants. It is impossible to do that. In many cases men come in who may appear to be all right. They possess the necessary qualifications, they possess the necessary amount of currency, and therefore they become citizens of the country. But we do not know what their real, inside motives may be.[99]

Conservative MP William Nickle of Kingston, Ontario, agreed with Carvell's statement, arguing that Canada was more in need of capital punishment than ever as the nation was being "flooded" with the "foreign element."[100] Many MPs expressed the view that Eastern Europeans were particularly in need of the death penalty to teach them about Canadian law and order. The same sentiments carried through Bickerdike's 1915 campaign for abolition as well. In that year's debate on the subject, Minister of Justice Charles Doherty blamed the nation's rising murder rate on the influx of immigrants.[101]

In the context of the CEF, the other example comparable to Oram's conclusions regarding the treatment of the Irish in the BEF would be the treatment of French Canadians. The two CEF battalions with the highest number of death sentences passed were the 22nd and the 14th Battalions, the former with twenty-one death sentences and the latter with twelve. Both units were raised in Quebec, the 22nd Battalion in Quebec City, the 14th Battalion in Montreal. Although only one man from the 14th Battalion, Fortunat Auger, was actually executed, five of the twenty-three men executed for desertion or cowardice came from the 22nd Battalion, the only fully French-speaking Canadian battalion. It was suggested in 1922 that prejudice was an important factor in this statistic. Sir Arthur Currie, at that time the principal of McGill University, wrote to Major General MacBrien that

> I have private and confidential information from Ottawa this morning that when the House [of Commons] meets some member is going to bring up the question of shooting deserters at the front and that stress will be laid on the shooting of

French-Canadians in the 22nd and one French-Canadian in the 42nd ... Apparently the aim will be to prove that French-Canadians were treated unfairly, whereas we both know they got a little more consideration than anybody else.[102]

Based on this information, Currie recommended that MacBrien gather evidence to disprove the point; however, the parliamentary inquiry into the matter never went any further.

Scholars who have researched the issue of executions in the 22nd Battalion, notably Jean-Pierre Gagnon, author of the history of the battalion, have found that the high incidence of executions in the battalion had less to do with ethnicity than with the decisions of one man, Lieutenant Colonel Thomas-Louis Tremblay. Although the battalion did contend with a disproportionate number of disciplinary issues, in part brought on by high casualty rates and the subsequent replacement with undisciplined reinforcements, Gagnon also presents evidence that in many cases the high command sought reasons not to confirm the death sentences that Tremblay recommended. While in actuality the 22nd Battalion might not have been held to higher standards of behaviour, Gagnon suggests that Tremblay's decisions regarding discipline might have resulted from either outside or self-imposed pressures. Gagnon writes that "the smallest fault evident in the 22nd Battalion could well assume disproportionate importance in comparison with similar faults in English-speaking units."[103] Tremblay was particularly quick to call for the death penalty to prove both his own sense of duty and loyalty and the worth of Canada's single French-speaking battalion. In this sense, he was faced with a unique set of pressures related to both culture and language with which other commanding officers did not have to contend. As a result, Tremblay proved at times to be tougher on his men than the superior officers who reviewed the cases and were more accepting of extenuating circumstances.

RATHER THAN DISCUSSING uniforms and locations, when writing of intention most commanders tended to focus on whether or not there had been a major engagement, work party, or any other particular duty that the soldier had avoided. For example, in the case of Karlampy Bozan, who deserted from the St. Lawrence Camp at Bois de la Haie, France, where his unit was practising for an attack in June 1917, Lieutenant Colonel A.H. Borden from the 85th Battalion stated that "my opinion based on this man's characteristics as advised by his Company is that, the accused went absent deliberately to avoid going over the top in the attack for which he had been practicing with his company."[104] Such comments were common in the letters of recommendation and help to illustrate the importance of the timing of an offence in helping commanders to decide when an execution was needed as an example.

Oram has suggested that death sentences were directly influenced by the phases of the war. His statistics indicate a direct correlation between an increase in the enforcement of death sentences and the planning and execution of a major British offensive. He cites two major reasons for this relationship: "Firstly, desertion increasingly was more prevalent as zero-hour approached: tensions were no doubt heightened as the usual preliminary bombardment intensified. Secondly, the courts martial may at such times have adopted a harsher line with alleged deserters, using the death sentence as a deterrent to prevent any evasion of front line duties."[105]

Certainly, timing was an important consideration when offences and courts martial coincided with major offensives, and Oram's statement proves to be true in the Canadian case. Of a total of seven executions in the CEF in 1917, four of them were of individuals who had deserted only days before the Battle at Vimy Ridge. They included the executions of Harold George Carter, tried for desertion on 5 April; Gustave Comte, who deserted on 4 April; Joseph LaLancette, who deserted on 6 April; and Eugene Perry, tried for desertion on 3 April.[106]

Preparations for the Vimy Ridge attack were extensive. Units underwent weeks of tactical training, and objectives were clearly laid out to every soldier. Full-scale models of the battlefield and topographical maps were also used in training. Soldiers were keenly aware of the importance of Vimy Ridge, especially in light of previous Allied defeats there.[107] But with this knowledge came fear. Soldiers understood that many lives would be lost in the attempt to capture the ridge. In the weeks of preparation that preceded the offensive, fear of the upcoming advance might have compelled some soldiers to desert. During this time, commanding officers would have been keenly aware of the need to maintain strict discipline and to impose harsh punishments in cases of absence and desertion in order to send clear messages to other potential deserters.

Offensives influenced the behaviour of the ordinary soldier as well as the decisions of high command. For example, half of the executions for cowardice in the British Army took place during the Battle of the Somme, which tested the wills of British soldiers to a previously unfathomable level.[108] Furthermore, high command was far less likely to forgive transgressions committed during major battles in which other soldiers endured. No doubt this was an influential factor in the decision to execute Edward Fairburn, a machinist from St. Catharines, Ontario. He was absent from the 18th Battalion from April 1917 to January 1918. He was originally believed to have died on 9 April 1917 but was later arrested in Bruay, France, on 29 January 1918. During his period of absence, Fairburn missed the major offensives at Vimy Ridge, Hill 70, and Passchendaele, an extremely important factor in the desperate days of 1917.[109] There was intolerance among commanders for desertion committed in the days preceding or during major Allied offensives. Of the twenty-two men executed for desertion in the CEF, three were deserters from the Somme, four deserted during or just prior to the advance on Vimy Ridge, two were deserters from Passchendaele, and three deserted during other emergency situations. Records show that commanders made a point of describing the situations under which soldiers fled. Commanders were inclined to show more leniency to soldiers who failed to return from leave than to those who fled in the midst of an engagement or when called on to perform a specific duty.

That the CEF showed a link between a rise in executions and the timing of an offence is of little surprise. Civilian statistics follow similar patterns of leniency and severity. For example, rates of execution traditionally increased after a year marked by a particularly high number of homicides.[110] In 1930, Canada experienced an unprecedented high of 214 murders, up from 120 murders only four years earlier.[111] In 1931, the rate of executions jumped from 55 to 75 percent.[112] Undoubtedly, this jump was a response to the increase in crime as well as the social anxieties invoked by the onset of the Great Depression. The actual crimes were no more severe in 1931 than they were in 1929; rather, increased use of the death penalty was a response to outside factors and not actual facts of a case. Therefore, in both civilian society and the military, a rise in executions could be linked more to the timing of an offence or other related factors than to the criminal or his crime.

AT THE LEVEL OF recommendations, it is surprising to learn that leverage was an important feature of the military disciplinary system. Commanders freely took advantage of opportunities to express their opinions on their soldiers and even on the judicial process where they saw fit. For example, Brigadier General Edward Hilliam of the 10th Canadian Infantry Brigade went beyond the typical letter of recommendation by questioning the very charges against Frederick Doyle of the 44th Battalion. On the night of 19-20 June 1917, Doyle was proceeding to a communication trench to take up his post in a front line when he left his Lewis Gun Section and remained absent until 26 June. Although he was found guilty of desertion, the court martial recommended mercy on the grounds that Doyle had been ill at the time of the offence. This recommendation was not in fact legally viable. Commenting on the case, the assistant adjutant wrote to the 10th Canadian Infantry Brigade that

> the recommendation to mercy is not consistent with the finding. If it is considered that the man was ill at the time the offence was committed, the man had a very good reason for not being at his post and cannot therefore be found guilty of desertion. On the other hand, if the Court consider[s] the man was fit and capable

of doing his duty they can find him guilty of the offence, but they cannot recommend him to mercy on the grounds that he was ill.[113]

Based on the recommendation of the assistant adjutant that the proceedings should not have been confirmed and that the court martial should reassemble for revision, the recommendation for mercy was scratched from the proceedings. Brigadier General Hilliam went even further in criticizing the circumstances of the case. In his letter of recommendation for commutation, Hilliam argued that Doyle's death sentence should have been commuted because Doyle had been on his first tour only twenty days after being released from hospital, where he had undergone treatment for shell shock and a gunshot wound to his leg sustained at Givenchy.[114] Furthermore, Hilliam argued, at no time had Doyle actually left the forward area; instead, Hilliam believed, according to the evidence, Doyle, rather than deserting, had simply been unable to keep up with the other men. Hilliam questioned the charges laid against Doyle: "In my opinion the wrong charge has been placed against this man, and instead of being tried for desertion, which he certainly did not do, he should have been crimed with and charged for the crime of 'Deliberately Deserting his post and Neglecting his Duty, in the face of the enemy.'"[115] In spite of Hilliam's protests, a new trial was not ordered, and Doyle's guilty verdict was upheld, though his death sentence was commuted to three years of penal servitude.[116]

Commanders such as Hilliam typically referred back to their own judgments when writing their letters of recommendation, and trial transcripts appear to have been of little relevance at this point in the disciplinary process. Commanders were far more concerned with proven records of service over the long term of the accused and their battalions than with a single disciplinary incident. Beyond the mere facts of the case, commanders used their letters of recommendation to address broader issues of importance such as the disciplinary state of a battalion as a whole. Letters of recommendation allowed commanders to voice their most pressing concerns and to negotiate on behalf of, or against, their own soldiers. For the most part, these letters show that commanding officers, especially battalion commanders, lobbied for commutation more often than confirmation of the death penalty. By commenting on the "fighting value" of a soldier, commanders were using their own leverage within the military disciplinary system, and their opinions counted the most. While it can be argued that the inconsistencies in punishment point to a disorganized system, I would contend that in fact the system was set up this way intentionally to give commanders power over their own troops. The power structure was broken up into various levels of authority to ensure that no one level dominated the issuance of discipline and that the responsibility of handing down punishments was diffused among various levels of command. Thus, the leverage in the military system was the result of calculated policy and not disorganization. Furthermore, it is worth asking whether or not consistency in punishment was even possible given the circumstances of court martial proceedings. Unlike the civilian court system, in which precedent was used to ensure a certain level of consistency in decisions, precedent was irrelevant in military law since every case was to be judged on its own, with no reference to any prior case. When decisions were made based on considerations of the battalion as a whole rather than individual records, the results of a case had much to do with outside factors, so there could be little expectation of consistency. The individual facts of a case or the record of an individual soldier became secondary to the state and needs of the battalion as determined by its immediate commanders. The voices of commanders and their expressed wishes comprised the most important factor influencing military discipline. Factors that had not been considered during a court martial were of importance when it came time to make recommendations for punishment.

6
Pardon Campaigns

ON 16 OCTOBER 1916, Private Harry Farr of the Yorkshire Regiment, British Expeditionary Force, was shot at dawn for the crime of cowardice. Prior to his execution, Farr had served two years with the BEF and had, over the course of three separate occasions, spent approximately five months in hospital for the treatment of shell shock. In 2006, ninety years later, the particulars of his case were under review by the British High Court when the daughter and granddaughter of Farr were notified by Des Browne, the British secretary of state for defence, that Farr was being granted a posthumous pardon for his 1916 conviction. The decision in this case became the catalyst in the decision to grant a blanket pardon for all other British and Commonwealth soldiers executed for military offences in the First World War.[1] In total, 361 men were tried and executed under the British Army Act between 1914 and 1918. This number pales in comparison to the 996,230 men of combined British forces who died in service during these years. Yet the stories of these 361 men managed to come under public scrutiny and became the centre of political debates and grassroots movements to pardon those soldiers who faced their last moments at the firing post.

From 1914 to 1920, a total of 3,080 men of the British and dominion forces were sentenced to death, but approximately 90 percent of all death sentences were commuted. Judicial executions were an extremely rare form of death among soldiers of the British Empire. Considering the vast number of men from Great Britain and its empire who served on the western front at any given time, that there were only 7,371 courts martial for desertion, resulting in 2,004 death sentences and 272 executions, clearly shows that courts martial were not necessarily the norm, that most military offences were dealt with in a soldier's own company, and that punishment was often left to the discretion of his commanding officer.[2]

The execution of British and Commonwealth soldiers was a more contentious issue between 1989 and 2006 than at any other time during or since the Great War. The subject raised complex moral debates regarding military justice, and it proved to be a deeply divisive issue among historians of the war, campaigners for pardons, members of government, and the media.

The beginning of the campaign for pardons can be traced back to 1985 and a call by the British Royal Legion for the government to review the cases of executed British soldiers of the First World War. This early request was denied by the sitting minister of defence, but the call remained legion policy even though the issue would not be raised again until the 1990s. The renewed vigour of the campaign was due primarily to two events. The first event was the 1989 publication of the highly influential *Shot at Dawn*.[3] Authors Julian Putkowski and Julian Sykes identified by name for the first time those who had been executed during the war. Unable to consult the British court martial records, closed to public research, they compiled their list by consulting war diaries, medal rolls, and other information available from the Public Record Office in Great Britain. Furthermore, their work relied on Judge Anthony Babington's *For the Sake of Example*, which did have the benefit of access to all available documentation.[4] Putkowski and Sykes called on the Ministry of Defence to admit to military injustices in the First World War and to exonerate all those men who had been executed by order of court martial. They called for a blanket pardon, making no distinction among the crimes of desertion, cowardice, murder, mutiny, and treason.[5] The second event that helped to ignite the pardons campaign was the opening of the British government's previously closed field general court martial files in 1990. In conjunction, these two events helped to launch the official Shot at Dawn campaign in December 1990. Led by retired school teacher and Second World War veteran John Hipkin, the campaign counted grassroots activists and amateur historians among its members.

An official political voice was given to the campaign when British Labour MP Andrew Mackinlay used his influence to introduce the issue in political circles and to urge the government to consider official pardons for the executed soldiers. In the course of correspondence with Conservative Prime Minister John Major on the issue, Major wrote to Mackinlay in 1993 that "no evidence was found to lead us ... to think that the convictions were unsound or that the accused were treated unfairly at the time."[6] Major rejected the request for pardons, arguing that the severe punishments were to be understood within the context of the conditions of the First World War, that it was misguided to believe that history could in any way be rewritten, and that shell shock had in fact been considered in court martial procedure. As Major went on to write to Mackinlay, "shellshock did become recognized as a medical condition during World War I. And, where medical evidence was available to the court, it was taken into account in sentencing and the recommendations on the final sentence made to the Commander-in-Chief. Most death sentences were commuted on the basis of medical evidence."[7] Without surviving records of commuted British death sentences in the Great War, it is unclear how Major arrived at the conclusion that most commutations had been based on medical evidence. The material simply did not exist to substantiate this claim. Furthermore, given the evidence produced in the Canadian cases, this would indicate a marked difference between the two disciplinary structures and the values of their commanding officers. Most letters of recommendation in the Canadian cases favoured commutation based on overall battalion discipline rather than any medical condition. To have such an important difference between two systems that were so closely linked in every way has no firm basis and runs contrary to every other example in which Canadian authority followed and mirrored the British example. Despite the prime minister's stance, Mackinlay continued to push the agenda for pardons forward, ultimately introducing a private member's bill arguing that most men had been executed in spite of claims that they had been suffering from the effects of shell shock.[8]

Following Major's decision, the pardons campaign received welcome news when in 1995 Tony Blair, then Britain's leader of the official opposition, indicated that a Labour government in power would consider the plea for pardons and do so "sympathetically."[9] With election to office in 1997, the new Labour government did reopen the question of pardons by calling for a formal review of court martial files. In 1998, John Reid, minister of the armed forces, formally announced that, once again, the request for pardons would not be granted. His statement to the House of Commons noted that there were few legal grounds for granting pardons:

> So, if we were to pursue the option of formal, legal pardons, the vast majority, if not all, of the cases would be left condemned either by an accident of history which has left us with insufficient evidence to make a judgment, or, even where the evidence is more extensive, by a lack of sufficient evidence to overturn the original verdicts. In short, most would be left condemned, or in some cases re-condemned, 80 years after the event.[10]

Like Major before him, Reid could find no conclusive evidence in existing files that shell shock had been ignored during trials, and he further noted that "it seems reasonable to assume that medical considerations may have been taken into account in the 90 per cent of cases where sentences were commuted."[11] Reid concluded his statement to the House of Commons by offering an expression of regret on behalf of the government.

His decision failed to put an end to the Shot at Dawn campaign. Activists continued to voice their opinions in the media and online, and the issue of posthumous pardons was brought forward in the Irish government and the Scottish parliament. In what was a powerful symbol, members of the Shot at Dawn campaign began laying wreaths in honour of the executed at community cenotaphs during Remembrance Day ceremonies. Furthermore, the Shot at

Dawn Memorial was dedicated at the National Arboretum Memorial in Staffordshire, England, in June 2001. The eight-foot statue of a blindfolded soldier set to face a firing squad is surrounded by over three hundred stakes, each intended to represent one soldier of the British Empire shot during the Great War. The memorial was funded by donations solicited from the public. In 2001, a Ministry of Defence spokesperson confirmed that "we wouldn't endorse or condone this memorial as it is a private matter."[12]

In October 2005, the issue of pardons entered a stage of renewed vigour with the announcement by the British government that, under advisement from the High Court, it would reconsider a posthumous pardon for the case of Private Harry Farr. His case stood out among those of his counterparts in that he had surviving family members willing to pursue litigation on his behalf. Furthermore, there was evidence that Farr had been suffering from shell shock, for which he had undergone treatment only five months prior to his execution.[13] His case came to a pre-emptive halt in the courts with the announcement in August 2006 that the British government would recommend that a pardon be granted to Farr in addition to all other troops of the British Empire executed during the First World War. Royal assent was given to the Pardons Bill in November 2006.

As part of the British Commonwealth, Canadian soldiers executed during the First World War were included in the bill. Prior to 2006, Canadian legislators had sought a middle ground on the issue. After considering the option of pardons, on 11 December 2001, Minister of Veterans Affairs Ronald J. Duhamel delivered a statement to the House of Commons in which he was careful to note that the twenty-three Canadian soldiers executed for desertion and cowardice had been "lawfully executed." Duhamel went on to note that "we can revisit the past, but we cannot recreate it."[14] Duhamel had not reviewed the trial transcripts from the court martial files because they no longer existed, having been destroyed by the Directorate of History before they could be transferred to Library and Archives Canada.[15] Following his statement, Duhamel offered an expression of regret, read the names of the twenty-three executed soldiers to the House of Commons, and announced their addition to the Official Book of Remembrance at Parliament Hill. Although there were actually twenty-five Canadian soldiers executed during the First World War, only twenty-three names were added. They were the names of the soldiers shot for cowardice and desertion. The names of Alexander Butler and Benjamin De Fehr, both convicted of murder, were omitted from both the expression of sorrow and the revised Official Book of Remembrance.

Duhamel's statement was not enough for advocates of pardons. Commenting on the action, John Hipkin stated that "an expression of sorrow is not a change of heart. It's a cover-up."[16] Although Duhamel's statement came down weakly on both sides of the pardons issue, it met with no opposition from his colleagues in Parliament. Surprisingly, especially in comparison to Great Britain, there was a lack of debate regarding Canada's decision to issue an official expression of sorrow. A search in the House of Commons Hansard from 1990 to 2001 failed to turn up any discussion on the matter leading up to the official statement by the government on 11 December 2001.[17]

Once the expression of sorrow was issued, the Veterans Affairs critics from each of the political parties spoke in favour of the minister's statement and congratulated the move. Louis Plamondon of the Bloc Québécois went so far as to condemn the entire war and suggest that the executed had been condemned for their belief systems as much as for their acts of desertion. He stated to the House of Commons that "they [the executed] took part in a cruel war, and one we realize today was completely pointless ... These young men came to question certain decisions, to wonder about the appropriateness of certain commands. For daring to think, for daring to question, the cruel law of war, instead of trying to understand them, had them executed."[18] Plamondon's remarks spoke volumes about the lingering resentments among some Quebecers who continued to associate the First World War with the 1917 conscription crisis. This crisis created cleavages between French and English Canadians that would last for decades. Many French Canadians lobbied against conscription, feeling that they had no part in what they believed was essentially a British imperial war. When the Military Service Act was passed, requiring eligible young men to register for conscription, many young French Canadian men (as well as other groups, including farmers, immigrants, and pacifists) continued to protest either by not registering or by applying for exemptions. These protests culminated in Easter weekend riots in Quebec City in 1918. The ensuing violence left four people dead and many more injured.[19] For many in Quebec, the memory of the war was fixed in terms of the power struggle between French and English Canada. They saw themselves forced to participate in a conflict that was never theirs. This version of the past suited the image of a rebellious yet morally upright soldier daring to question the actions of a much more dominant power. However fabricated this image might have been, it served a political purpose for individuals such as Plamondon who continued to use the war as political capital for the sovereignist agenda.

Furthermore, the fact that there was an absence of debate in Parliament regarding the refusal to grant full pardons to executed Canadians says much about the views of Canadians on the subject. The small number of Canadians executed contributed, of course, to the lack of debate, while the length of time that had passed made the issue even less relevant to Canadians. Furthermore, most

Canadians would likely agree that executing soldiers in the First World War was simply wrong, and thus no opposition was warranted when the expression of regret was announced. Unlike other redress campaigns in Canada, this issue caused very little debate and produced little or no media scrutiny. The lack of debate and media coverage can also be attributed to the fact that, unlike other Canadian redress campaigns, the pardons campaign did not call for any financial compensation for the victims' families to be paid by the government and ultimately borne by the Canadian taxpayer. Without financial compensation, the call for pardons never became an engaging topic for the media or the public.

Debate in Canada on the pardons issue seems to have remained confined to a small circle of historians. In 2007, after the issue had been resolved, the debate re-emerged on *H-Net Canada*, an Internet site devoted to queries and debates among those interested in Canadian history. Although the site is not limited to professional historians, debate on the issue of posthumous pardons that took place from 9 to 11 January 2007 was addressed only by them. Most postings argued against blanket pardons for Canadian soldiers executed during the First World War.[20]

While Great Britain and Canada were engaged in debate on the issue, the New Zealand pardons campaign had already reached a successful conclusion. In April 2000, initiated by the Pardon for Soldiers of the Great War Bill presented by Labour MP Mark Peck of Invercargill, the government of New Zealand announced a formal review of the case files of five New Zealand soldiers executed in the war. By June 2000, pardons had been granted for all five soldiers, four of whom were executed for desertion and one for mutiny. While the original bill presented by Peck called for pardons on the basis of shell shock, as in the British example, no clear evidence could be found to substantiate the claim that all of the soldiers had been suffering from it. Instead, the original bill was redrafted, and pardons were granted to the five soldiers based on the belief that their fates had been undeserved, the result of harsh discipline perceived as necessary at the time.[21] Furthermore, a select parliamentary committee assigned to research the case for pardons stated in its report that "we have given weight to the effect that the executions had, and continue to have, on the families of the soldiers." The committee went on to note that "we have also accepted that the executions did a dishonour to our national history, as well as to the soldiers."[22] Royal assent to the pardons for New Zealand's executed was granted in September 2000. One can surmise that a New Zealand pardon came much sooner than a British or Canadian counterpart since there were only five soldiers in question, and with full archival evidence available it was simply easier for the government of New Zealand to review the evidence and come to a quick decision. This, combined with a government receptive to the idea of full pardons, sped up a decision that took Great Britain and Canada six more years to reach.

From its inception, the pardons debate was infused on both sides with highly emotive language as well as heavy reliance on myths regarding the First World War by those who demanded pardons. A prevailing view of the Great War as a war of futility easily lent itself to the debate. In the words of historian Peter Leese, "the injustice of the capital courts-martial becomes the injustice of the Great War itself."[23] To begin to discuss the use of such myths by the pardons movement, it is instructive to explore the dominant view of the First World War and the development of this social memory. Without this social memory of a "bad war," it is less likely that a pardons debate would have emerged, let alone garnered the support that it did.

When most individuals conjure up an image of the First World War, they are likely to see the grey and barren landscapes of the western front. In *Fallen Soldiers: Reshaping the Memory of the World Wars,* George Mosse writes that "the Western Front with its peculiar and unique style of warfare dominated the prose and poetry, as well as the picture books and films about the war; it decided what contemporaries and future generations would make of it."[24] Yet this image of barren landscapes and wasted youth that dominates the social memory has not been static; rather, the meaning and the memory of the Great War have changed over time. Evidence suggests that there was widespread support for the war effort in the British Empire that remained steady from 1914 to 1918.[25] Most historians have argued that the negative connotations associated with the war developed in its aftermath, though there is some disagreement over when and why this interpretation of the war developed.

A major turning point in the social memory of the war occurred in the late 1920s and early 1930s, which saw the publication of memoirs and other works of literature devoted to the First World War. For the first time, major works such as Erich Maria Remarque's *All Quiet on the Western Front,* published in 1929, and *Poems of Wilfred Owen,* published in 1931, contributed to the modernist tradition and popularized the view of the war as tragedy and the soldier as victim.[26] Yet, if this were the reality of the war, why did this voice take ten years to develop? Some have suggested that nations remained emotionally numb following the war's end and that a full decade was required to process the extent of the casualties and for the survivors to articulate their experiences.[27] It has been further suggested that postwar literature emerged less as a response to the war than as a response to the postwar world. A generation of physically and emotionally scarred survivors, unemployment, and economic depression helped to foster a climate of disillusionment and to create the concept of the "lost generation." As historian Janet Watson states of this era, "the war was culturally important, now, not for what it had achieved, but for what it had cost."[28]

Yet, in citing the changing perception of the war in the late 1920s and early 1930s, one must exercise caution. Many veterans held on to their war experiences as mostly positive and full of purpose. For these men, the high literary tradition of the war poets was of little consequence, and the view that the First World War and tragedy were synonymous was not yet widely accepted. According to historian Jonathan Vance, long into the postwar era, many veterans continued to celebrate the spirit of victory and camaraderie while downplaying the more negative aspects of trench warfare.[29] This attitude is further seen by the reaction of Canadian veterans to a visit by Sir Douglas Haig to Canada in 1925. In a visit meant to unite disparate veterans' organizations, Haig received warm and enthusiastic receptions in Quebec City and Ottawa from veterans, the Canadian media, and the general public.[30]

It might be argued that the view of the First World War as needless tragedy did not become widely accepted until the late 1950s and the 1960s, with a resurgence of interest in the war. Several factors can account for this renewed interest and refashioned perception. First, the fiftieth anniversary forced historians and the media to take a new look at the past, and they did so through the lens of the increasingly popular field of working-class history. The coincidence of these two trends, along with a growing distrust of authority in the 1960s, contributed to an understanding of the war in terms of class – soldiers versus generals – a notion that easily lent itself to the "lions led by donkeys" thesis.

Beginning in the late 1950s, a number of histories were published that provoked a reassessment of the First World War's battles and leaders. Among the first of these histories was Leon Wolff's *In Flanders Fields,* published in 1958. Using the backdrop of the Passchendaele campaign and highlighting its failures, Wolff commented on what he perceived as the almost criminal generalship of the war and on the futility of the war in general. Wolff, an officer of the US Army, based his research on primarily secondary material and offered little archival evidence in his work.[31] His work was followed by similar histories, which included Alan Clark's 1961 *The Donkeys* and A.J.P. Taylor's 1963 *The First World War.*[32] These works contributed to a clear historiographical trend in the 1960s that focused primarily on attacking the supposedly outdated and even ruthless leadership of the First World War. With the exception of Taylor, many of the works of this time were written by popular historians, and like Wolff's work they were particularly weak in their archival evidence.

Furthermore, cultural historian Modris Eksteins argues that the renewed interest also coincided with the growing popularity of irony and satire. Eksteins points to the satirical anti-war play *Oh! What a Lovely War,* which opened to large audiences in London in 1963.[33] Beyond these cultural changes, in Britain the national curriculum began to allow for the teaching of war poets in state schools, which, historian Gary Sheffield argues, meant that English teachers, not history teachers, began to have the greatest impact in creating the British understanding of the Great War. Furthermore, national television in Britain began by the 1960s to air documentaries such as *The Great War* that reinforced existing perceptions of war through carefully edited commentaries and grainy black-and-white archival footage of mud and slaughter, which had a deep impact on the public.[34] Against such an onslaught of images, Sheffield argues, the political and military realities of the war faded to the background, and the victory of 1918 had been all but forgotten by the public.[35]

This perception of the war holds true for the Commonwealth as well. In the case of Australia and New Zealand, the slaughter at Gallipoli, where the Australian and New Zealand Army Corps suffered 35,623 casualties in a failed campaign, has come to represent the dominant image of the war.[36] For Canadians, several competing images exist. There is the divisiveness of the war brought on by conscription, an issue that created lasting cleavages between French and English Canada. This image of the war is especially dominant in French Canada and remains relevant in the historical memory. There is also the myth of the birth of the nation at Vimy Ridge. This perception purports that Canada's victory at the Battle of Vimy Ridge on 9 April 1917 was the defining event of a young nation. This battle, which marked the first time that all four divisions of the Canadian Corps fought together, has often been referred to as Canada's "baptism by fire" and the moment when Canada truly became a nation. Finally, there is the overwhelming representation of the First World War as one of futility and a loss of innocence. It is this image of wasted youth, shell-shocked soldiers, desperate conditions, and archaic leadership mired in a needless war that has most managed to capture the popular imagination.

It was this view of the war, developed throughout the 1960s, that I believe was the cornerstone of the movement to pardon the executed soldiers of Great Britain, Canada, and New Zealand. Enduring myths of the war easily fed into myths of the courts martial themselves. In the words of one writer, "a mythology had grown up about the supposed injustice done to these young men [the executed] which has more to do with modern sentimentality than contemporary reality."[37] Helping to create these myths was the fact that official British courts martial files were shrouded in secrecy until 1990. In 1919, the files were ordered sealed for a period of 100 years. Sealing files is a customary practice in national archives, and in many cases thousands of sealed records contain information that is innocuous. However, this common government practice was later reinterpreted by campaigners for pardons and purposefully portrayed in a way to leave the British government open to accusations of a cover-up. Yet it seems evident that, if there was any ulterior motive in closing the files, it was because the government had more than its own interests in mind. During the war and in its immediate aftermath, the families of soldiers executed for desertion and cowardice were subject to a strong social stigma. Next of kin were usually notified of the circumstances of death, but most families chose to keep this information private. Harry Farr's daughter, Gertrude Harris, recalled her mother receiving the letter notifying her of the circumstances of her husband's death: "She was so ashamed of the letter when it came and the stigma that it carried that she never told any one of the family."[38] If the government was truly intent on covering up gross injustices, the files could have been destroyed following the war. Providing further evidence of the government's difficult task in protecting both privacy and history, in 1972 a British MP, Don Concannon, requested that the court martial files be destroyed to prevent the names of the executed from becoming public knowledge. In response to the request, the sitting minister of defence stated that "the present policy ... attempts to strike a balance between the protection of the innocent from unnecessary pain and the preservation of material that is part of our history."[39] The minister went on to deny the request for destruction. It was not until 1990, after the names of all of the executed soldiers had been published in *Shot at Dawn* and after repeated requests for transparency, that the court martial files were opened for public research.

In addition to myths of conspiracy, the pardons debate was plagued on all sides by misinformation. One persistent image of the campaign was that of an underage soldier crumbling under the pressure of combat. In a press interview on Remembrance Day 2000, John Hipkin stated that "those who were shot were boy soldiers, immature and confused. They were of the same age group as those who nowadays commit suicide in remand centres. They did not understand."[40] The reality was that most soldiers executed during the First World War were, like many soldiers, young; however, in the eyes of the law, they were not minors. The great majority of British soldiers were over twenty-one years of age, while the average age of executed Canadians was twenty-three.[41] A twenty-three-year-old male in the early twentieth century would have had vastly different life experiences from a twenty-three-year-old male today. At twenty-three in 1914, many men would have held full-time jobs and helped to care for their families, whether their aging parents or their wives and children. A twenty-three-year-old male in 1914 would have been accustomed to having far more responsibility.

Closely related to the image of the young soldier has been that of the shell-shocked soldier. Shell shock has come to be one of the defining images of the Great War, and the Shot at Dawn campaigns expertly used it to their advantage. Commenting at a Remembrance Day ceremony in London, England, in 2002, one unidentified campaigner stated that "we don't want pardons for villains. We want justice for people who were shot for insubordination because they refused to put on a hat, or who fell asleep at their post, or were just so terrified they simply could not cope."[42] The British *Shot at Dawn* website contained powerful phrases such as "medical excuses were not to be tolerated." The site stated that "over three-hundred innocent British and Commonwealth soldiers were brutally gunned down by the authorities, not in the name of justice, but as a stupid, spiteful and shameful example to others. Most were clearly suffering from shell-shock." A number of factors are inherently incorrect about this statement. In not one case has it been proven that a soldier was innocent of the military crime for which he was found guilty. While our understanding of extenuating circumstances might have changed over time, this does not erase the fact that soldiers were guilty of their crimes under the law in force at the time. As I have shown here, no soldier was the victim of a summary execution. In defence of the military's actions during the war, in 1922 the chief of the general staff of the CEF wrote that

> it can be confidently asserted that no man suffered the extreme penalty except after a fair trial and after due consideration had been given to all extenuating circumstances. This is certainly true of all cases occurring in the Canadian Corps and there is no reason whatever to doubt that it is not equally true of the cases outside the Corps.[43]

Finally, as stated earlier, reviewed courts martial files of Great Britain and New Zealand do not show that medical evidence was ignored in courts martial as a matter of protocol. This point has also been abused by those who argue against pardons. Medical evidence from courts martial is scant, and there is little to prove that evidence was thoughtfully considered or wilfully ignored. Both sides of the debate have used this lack of evidence conveniently to construct their own conclusions. What can be said with more certainty is that most desertions took place outside the trenches rather than under the pressure of intense bombardment. Most deserters absented themselves when their units were coming out of the line or moving up to the front. Also, many deserters simply failed to return from leave in Britain. Finally, some were such habitual absentees that they saw little time in the front lines.

The final myth worth dispelling regarding military executions concerns the structure of the military judicial system. It has often been argued by campaigners for pardons that the military judicial system was a form of class-based warfare in which public school-educated officers punitively imposed their will on working-class soldiers. In particular, this view was advanced by author Julian Putkowski, who wrote in 1989 that, "assuming that death sentences were imposed by officers overwhelmingly drawn from the upper classes, on soldiers who were predominantly of working class origin, the taint of class justice which accompanied the Edwardian civil magistracy cannot have been absent from courts martial."[44] Furthermore, an article by Putkowski on the *Shot at Dawn* website stated that "the influence of public schools and consequently the perspectives of a narrow social elite dominated the wartime military hierarchy." However, this view fails to account for a system of promotion from within the ranks that would have been in place by 1916, helping to create greater class diversity in the officer corps. While university graduates could still receive direct commissions, demand for officers might have outpaced supply, allowing for greater inclusion of middle-class soldiers in the officer corps. Historian G.D. Sheffield argues that the officer-man relationship in the British Army was essentially a good one rooted in trust. He attributes the high morale of the British forces throughout the war to a paternalistic officer-man relationship. However, he also notes that there was a recognized need for balance in such relationships: "In many units good officer-man relations and harsh discipline existed side-by-side." Sheffield goes on to say that "regimental officers helped to protect their men from some of the excesses of military discipline," but he also concludes that, "if officers identified too closely with their men, this could lead to a reluctance to take aggressive action and thus put the group at risk."[45]

In its everyday application, military law was certainly filled with more rules and regulations than its civilian counterpart, but like civilian law it was also dependent on consent. Just as citizens who choose to obey the laws grant legitimacy to a government, so too did soldiers legitimize military authority by choosing to follow the rules. Commanders required obedience from their soldiers, but their legitimacy to lead was dependent on soldiers' willingness to follow. For the most part, soldiers followed because they knew it was in the best interests of their units to do so and because it represented the best chances for survival of themselves and their comrades. Military law in the CEF was not an authoritative anomaly but sprang directly from a Canadian society firmly rooted in British ideals of governance and order.

Further complicating the granting of pardons is the issue of blame. To state emphatically that a soldier was wrongfully executed implies that a wrong decision was made and that someone should be blamed for it. Following the official expression of sorrow offered to the twenty-three Canadian soldiers executed for desertion and cowardice in the First World War, Desmond Morton called the government's decision "self-indulgent rubbish" and claimed that it shifted the blame for the executions to those officers who sat on the courts martial and ordered the punishments. Morton went on to ask of the executed soldiers, "does it deny their responsibility for their actions?"[46] Responding to such statements, Minister of Defence Ron Duhamel stated that the government's expression of sorrow was meant to help heal the surviving family members of the executed, not to "condemn the culture of military justice that prevailed during the First World War."[47] But, with the exception of a few soldiers, including Britain's Harry Farr, one would be hard pressed to find family members of executed soldiers involved in the pardons campaign. Instead, the campaigns were dominated mostly by politicians and lobbyists.

In the Canadian example, the relatives of Stephen Fowles were the only family members to appear consistently in media interviews from the mid-1990s to 2006. As a result of their involvement, and the participation of Duhamel, who during a 2000 election in Manitoba promised Ruth Duncan, the surviving sister of Fowles, that he would work toward a full pardon for Fowles and his fellow soldiers, Fowles became the face of the Canadian campaign.[48] His image was reproduced many times over, and his story was told in multiple media outlets, including many news articles. In the majority of these stories, Fowles was portrayed sympathetically. For example, in a 2001 article following the addition of the names of the executed to the Book of Remembrance, Paul Samyn of the *Winnipeg Free Press* wrote that "eighty-three years after a bullet from a British firing squad took the life of Pte. Stephen McDermot Fowles, the sacrifice of the young Manitoba soldier was finally recognized by his country."[49] However, problematic about such sympathetic portrayals was that, unlike Harry Farr, who likely suffered from shell shock and should never have been executed even in the context of his time, Fowles represented the worst of the CEF. He was a chronic deserter who had numerous offences on his record, including two previously commuted death sentences, before he was ultimately executed on 19 June 1918, following his third FGCM conviction for desertion.[50] Although several newspaper articles indicate that Fowles was executed following a late return from leave after visiting his girlfriend in France, archival records show this story to be completely false and nothing more than family lore.[51] Instead, records show that his final desertion occurred on 25 April 1918 when he was released from prison and proceeding under escort to the front lines. Fowles was released early from his sentence and allowed to rejoin the 44th Battalion. Instead of rejoining his unit, he fled once again when he was given an order to obtain a gas respirator and join the ration party proceeding up the line. Fowles was not seen again until 2 May, when he turned himself in to authorities at Albain-Saint-Nazaire, north of Arras.[52] Why he surrendered of his own volition is unclear. While his niece, Linda Ballard, stated in 2001 that his surrender proved that he had never intended to desert, this claim is hard to believe given his disciplinary record and pattern of behaviour.[53] As issues of guilt and innocence are reconsidered, it is interesting to reflect on a point raised in regard to the pardons in a British House of Commons debate in July 1998: in granting a pardon, does that not imply guilt in the first place? If this is so, then is a full pardon really the answer that campaigners for pardons were seeking?[54]

Yet, for all of the arguments regarding what was fact and what was fiction in the campaign for pardons, one issue pervaded the movement: whether the move to provide pardons was an attempt to rewrite history and, if so, should even be done. Did the provision of pardons provide a service or a disservice to historical memory and historical truth? Was it an honest attempt to amend past wrongs (if, indeed, one believes that wrongs were committed) or an attempt simply to appease surviving family members and campaigners? Did the campaign to grant full pardons have more to do with contemporary politics than past wrongs? Arguing against pardons in 1999, Conservative British MP Ben Wallace stated that "this is history we are tinkering with. The crime of desertion is serious, but we cannot judge the severity of the punishment by our values. Do we pardon those that were flogged by Lord Nelson?"[55] Referring to the decision to grant full pardons to the executed soldiers of the First World War, in April 2000 New Zealand's prime minister, Helen Clark, stated that "our conscience wouldn't rest if we didn't do something to retrospectively pardon those soldiers."[56] Was this an issue, over eighty years later, that should even have bothered the modern conscience? Was it a problem in need of fixing, or was it simply a fact of history that we should have accepted, learned from, and quietly moved on from? This proved to be a deeply divisive question among historians and others interested in the issue. Many believed that, even if executed soldiers did not necessarily deserve their fate, granting pardons was not the best way to honour their memory. In the words of John Hughes-Wilson, "if these men were alive today, we would not kill them. But we must be very wary about applying our modern sentiments and values to the 1914-18 war. We cannot re-invent the past to suit ourselves today."[57]

Is it not true that the historian's role is to explain rather than to judge? Answering to accusations of applying today's standards of justice to the past, the *Shot at Dawn* website countered that public opinion between 1914 and 1918 did not officially support the executions. There is little proof to support this statement, and the argument is weak given that, as previously mentioned, most families of executed soldiers were notified of the details of the deaths, and the

Army Act, which contained guidelines for executions, was reviewed on an annual basis. Responding to an accusation that the New Zealand pardons were part of a concerted attempt to rewrite history, a New Zealand editorial in the *Evening Post* wrote, "oh, that we could. To pardon those men is not to rewrite history. It is merely to acknowledge that, by necessity, one of the casualties of wartime is forgiveness."[58]

Although the campaigns have now concluded, the topic is still important to consider because of the broader trends to which it speaks. The rise of the pardons movement is just one example of a growing number of campaigns that call for redress for past wrongs. In Canada alone in recent memory, there have been multiple ongoing campaigns calling for redress, apology, or compensation for past wrongs. These campaigns have included calls for compensation for Chinese immigrants forced to pay a head tax in the early twentieth century under the Chinese Head Tax and Exclusion Act; for recognition of and compensation for the abuses suffered by Aboriginals subjected to the Indian residential school system; for redress for Ukrainian Canadians interned during the First World War; and for redress of and compensation for Japanese Canadians interned during the Second World War. All of these groups have obtained some level of success. In 1988, a formal apology was issued to Japanese Canadians, and a fund was created for compensation, including compensation for property confiscated and sold during their internment. In 2006, an apology and compensation were offered to survivors forced to pay the Chinese head tax. A final settlement agreement was reached in 2006 that provides payments to survivors of the Indian residential school system, and a formal government apology was publicly offered in 2008. Also in 2008, an agreement was reached with the Ukrainian Canadian community that included developing a fund to commemorate their experiences during the First World War.

The pardons movement was part of a larger trend to revisit and redress government and military policies of the past. Acceptance of this trend, newly opened court martial files in 1990 that reinvigorated research and interest, as well as existing myths of the First World War all contributed to the emergence and sustained popularity of the pardons campaign. However, there are some key differences between this campaign and the redress campaigns noted above. First, of course, there were no survivors to speak on their own behalf. Second, there was no racial or ethnic motivation behind the executions, and those lobbying for pardons were, in most cases, unrelated to the victims. Furthermore, in no case was one of the men innocent of the crime of which he was convicted. In each case, the soldier was guilty of desertion or cowardice as defined by military law at that time. Finally, though the campaigns advocated by former residential school students, Japanese Canadians, Chinese Canadians, and

Ukrainian Canadians all gathered and relied on historical evidence to further their causes, the campaigners for pardons often relied on ahistorical evidence.

What was so problematic about the pardons campaign was that, as my research has demonstrated, it was based on a series of historical fallacies. Whether the activists involved were misinformed, or whether they purposefully misrepresented the facts, they had an incomplete understanding of the major issues involved, such as shell shock and military law during the First World War. Campaigners routinely portrayed the majority of the executed soldiers as shell-shocked and under-aged victims of callous military authority while conveniently ignoring the long disciplinary records of many of these men and the neglect of duty for which they had volunteered. Commenting on the expression of sorrow granted to executed Canadians in 2001, historian Jack Granatstein stated that, "in many of these cases, you don't have the sense that people broke down under terrible fire; you have the sense that they deserted in order to avoid a dangerous duty." He went on to note that, "for soldiers, the greatest fear – the one that allows them to overcome all others – is that they don't want to let down their friends under fire. And these people, however you slice it, did."[59] In regularly describing the executed as innocent, when they were in fact guilty of the crimes of which they had been convicted, the campaigners for pardons proved themselves to be far more interested in creating a sense of collective injustice than in examining the facts of the individual cases.

In addition to their incorrect assumptions about the nature of military law and the convicted soldiers, the campaigners routinely used incendiary language to drive home their points. For example, the introduction to the *Shot at Dawn* website stated that "this website exposes the farce of so-called military justice," and it went on to describe courts martial as "show trials," yet in no instance were courts martial public events at which the outcomes of the proceedings were already determined. In fact, court martial transcripts reveal a far different story, for each soldier was given multiple opportunities to present his side of the story and call witnesses to his defence as well as to his character. Furthermore, in cases in which court martial proceedings did not follow the correct protocol, a member of the Adjutant General Corps could dismiss the findings of the case and call for a new trial. Myriad facts such as these undermine the rhetoric of the pardons movement and reveal the misinformation under which the pardons were ultimately granted.

While the question of posthumous pardons for soldiers of the First World War might now be answered, some of the core issues that go beyond the details of the campaign are not. The prudence of applying modern-day standards to history is worth considering not only by historians but also by national governments, victims of abuse, and their ancestors. Should these issues be decided on a case-by-case basis, or are we resolute in that the past is the past and what has been done cannot be changed? This is the core of the debate, the question still to be answered. In addition to a collective memory of the past, we are burdened by a collective conscience.

Conclusion

LATE IN 1919, ALMOST a year after the armistice was signed, the Canadian Expeditionary Force still found itself dealing with the issue of discipline and punishment among soldiers. Writing to the minister of militia and defence, Sydney Chilton Mewburn, on 15 September 1919, the judge advocate general (JAG) detailed the policy of dealing with imprisoned CEF soldiers:

> In the case of short term sentences, the practice has been to recommend that the sentence be commuted to detention, and the men in question transferred to detention barracks. Allotment of a certain amount of accommodation in each sailing to Canada was then made to these detention barracks, the selection of the men to be so returned home being left to the discretion of the Officers Commanding the barracks. A considerable number have been so returned. As regards men sentenced to long terms of imprisonment and penal servitude, on the proceedings of their respective trials being reviewed it was not thought advisable to remit or commute their sentences at the present time, as the overseas authorities felt that they should not be returned to Canada at the same time, or sooner, than their comrades who had clean Conduct Sheets. Consequently, the overseas authorities have recommended in each case that the sentence be remitted after a period of six months', or less, has been served, so as to enable such men to be returned to Canada during November and December of this year. Colonel Dennistoun states that the last of such men should be returned to Canada before the new year. The offences in these cases are, in the main, purely military, such as desertion, mutiny, etc.[1]

No general amnesty was offered to the soldiers since there remained twenty cases said to require "special consideration." These cases involved crimes such as murder, rape, manslaughter, and indecent assault, so they could not be dealt with in the same manner as purely military offences. However, though imprisoned men might have been forced to stay behind a little longer while their comrades were demobilized and returned to Canadian soil, in the end all but twenty of these soldiers were back in Canada by the end of 1919.[2] In most cases, the men returned to Canada, went on to live normal lives, and were quick to leave their past actions behind them in Europe. While spouses or other dependants at home might have been aware of a soldier's disciplinary troubles during the war because of stoppages in pay, veterans who had been court martialled, sentenced to death, and subsequently received commuted sentences could easily leave this information behind them and go on to be productive civilian citizens after the war.

The names of executed soldiers remained unknown for many years partly because of the shame that the executions could have brought on family members in Canada. Although each executed soldier was given a proper burial and gravestone in a military cemetery in France or Belgium, the gravestones bear no indication of the extraordinary circumstances under which they died. In addition, the names of executed soldiers often do not appear on local memorials or in regimental rolls of honour. For example, Fortunat Auger of the 14th Battalion is not mentioned in his regimental history, while Wilson Norman Ling of the 2nd Battalion is listed but classified under accidentally killed or death from sickness.[3]

Attempts were made to keep news of the executions within the immediate families of the executed soldiers. The Canadian government sought the help of parish priests to deliver the news of an execution to family members, and in some instances these clergymen, using their own discretion, decided that it was not in the best interests of the family to be informed of the circumstances of death.[4] The parents of Frederick Stanley Arnold and Wilson Norman Ling were never notified about the true circumstances of their sons' deaths. Throughout 1919 and 1920, the issue of notifying Ling's parents in Toronto of the facts of their son's death was debated within the Department of Militia and Defence. Ling had been executed on 12 August 1918 following his second FGCM conviction for desertion. A member of the 2nd Battalion, he had deserted his unit on 21 June 1917 while at Neuville St. Vaast, France. He had been arrested by military police almost one year later, in May 1918, after trying to fool authorities by giving false information. Ling was the last member of the CEF to be executed.[5] In 1919, James and Fanny Ling began inquiring into the cause of their son's death as well as into his remaining estate. In correspondence with the Canadian Records Office on 16 January 1919, Fanny Ling wrote that

> it is a great injustice not to inform the parents of a serious illness or wounds which result in the death of our boys who have risked their lives, in the "Great Cause" and consider that I (his mother) am entitled to know what has caused his death. If you will kindly investigate this and let me know as soon as possible you will confer a favour on me his heart-broken Mother.[6]

In response to her letter, a clergyman from her parish was assigned the sad task of delivering the news to the family. An internal memorandum from the Department of Militia and Defence written on 5 September 1919 revealed that the truth was never actually conveyed to Ling's parents. Describing the situation, a district records officer informed the director of records that

> the Curate of the Parish took the matter in hand and interviewed Mrs. Ling, explaining the circumstances of the death of her son, telling her that he was buried somewhere in France, making the case as mild as possible, and leaving Mrs. Ling in a comforted and happy state of mind. It was not believed to be necessary to tell Mrs. Ling that her son was executed by the Order of Field General Court Martial.[7]

Almost one year later the secrecy surrounding Ling's death continued to pose problems for the Department of Militia and Defence. Because his parents continued to ask questions regarding their son's estate, including the issuance of his Memorial Cross, the department found itself in the awkward position of either issuing a medal to the family of an ineligible candidate or telling the Lings of the true circumstances of their son's death two years after the event. As the director of records at Militia and Defence wrote to Captain E. Bunfield in the Legal Section in 1920,

> a Memorial Cross would not ordinarily be issued on account of this man, but if a Memorial Cross is not issued, the question will in all probability be raised by his parents. Should, therefore, a Memorial Cross be issued in this case? The Pay Account in this case showed that a large proportion of the pay had been forfeited, and it was thought that to inform the parents of the state of the pay account would lead to the disclosure of the facts to them concerning their son's death.[8]

Correspondence related to Ling stopped in July 1920, and it is unclear whether Ling was ever issued a Memorial Cross by the department.

For those families aware of their executed kin, there is a limited number of responses in the court martial records, and these few examples convey emotions ranging from anger at military protocol to sad acceptance of it. For example, Joseph Comte, father of the executed Gustave Comte, wrote to the secretary of the Militia Council in March 1918 requesting further details of his son's execution. Comte based his request on what he termed "the proverbial 'British Fair Play'":

> It is very sad for the father and mother to hear of the death of their son, whom we thought was doing well in going away for the service of his country; and all

the more sad was his condemnation June 6th, and his death July 3rd, abandoned by all, without any natural protector, not even a telegram immediately after his condemnation; is this not cruel?[9]

In a letter with a very different tone, Rhoda Moles wrote to request further information on the execution of her brother, Thomas Moles. Although writing only two months after the shooting of her brother, she appeared to be resigned to the army's decision: "If cowardice was the cause, my mother will not look upon it as such knowing him to have had head weaknesses from birth ... Had my brother been killed in battle we should have been proud of him, but we make allowances for him, but trust he is now in the hands of a Righteous Judge."[10]

The letters of Joseph Comte and Rhoda Moles not only exemplify the feelings of families directly affected by the martial execution of a loved one but also give insights into some of the contrasting ideas in Canadian society during this era. On the one hand, there was the belief that any soldier who willingly volunteered to serve his country but was then executed was betrayed in the most vulgar way by the very country that he loved. On the other hand, the letter of Rhoda Moles, in its acceptance of the circumstances of her brother's death, reveals the deference to authority common at the time. Also contributing to familial reactions to executions were ideas of manhood and bravery ingrained in early-twentieth-century society. These ideals helped to keep the news of an execution hidden within the immediate family to prevent the gossip and judgment of the larger community. Perhaps for some, not to have died nobly in battle negated Thomas Moles's sacrifice completely, for Moles had failed to live up to the masculine ideals of strength and steadfast bravery. Although the policy of secrecy was meant to protect families, it also helped to encourage a sense of shame.

In part because of the practice of keeping news of executions within the family, the level of awareness among the Canadian public regarding executions in the CEF is unclear, and thus it is difficult to gauge feelings about the practice. I have found no evidence to suggest that there were enough references in letters home to fuel public sentiment on the issue. Perhaps references to the death penalty did not make it past the censors or, if they did, that soldiers did not speak negatively of its use. Furthermore, capital punishment during wartime was not an issue taken up by Canadian churches or the media, the two major sources of information and community organization during this era.

The soldiers who served on the firing squads also spoke very little of their experiences. Some saw it as an unenviable duty but a duty nevertheless. Deward Barnes of the 19th Battalion was assigned to the firing squad of convicted deserter Harold Lodge and described his assignment as "a job I never wanted."[11]

Captain Georges Vanier of the 22nd Battalion similarly described his duty commanding the troops called to take part in the execution of Arthur Charles Degasse as "a sad task, a sad command."[12] Recalling his experience on the firing squad of Charles Welsh over forty years earlier, veteran C.E. Barnes of the 8th Battalion stated that "they should never have picked our boys to do it."[13] George Coppard, a machine gunner for the BEF, speculated on what he would have done if confronted with the task of serving on a firing squad, and he wrote with searing honesty in his memoir *With a Machine Gun to Cambrai: The Tale of a Young Tommy in Kitchener's Army, 1914-1918*:

> Would I be able to shoot straight at another Tommy? To be honest, I don't think I would have refused. The code of slavish obedience to orders given, no matter what, was as strong in me as in all volunteers then. That was the important thing about the volunteer system fifty years ago. A man was challenged, not compelled, to fight for his country and all that it entailed. A volunteer seldom failed to meet the challenge because of an inborn pride at being a volunteer. It worked that way.[14]

While assignment to a firing party was obviously not desirable, there is no record of open rebellion among those chosen to perform the task; however, among the files of the executed soldiers is one incident of interest that might be construed as a silent form of protest. During the execution of John Maurice Higgins in December 1916, one member of the firing party failed to fire his gun. Documents found in the Higgins court martial file state that, "upon examining the rifles after the volley had been fired, it was found that one had not been fired. This rifle belonged to No. 177293 Pte. O'Brien. M.P."[15] A follow-up memorandum confirms the incident and notes that O'Brien was placed in close arrest as a result of his action.[16] Following this, the paper trail runs out. A search through Michael O'Brien's personnel file gives no indication of any crime, punishment, or even duty to serve on a firing party, and no record of a court martial exists for O'Brien. Without further documentation, the motivation behind his action remains unclear. Was his action meant as a statement of protest, or did it simply grow out of a loss of nerves? Was his failure to fire a reflection of more widespread feelings among members of the CEF?[17]

That soldiers might have been uncomfortable being part of a firing squad does not necessarily indicate that they were against the death penalty. In fact, there is very little evidence that this was the predominant sentiment. Desmond Morton writes that veterans were furious over a military judicial system that allowed executions. In *When Your Number's Up,* he quotes a letter that he received from veteran D.E. Pearson: "The feeling was that we were all volunteers ... and that no volunteer deserved the death sentence if he was unable to face the enemy in battle."[18] While one should take the opinions of men such as Pearson at face value, one should also acknowledge that many veterans might have revised their views on executions with the urgency of warfare gone and overall views on executions having generally shifted in Canadian society.

In April 1919, the Army Council of Great Britain established the Darling Committee, named for its chairman, Sir Charles Darling, to examine court martial procedures and use of the death penalty in the First World War. At the time of his appointment, Darling was a senior judge on the British High Court. In total, ten members were appointed to the Darling Committee, none of whom had any experience serving on or attending a court martial in the field. After twenty-two days of oral evidence, and after examining multiple written submissions, the committee found that overall the system of military discipline, including application of the death penalty, had been fair during the war and should be maintained in the future.[19] As stated in the final report,

> the results of our investigation into a limited number of cases put before us as typical lead us to the conclusion that, having regard to all the circumstances, the work of courts martial during the war has been well done. We are satisfied not only that the members of courts martial intend to be absolutely fair to those who come before them, but also that the rank and file have confidence in their fairness.[20]

Despite their support for the existing system, members of the Darling Committee did go on to make several recommendations for improvement. They agreed that, when possible during courts martial, officers with legal training should be used and that a greater emphasis should be placed on legal training. No specific recommendations were given on how to achieve this training during wartime when both manpower and time were in short supply. Members also agreed that soldiers who faced trial should be informed of the initial verdict as soon as it was pronounced rather than being kept in the dark during the process of confirmation. Finally, when it came to the subject of appeals, members were in agreement that the status quo should remain (i.e., soldiers should not have the right to appeal) and that the power of the commander-in-chief should not be subject to questioning.[21]

In addition to the official report of the Darling Committee, some members of the committee signed on to a special minority report. While in agreement with the major conclusions reached by the committee, the signatories to the minority report also thought that a number of other issues were worth addressing. Among these issues was an increase in power for commanding officers. In response to complaints such as those raised by Brigadier General John Kentish, some members of the committee thought that the number of courts martial could be decreased significantly if commanding officers were given greater powers of punishment. Interestingly, this report also advocated abolition of the confirmation process in favour of the court martial being made up entirely of officers with legal training. A more professional trial, it was believed, would render the confirmation process redundant.[22]

By the time of the Second World War, the death penalty had been abolished in the military for the crimes of desertion and cowardice. Murder, mutiny, and treason were the only crimes still subject to the punishment. Several attempts were made by various British military leaders between 1940 and 1944 to have the death penalty reintroduced for the crime of desertion on active service, but all of these attempts failed.[23] The reasons for this failure are speculative but many. Historian David French argues that the Army Council and the British government refused to reintroduce the death penalty because desertion rates were never high enough to justify it during the Second World War. French also states that there was an inability among medical professionals to distinguish true psychological symptoms from malingering, and authorities were unwilling to risk shooting the wrong soldiers. There also might have been political reasons for the decision. The case for reintroduction was not presented strongly enough by the British military to garner the necessary support from British politicians and the public. Furthermore, the disclosure of poor morale necessary to pass the legislation would have played directly into enemy propaganda. Finally, French argues, the decision to reintroduce the death penalty would never have been supported by dominion governments such as that of Canada.[24]

Only one Canadian soldier, Harold Pringle, was executed during the Second World War. He was executed in Italy for the crime of murder on 5 July 1945, almost two months after the end of the war in Europe.[25] Historian Andrew Godefroy has written that "by not using the Death Penalty in the Second World War the Canadian Government was admitting it had erred in the First."[26] I would disagree with this interpretation. The military's decision had far less to do with any perceived failure in the First World War than it did with shifts in the attitudes of civilian society. By the time of the Second World War, though not yet abolished, the death penalty had become a far less acceptable form of punishment in modern society. The military, as an institution of Canadian society ultimately directed by a civilian government, inevitably reflected the changing values of society. Although change might come slowly to the military, inevitably it comes. The military was not an institution opposed to change, as evidenced during the First World War when measures such as a mandatory guilty plea, medical exams, and court martial officers were introduced to improve the court martial system and ensure fair trials. These changes reflected a military system willing to acknowledge mistakes and open to improvements that would better the lives of its soldiers. This willingness to adapt and modernize went beyond the tactical side of the war and slowly made its way into the medical tents and courts martial.

While military law's primary concern might have been discipline rather than justice, this does not mean that military law did not reflect the civilian values of Western society when it came to legal practice and the right to a fair trial. In fact, military law made ample reference to its civilian counterpart. Although there were some obvious differences, such as the absence of precedents or the irrelevance of one's past disciplinary record in military law, there were many similarities between the two systems. For the most part, trials followed the same procedural rules. The roles laid out for the prosecution, the defence, and the witnesses in an FGCM mirrored those in the civilian process. Furthermore, in the period 1914-18, a formal right to appeal was a privilege not automatically granted to soldier or civilian. Although I have argued that the process of confirmation that followed a military death sentence in many ways acted as an appeal process, the formal right was not enshrined until 1923 in Canadian criminal law and in 1950 in the Canadian military.[27] The Court Martial Appeal Board was created by amendment to the National Defence Act, allowing soldiers to bring appeals of court martial decisions to a civilian tribunal.[28]

In the era of the First World War, issues of mental health were also treated in an inconsistent way in both military and civilian courts. Beginning in the nineteenth century, criminal law recognized a defence based on a mental disorder that prevented a person from distinguishing right from wrong or from understanding the nature of a crime. Juries were not always receptive to the defence, especially when it came to capital offences such as murder. In military law, issues of mental health such as shell shock could save a soldier sentenced to death, while at other times clear evidence of the condition was ignored. The inconsistency with which medical examinations were administered was reflective of a larger misunderstanding of mental health issues that was as much a part of the military as it was of civilian society.

In terms of application of the death penalty, there were many similarities between civil society and the military. In both cases, the expressed purpose of the penalty was twofold: to punish and to deter. Also in both cases, use of the death penalty ebbed and flowed in relation to outside circumstances. Evidence shows that the death penalty was more readily applied in civilian society in years that followed rising crime rates.[29] Similarly, during the First World War, the death penalty was used to serve as an example when crimes such as desertion had become particularly pronounced in a battalion. In both cases, timing was everything.

There is evidence suggesting that in some ways military law was actually more advanced than civilian law. In terms of representation, the "prisoner's friend" offered to every soldier, regardless of rank, preceded the development of mandatory representation for any person charged with a crime in civilian society. Although one must acknowledge that many of these prisoners' friends lacked legal training, the offer of representation came well before the establishment of legal aid. Finally, the application of mercy in the military should be weighed against its application in civil society. Although one might have been more likely to receive a death sentence for a military crime committed during wartime than at any time in civilian society, the chance of having a military death sentence commuted was much better. Although the army gained marked advantages such as meeting its manpower needs by showing mercy, 197 commuted death sentences in a corps of 100,000 troops were not enough to comprise the basis for a policy of commutation.

On 10 December 1998, use of the death penalty in the Canadian military was abolished when legislation was passed to remove it from the National Defence Act. It had been over fifty years since any Canadian soldier had been executed for crimes committed in wartime and twenty-two years since the death penalty had been abolished in civilian society.[30]

The research into commuted death sentences of the First World War reveals many things about discipline and punishment during the conflict, and this research provides much more insight than twenty-five executions ever could. While martial executions are undoubtedly an essential part of the story of discipline and authority in the CEF, they are by no means the whole story, as many past studies on the topic would have us believe. After all, how could twenty-five executions tell us everything that there is to know about an army of 620,000 men? Although the number of commuted death sentences also represents only a fraction of the disciplinary incidences in the CEF, at least they offer a broader view of the military's most serious offences and its legal system's treatment of them. Perhaps most importantly, most of the evidence remains in the commuted cases – a clear advantage over the confirmed cases, for which files remain devoid of the most important material, including court transcripts and letters of recommendation.

The commuted death sentences of the First World War that I have discussed throughout this book reveal several important conclusions regarding discipline, punishment, and authority in the CEF. Foremost among these revelations has been the surprising amount of flexibility in the army's disciplinary structure. Of course, there is always some flexibility in the army that arises as a result of unofficial actions and the individual wills of battalion and company commanders. Such flexibility is necessary in a large military organization, especially during wartime, when discipline needs to be more carefully considered because of the requirement for manpower. When the severity of the crime allowed for it, company and battalion commanders preferred to deal with discipline on their own because doing so was easier and quicker than funnelling errant soldiers through official routes of discipline and played a useful part in sustaining good officer-men relations. At the lowest level of authority, discipline was the most fluid. Company and battalion commanders had the authority to make executive decisions regarding severity and leniency in punishment. Depending on a soldier's relationship with his commander, this could be either positive or negative. In addition to minor crimes, more serious offences, such as desertions, were also likely dealt with in the battalion and recorded as less serious offences, such as absence without leave. This practice had obvious benefits for the errant soldier as well as the battalion officer. It also saved both time and resources because a court martial required organization and the time of officers who could better occupy themselves with running the war.

More surprising than these unofficial disciplinary measures was the amount of flexibility built into the official military legal system at each echelon of power and authority. It has been a common perception that military discipline during the First World War, and to some extent even now, has been both rigid and oppressive. It has also been assumed that authority was concentrated at the top. Yet the commuted death sentences provide us with a very different view. During the First World War, there was a great amount of leverage in the military judicial system. While courts martial themselves were run according to a protocol, in their letters of recommendation for punishment commanding officers from various levels, while given an outline of factors to cover in their letters, were also keen to elaborate their views and voice personal opinions. These opinions, more often than not, were sympathetic to the errant soldier. Furthermore, the commuted cases reveal that the opinions of battalion officers were of just as much value as the opinions of brigade and division commanders. In fact, I would argue, the opinions of battalion commanders were actually more influential since they were usually based on more personal knowledge of a soldier and because they were the first letters to be written and were thus highly influential in shaping the letters of recommendation of the brigade, division, and sometimes corps commanders that followed. In contrast to the popular perception that military justice was brutal and that the commander-in-chief's power was absolute, power was actually diffused in this system. Commanders at every level of authority had a role in negotiating on behalf of or against the soldiers under their command, and they were not discouraged from sharing their general concerns regarding discipline. Their opinions were valued and thoughtfully considered.

From my research, I have certainly found that the punishments handed down in lieu of executions could be erratic. I found no pattern to account for a sentence of fifteen years of penal servitude versus a two-year sentence. I would argue that in fact these sentences meant little. In all likelihood, these sentences would ultimately be suspended and the offending soldier sent back to the front, so they carried little weight among those who assigned them. They seem by all accounts to have been arbitrary, and they provide another example of the degree of flexibility available to commanding officers in the army.

In addition to revelations about military law in the era of the First World War, my research has provided important insights into the soldiers who committed acts of desertion and cowardice. Deserters in the CEF were motivated by both internal and external factors. Many soldiers chose to flee, simply because they had nothing left to give. Suffering from battle exhaustion, men deserted by making quick decisions to run or simply by failing to return from leave. Prolonged service had a profound effect on a soldier's psyche and was one of the primary motivations behind desertion. A soldier mentally worn down by war was often diagnosed with shell shock. Because this condition was still imperfectly understood, it remains unclear how many soldiers were actually suffering from this condition when they chose to desert.

In addition to mental exhaustion, men broke down physically or were influenced to desert by any number of other personal circumstances, including family problems at home or an inability to fit in with peers in their battalions. For some soldiers, acts of desertion or cowardice were based on little more than an unwillingness to fight. A number of soldiers were constant disciplinary problems in their units; some had to face firing squads, and some did not.

Desertion could also be an expression of dissatisfaction with military life or the running of the war. Unlike the French military, plagued by mutinies in 1917, the CEF managed to avoid any major rebellions among its soldiers. It is important to remember that in 1916 the French Army had come off staggering losses incurred during the ten-month Battle of Verdun, only to follow up with more devastating casualties during the failed Nivelle Offensive. For Canadian soldiers, the horrible losses suffered during the Battle of the Somme in 1916 were at least followed by the successful capture of Vimy Ridge in 1917.

The paternalistic relationship between private soldiers and officers in the BEF and CEF also helped to prevent a scenario similar to that of the French mutinies, but dissatisfaction with military life was expressed at times through individual acts of desertion or disobedience. Desertions were also influenced by heavy casualties, which provoked fear, and other conditions of the war, for example before major offensives or during times of especially low morale among soldiers.

Strong leadership and the provision of creature comforts were important in sustaining morale and keeping soldiers loyal to their units.

The prevailing historiography regarding executed soldiers of the First World War has been dominated by two opposing views. On the one side are those who believe that the executed men represented the worst elements of the BEF and CEF, rogue soldiers who failed to honour their commitments to the army and, more importantly, their fellow soldiers. On the other side are those who believe that these soldiers deserve great sympathy and even pardons. This group believes that the deserters were primarily motivated by intense fear and cracked under the strain of warfare. Proponents of these arguments are quick to use the term "shell shock," but moving beyond the scope of the executions to include the evidence produced by the commuted death sentences uncovers a much more nuanced reality.

There was nothing particularly special about the executed soldiers. Generally, they were not particularly bad or particularly scared compared with those whose sentences were commuted. Habitual offenders can be found in both the executed and the commuted cases. Some of these men deserted so often that they barely saw service in the front lines. Shell-shocked soldiers can also be found in each category. In fact, executions had far less to do with individuals than with the circumstances of the war. Outside factors were the greatest influence in a decision to execute a soldier. The state of discipline in the battalion and the timing of an offence dictated who would be executed more than any other factors. A personal disciplinary record was not an accurate predictor of whether a death sentence would be confirmed or commuted. Although one's overall record of service was considered in the letter of recommendation that followed the court martial, one's past disciplinary record was never a factor in sentencing.

Instead, what mattered most when making decisions on sentencing were the state of behaviour in the battalion and the timing of the offence. Letters of recommendation prove over and over that the primary concern of commanders at every level of authority was the discipline of the battalion. Where behaviour was faltering, commanders did not hesitate to call for an example to be made, even if the particular soldier was not the worst among his peers. This need for an example also manifested itself during particularly important phases of the war, such as immediately prior to or during major offensives, when executions were more likely to be ordered. A soldier who fled before or during a major offensive also took a particular risk in contrast to a soldier who fled during a quiet period or failed to return from his leave.

Ironically, opening up the files of the almost two hundred commuted death sentences in the CEF during the First World War has helped to make clear the individuality of each case. Each death sentence represents a unique soldier, and each archival file contains a unique story. It was easier to conjure up sympathy for some men than others. Every coward and every deserter found himself in a situation that he had likely never imagined, and possibly he responded in a way that he could never have foreseen. Since the mid-1980s, the cases of executed soldiers of the Great War have become highly politicized, while the records of reprieved soldiers have remained largely undisturbed and their stories mostly forgotten. Yet, while these cases prove far less compelling to some, to the historian they are invaluable for the insights that they offer into the realities of war, discipline, and authority. These files have shown that military justice in the CEF, and by extension in the BEF, was never black and white but always filled with shades of grey. Commanders could be brutal in their calls for execution, but they were just as likely, or even more likely, to be sympathetic toward their men. Many commanders found themselves in an unenviable position, torn between the needs of a single soldier and those of an entire battalion. Furthermore, soldiers could be just as nuanced as the situations in which they found themselves. Young men responded in myriad ways to the conditions of war and to army authority once they found themselves on the receiving end of martial justice. Here, I have questioned the validity of many of the assumptions about military justice in the First World War. Although the main purpose of military law was to enforce discipline, in practice the system was also designed to afford second chances and mercy. Commanding officers were given much leeway in assigning punishments, and, when punishments were out of their hands, they were granted the opportunity to voice their opposition to the death penalty. The military justice system was much more dynamic than one might typically imagine. Military justice was a complex matter, and only by fully acknowledging this can we move toward a real understanding of discipline and punishment during the First World War.

Notes

Introduction

1. The weather is confirmed in the war diary of the 3rd Canadian Division, General Staff, which was stationed in the same area that day. Library and Archives Canada (hereafter LAC), RG 9, Militia and Defence, Series III-D-3, Vol. 4853, File 139, Reel T-1934, 27 March 1917.
2. LAC, RG 150, Ministry of the Overseas Military Forces of Canada, Acc. 1992-93/166, Box 5564.
3. LAC, RG 150, Series 8, File 649-L-7462, Reel T-8671, and RG 150, Acc. 1992-93/166, Box 5564.
4. Ibid.
5. See Erich Maria Remarque, *All Quiet on the Western Front,* trans. A.W. Wheen (New York: Fawcett Crest, 1928); Charles Yale Harrison, *Generals Die in Bed* (New York: William Morrow, 1930); Frederic Manning, *Her Privates We* (New York: G.P. Putnam's Sons, 1930); and Wilfred Owen, *The Poems of Wilfred Owen* (London: Chatto and Windus, 1930).
6. Remarque, *All Quiet on the Western Front,* 240.
7. Manning, *Her Privates We,* 109-10.
8. Chris Madsen, *Another Kind of Justice: Canadian Military Law from Confederation to Somalia* (Vancouver: UBC Press, 1999).
9. Desmond Morton, "The Supreme Penalty: Canadian Deaths by Firing Squad in the First World War," *Queen's Quarterly* 79, 3 (1972): 345-52.
10. Andrew Godefroy, *For Freedom and Honour? The Story of 25 Canadian Volunteers Executed in the First World War* (Nepean, ON: CEF Books, 1998).
11. Official statistics quote a total of 3,080 death sentences; however, historian Gerard Oram suggests that the actual number is 3,118. I have decided to quote here the number given in official statistics. See Gerard Oram, *Military Executions during World War I* (New York: Palgrave Macmillan, 2003), 3; and Gerard Oram, *Death Sentences Passed by Military Courts of the British Army, 1914-1924,* ed. Julian Putkowski (London: Francis Boutle Publishers, 1998), 13-14.
12. Oram, *Death Sentences Passed by Military Courts of the British Army, 1914-1924.* The CEF was the designated name of Canada's field force and did not include navy or airmen. The CEF was composed primarily of volunteers.
13. Cathryn Corns and John Hughes-Wilson, *Blindfold and Alone: British Military Executions in the Great War* (London: Cassell, 2001), 104; Oram, *Death Sentences Passed by Military Courts of the British Army, 1914-1924,* 15.
14. William Moore, *The Thin Yellow Line* (New York: St. Martin's Press, 1975).
15. Julian Putkowski and Julian Sykes, *Shot at Dawn: Executions in World War One by Authority of the British Army Act* (1989; rev. ed., London: Leo Cooper, 1992).
16. Ibid., n.p. Although Putkowski and Sykes cite 351 executions among British and dominion forces, later studies, notably by Oram, cite 361 executions.
17. Ibid., 10.

18 Franca Iacovetta and Wendy Mitchinson, introduction to *On the Case: Explorations in Social History*, ed. Franca Iacovetta and Wendy Mitchinson (Toronto: University of Toronto Press, 1998), 4.
19 Tim Cook, *Clio's Warriors: Canadian Historians and the Writing of the World Wars* (Vancouver: UBC Press, 2006), 245. The Directorate of History became the Directorate of History and Heritage on 1 September 1996.
20 Lord Moran, *The Anatomy of Courage*, 2nd ed. (London: Constable, 1966).
21 Desmond Morton, *When Your Number's Up: The Canadian Soldier in the First World War* (Toronto: Random House, 1993), 248.
22 Tim Cook, *At the Sharp End: Canadians Fighting in the Great War, 1914-1916*, vol. 1 (Toronto: Viking Canada, 2007); Tim Cook, *Shock Troops: Canadians Fighting in the Great War, 1917-1918*, vol. 2 (Toronto: Viking Canada, 2008). Notable chapters on combat motivation and military discipline include "Chapter 13: Camaraderie of the Damned" and "Chapter 15: The Breaking Point" in *Shock Troops*.
23 Ken Leyton-Brown, *The Practice of Execution in Canada* (Vancouver: UBC Press, 2010).
24 Jonathan F. Vance, *Death So Noble: Memory, Meaning, and the First World War* (Vancouver: UBC Press, 1997).
25 *Paths of Glory*, prod. James B. Harris, dir. Stanley Kubrick, 86 minutes, United Artists, 1957; *A Very Long Engagement*, prod. Francis Boespflug et al., dir. Jean-Pierre Jeunet, 133 minutes, Warner Independent Pictures, 2004; *Passchendaele*, prod. Paul Gross et al., dir. Paul Gross, 114 minutes, Alliance Films, 2008.
26 *Oh! What a Lovely War*, prod. Brian Duffy and Richard Attenborough, dir. Richard Attenborough, 144 minutes, Paramount Pictures, 1969; *Blackadder Goes Forth*, prod. John Lloyd, six episodes, BBC One, 1989.
27 This website has since been dismantled.
28 War Office, *Manual of Military Law* (London: His Majesty's Stationery Office, 1914), 6.

Chapter 1: Competing Ideologies
1 For an example of this view, see John Peaty, "Capital Courts-Martial during the Great War," in *Look to Your Front: Studies in the First World War by the British Commission for Military History*, ed. Brian Bond et al. (Staplehurst, UK: Spellmount Publishers, 1999), 89-104.
2 For an example of this view, see Julian Putkowski and Julian Sykes, *Shot at Dawn: Executions in World War One by Authority of the British Army Act* (1989; rev. ed., London: Leo Cooper, 1992).
3 Lord Moran, *The Anatomy of Courage*, 2nd ed. (London: Constable, 1966).
4 The most notable British mutiny occurred in September 1917 at Étaples, which acted as a base, training, and transit camp before soldiers proceeded to the front. The troubles actually began in late August when a member of the Australian Imperial Force verbally abused a British non-commissioned officer and later resisted arrest. Following this incident, relations continued to worsen, and in September altercations broke out between soldiers and military police and resulted in the eventual arrest of 300 men. For further information on the Étaples mutiny, see D. Gill and G. Dallas, "Mutiny at Étaples Base in 1917," *Past and Present* 69, 1 (1975): 88-112. For Canadian examples, see Craig Leslie Mantle, "Polished Leathers and Gleaming Steel: Charges of Mutiny in the Canadian Army Service Corps at Bramshott Camp, England, November 1917," and Ian McCulloch, "Crisis in Leadership: The Seventh Brigade and the Nivelles 'Mutiny' 1918," both in *The Apathetic and the Defiant: Case Studies of Canadian Mutiny and Disobedience, 1812-1919*, ed. Craig Leslie Mantle (Kingston: Canadian Defence Academy Press, 2007), 261-95, 373-403; also see Desmond

Morton, "Kicking and Complaining: Demobilization Riots in the Canadian Expeditionary Force, 1918-19," *Canadian Historical Review* 61, 3 (1980): 334-60, which deals with the 1919 riots at Kinmel Park in Wales as Canadian soldiers waited to be demobilized.
5 John Keegan, "Towards a Theory of Combat Motivation," in *Time to Kill: The Soldier's Experience of War in the West, 1939-1945*, ed. Paul Addison and Angus Calder (London: Pimlico, 1997), 3.
6 John Baynes, *Morale: A Study of Men and Courage: The Second Scottish Rifles at the Battle of Neuve Chapelle* (New York: Frederick A. Praeger, 1967), 253-54.
7 Richard Holmes, *Firing Line* (London: J. Cape, 1985), 244-46.
8 Tim Cook, "'More a Medicine than a Beverage': 'Demon Rum' and the Canadian Trench Soldier of the First World War," *Canadian Military History* 9, 1 (2000): 7-22.
9 J.G. Fuller, *Troop Morale and Popular Culture in the British and Dominion Armies, 1914-1918* (Toronto: Oxford University Press, 1990).
10 David Englander, "Discipline and Morale in the British Army, 1917-1918," in *State, Society, and Mobilization in Europe during the First World War*, ed. John Horne (New York: Cambridge University Press, 1997), 137.
11 Eric J. Leed, *No Man's Land: Combat and Identity in World War I* (New York: Cambridge University Press, 1979), 164.
12 Ben Shephard, *A War of Nerves: Soldiers and Psychiatrists, 1914-1994* (London: Pimlico, 2002), 327.
13 As examples of this "lions led by donkeys" thesis in the literature, see Leon Wolff, *In Flanders Fields: The 1917 Campaign* (New York: Viking, 1958); Alan Clark, *The Donkeys: A History of the British Expeditionary Force in 1915* (London: Pimlico, 1991); and A.J.P. Taylor, *The First World War: An Illustrated History* (London: Hamish Hamilton, 1963).
14 No year of publication is listed, and various sources put its publication between 1918 and 1924. Ernest Thurtle, *Shootings at Dawn: The Army Death Penalty at Work* (London: Victoria House Printing Company, n.d.).
15 Parliament of the United Kingdom of Great Britain, *Chp. 22, An Act to Provide, during Twelve Months, for the Discipline and Regulation of the Army and Air Force, Pt. 2, Amendment of Army Act Applicable Also to Air Force Act*, 29 April 1930, 1st Session, 35th Parliament (London: Eyre and Spottiswoode, 1930), 198.
16 An example of a factual error is Thurtle's citation of 264 executions. In total, there were 361 British executions. Thurtle, *Shootings at Dawn*, 3; Gerard Oram, *Death Sentences Passed by Military Courts of the British Army, 1914-1924*, ed. Julian Putkowski (London: Francis Boutle Publishers, 1998), 13.
17 William Moore, *The Thin Yellow Line* (New York: St. Martin's Press, 1975).
18 Anthony Babington, *For the Sake of Example: Capital Courts-Martial, 1914-1920* (New York: St. Martin's Press, 1983).
19 Peaty, "Capital Courts-Martial during the Great War," 97.
20 Ibid., 101.
21 Cathryn Corns and John Hughes-Wilson, *Blindfold and Alone: British Military Executions in the Great War* (London: Cassell, 2001).
22 Gerard Oram, *Military Executions during World War I* (New York: Palgrave Macmillan, 2003), 2.
23 Ibid., 164-65.
24 Gerard Oram, *Worthless Men: Race, Eugenics, and the Death Penalty in the British Army during the First World War* (London: Francis Boutle Publishers, 1998), 16.
25 Christopher Pugsley, *On the Fringe of Hell: New Zealanders and Military Discipline in the First World War* (Toronto: Hodder and Stoughton, 1991).

26 Guy Pedroncini, *Les mutineries de 1917* (Paris: Presses Universitaires de France, 1967).
27 Leonard V. Smith, *Between Mutiny and Obedience: The Case of the French Fifth Infantry Division during World War I* (Princeton: Princeton University Press, 1994).
28 John Gooch, "Morale and Discipline in the Italian Army, 1915-1918," in *Facing Armageddon: The First World War Experienced*, ed. Hugh Cecil and Peter Liddle (London: Leo Cooper, 1996), 440.
29 Gerry Oram, "The Greatest Efficiency: British and American Military Law, 1866-1918," in *Comparative Histories of Crime*, ed. Barry Godfrey et al. (Portland: Willan Publishing, 2003), 170-71.
30 Mark Cornwall, "Morale and Patriotism in the Austro-Hungarian Army, 1914-1918," in *State, Society, and Mobilization in Europe during the First World War*, ed. John Horne (Cambridge, UK: Cambridge University Press, 1997), 188.
31 Ibid., 189.
32 This statistic is quoted in Peaty, "Capital Courts-Martial during the Great War," 97.
33 Peaty, "Capital Courts-Martial during the Great War," 97. A summary execution was one that proceeded without a trial.
34 Oram, *Military Executions during World War I*, 14.
35 Quoted in Holmes, *Firing Line*, 338.
36 Nicolas Offenstadt, *Les fusillés de la Grande Guerre et la mémoire collective: 1914-1999* (Paris: O. Jacob, 1999).
37 *Oh! What a Lovely War*, prod. Brian Duffy and Richard Attenborough, dir. Richard Attenborough, 144 minutes, Paramount Pictures, 1969; *Blackadder Goes Forth*, prod. John Lloyd, six episodes, BBC One, 1989.
38 "Corporal Punishment," Series 4, Episode 2, *Blackadder Goes Forth*, dir. R. Boden, BBC One, 5 October 1989.
39 *Paths of Glory*, prod. James B. Harris, dir. Stanley Kubrick, 86 minutes, United Artists, 1957; *A Very Long Engagement*, prod. Francis Boespflug et al., dir. Jean-Pierre Jeunet, 133 minutes, Warner Independent Pictures, 2004.
40 Humphrey Cobb, *Paths of Glory* (New York: Viking Press, 1935).
41 Sébastien Japrisot, *A Very Long Engagement*, trans. Linda Coverdale (New York: Picador, 1991); *A Very Long Engagement*, prod. Francis Boespflug et al.
42 Anthony Clayton, *Paths of Glory: The French Army, 1914-1918* (London: Cassell, 2003), 94-95.
43 *Passchendaele*, prod. Paul Gross et al., dir. Paul Gross, 114 minutes, Alliance Films, 2008.
44 John Wilson, *And in the Morning* (Toronto: Kids Can Press, 2003), 116.
45 Colin McDougall, *Execution* (Toronto: Macmillan, 1958).
46 Andrew Clark, *A Keen Soldier: The Execution of Second World War Private Harold Pringle* (Toronto: Alfred A. Knopf, 2002), 296.
47 Desmond Morton, "The Supreme Penalty: Canadian Deaths by Firing Squad in the First World War," *Queen's Quarterly* 79, 3 (1972): 345-52.
48 Andrew Godefroy, *For Freedom and Honour? The Story of 25 Canadian Volunteers Executed in the First World War* (Nepean, ON: CEF Books, 1998).
49 Jean-Pierre Gagnon, *Le 22ᵉ Battaillon (canadien-français), 1914-1919* (Ottawa: Les Presses de l'Université Laval et le Ministère de la Défense Nationale, 1986).
50 Patrick Bouvier, *Déserteurs et insoumis: Les Canadiens français et la justice militaire (1914-1918)* (Outremont, QC: Athéna Éditions, 2003).

Chapter 2: Military Law
1 Lieutenant Colonel S.T. Banning, *Military Law Made Easy*, 11th ed. (London: Gale and Polden, 1917).

2. For a more thorough discussion of nineteenth-century training in military law, see Chris Madsen, "Military Law, the Canadian Militia, and the North-West Rebellion of 1885," *Journal of Military and Strategic Studies* 1, 1 (1998): n.p., http://www.jmss.org; and Chris Madsen, *Another Kind of Justice: Canadian Military Law from Confederation to Somalia* (Vancouver: UBC Press, 1999), Chapter 1.
3. Gordon Corrigan, *Mud, Blood, and Poppycock: Britain and the First World War* (New York: Cassell, 2003), 216.
4. A complete list of offences punishable by death can be found in the Army Act in Part Two of the *Manual of Military Law*. Of particular importance are Section Four, "Offences in Relation to the Enemy Punishable with Death," and Section Six, "Offences Punishable More Severely on Active Service than at Other Times."
5. Andrew Godefroy, *For Freedom and Honour? The Story of 25 Canadian Volunteers Executed in the First World War* (Nepean, ON: CEF Books, 1998), 21-23.
6. Gerard Oram, *Death Sentences Passed by Military Courts of the British Army, 1914-1924*, ed. Julian Putkowski (London: Francis Boutle Publishers, 1998).
7. War Office, *Manual of Military Law* (London: His Majesty's Stationery Office, 1914), 18.
8. Ibid., 454.
9. Quoted in Leonard Sellers, *For God's Sake Shoot Straight! The Story of the Court-Martial and Execution of Sub. Lt. Edwin Dyett* (London: Leo Cooper, 1995), 66.
10. Cathryn Corns and John Hughes-Wilson, *Blindfold and Alone: British Military Executions in the Great War* (London: Cassell, 2001), 176.
11. Library and Archives Canada (hereafter LAC), RG 150, Series 8, File 649-J-10612, Reel T-8670.
12. Ibid.; RG 150, Acc. 1992-93/166, Box 4765.
13. LAC, RG 24, National Defence, Series C-1-b, Reel C-5053; RG 150, Acc. 1992-93/166, Box 5322.
14. LAC, RG 24, Vol. 2538, File HQS 1822-2, "Record of Courts Martial on Members of the Canadian Expeditionary Force on Whom the Death Penalty Was Awarded and Inflicted during the Great War."
15. LAC, RG 41, Canadian Broadcasting Corporation (hereafter CBC), Series B-III-1, *In Flanders' Fields*, Vol. 10, 18th Battalion, M.A. Searle, Tape 2, p. 3.
16. Bruce Crane, *It Made You Think of Home: The Haunting Journal of Deward Barnes, Canadian Expeditionary Force: 1916-1919* (Toronto: Dundurn Group, 2004), 165.
17. General Staff, War Office, *Field Service Regulations, Part II, Organization and Administration, 1909* (London: His Majesty's Stationery Office, 1914), 135-36.
18. References to the nickname can also be found in letters and memoirs; see, for example, Robert Graves, *Goodbye to All That* (London: Penguin Books, 1960), 147.
19. Banning, *Military Law Made Easy*, 16.
20. Canadian War Museum (hereafter CWM), Collection of William Antliff Shaw, Call No. 58A 1 182.5, Letter 98, 8 April 1917, p. 3. Shaw survived the war, was awarded the Military Medal in 1918, and died in 1985.
21. Ernest Sheard, "Manuscript Memoirs," Vol. 1, 51, Imperial War Museum, p. 285, as quoted in Joanna Bourke, *Dismembering the Male: Men's Bodies, Britain, and the Great War* (Chicago: University of Chicago Press, 1996), 100.
22. Public Records Office, WO32/5461, Haig to Secretary, War Office, 2 June 1919, as quoted in David Englander, "Discipline and Morale in the British Army, 1917-1918," in *State, Society, and Mobilization in Europe during the First World War*, ed. John Horne (New York: Cambridge University Press, 1997), 132.
23. LAC, Acc. 1992-93/166, various boxes.
24. Godefroy, *For Freedom and Honour?*, 10.

25 LAC, RG 150, Series 8, File 649-A-2567, Reel T-8651; RG 150, Acc. 1992-93/166, Box 6783 (MacDougall); RG 150, Acc. 1992-93/166, Box 990 (Bradburn); RG 150, Acc. 1992-93/166, Box 2913 (England); RG 150, Acc. 1992-93/166, Box 6814 (McFall). Lieutenant Robert England went on to become an important voice in veterans' rehabilitation after the war. He published *Discharged: A Commentary on Civil Re-Establishment of Veterans in Canada* (Toronto: Macmillan, 1943), and he was instrumental in the creation of the Veterans Rehabilitation Act.
26 Banning, *Military Law Made Easy*, 141.
27 Corns and Hughes-Wilson, *Blindfold and Alone*, 293-94.
28 Quoted in ibid., 294. In his reference to "both Death Sentences," Smith-Dorrien was also referring to the case of Andrew Evans, sentenced to death on the same day for an offence unrelated to Byers.
29 Ibid., 293-94.
30 War Office, *Manual of Military Law*, 46.
31 Ibid.
32 There were a number of trained lawyers serving in the army; however, their skills were not always taken advantage of, especially in the first two years of the war. According to *The Times*, as of 12 December 1914, 1,150 solicitors and articled clerks were serving in the British ranks as well as 726 credited barristers as of 18 December 1914. "Law in the Fighting Line," *The Times* [London], 12 December 1914, 12; "Barristers-at-Arms," *The Times* [London], 18 December 1914, 4. In a representative Canadian example, according to the Law Society of Upper Canada, 300 of its lawyers and a large number of law students served in the CEF during the First World War, with a total of 113 dying and many more being wounded. Christopher Moore, *The Law Society of Upper Canada and Ontario's Lawyers, 1797-1997* (Toronto: University of Toronto Press, 1997), 193.
33 James L. Wilkins, *Legal Aid in the Criminal Courts* (Toronto: University of Toronto Press, 1975), 8.
34 Karen Hindle, Philip Rosen, and Law and Government Division, *Legal Aid in Canada* (Ottawa: Library of Parliament, 6 August 2004), 2.
35 Wilkins, *Legal Aid in the Criminal Courts*, 6.
36 LAC, RG 150, Series 8, File 649-M-12799, Reel T-8675; RG 150, Acc. 1992-93/166, Box 6178.
37 Burtch went missing from his unit on 20 August 1917 when he was scheduled to be in the support trenches of the Avion sector. He was arrested on 4 September. At his trial, he said that he had felt ill and thought he would feel better if he could get away for a day or two. He stated that he had intended to return when he felt well enough. He also stated that he had been unaware that his battalion was scheduled to move up the line. Burtch was found guilty and sentenced to death. Although he received recommendations for death and Major R. Parkinson, commander of the 38th Infantry Battalion, believed that the crime had been committed deliberately, his death sentence was commuted to five years of penal servitude. In February 1918, Burtch suffered a nervous breakdown and was discharged as medically unfit. LAC, RG 150, Series 8, File 649-B-10263, Reel T-8654; RG 150, Acc. 1992-93/166, Box 1321.
38 LAC, RG 150, Series 8, File 649-C-5522, Reel T-8653.
39 In an interesting side note, Campbell's personnel file contains a letter from his daughter stating that her father had saved a man in the trenches and carried him to safety. She stated that, while her father never talked of the war, a man in a grocery store had approached her and told her the story. LAC, RG 150, Series 8, File 649-C-5522; RG 150, Acc. 1992-93/166, Box 1445.
40 Anthony Babington, *For the Sake of Example: Capital Courts-Martial, 1914-1920* (New York: St. Martin's Press, 1983), 15.

41 Some cases that I studied were missing the three letters of recommendation, perhaps because they never existed or were lost.
42 Corns and Hughes-Wilson, *Blindfold and Alone*, 450. This statistic is derived from Gerard Oram, *Worthless Men: Race, Eugenics, and the Death Penalty in the British Army during the First World War* (London: Francis Boutle Publishers, 1998), 113.
43 Capital punishment was abolished in Great Britain in 1969 and in France in 1981. Gerard Oram, *Military Executions during World War I* (New York: Palgrave Macmillan, 2003), 33.
44 Use of the death penalty increased dramatically in Germany under the Third Reich, and it was not until 1987 that capital punishment was abolished in what was then East Germany. Richard J. Evans, *Rituals of Retribution: Capital Punishment in Germany, 1600-1987* (Oxford: Oxford University Press, 1996).
45 Ken Leyton-Brown, *The Practice of Execution in Canada* (Vancouver: UBC Press, 2010), 9.
46 David B. Chandler, *Capital Punishment in Canada: A Sociological Study of Repressive Law* (Toronto: McClelland and Stewart, 1976), 13.
47 Kenneth L. Avio, "The Quality of Mercy: Exercise of the Royal Prerogative in Canada," *Canadian Public Policy* 13, 3 (1987): 368.
48 Statistics Canada, Historical Statistics of Canada, "Section Z: Justice," http://www.statcan.gc.ca/.
49 Chandler, *Capital Punishment in Canada*, 17.
50 Quoted in T.M. Hunter, *Some Aspects of Disciplinary Policy in the Canadian Services, 1914-1946*, Canadian Army Historical Section Report 91 (Ottawa: Army Headquarters, Historical Section, 1960), 22.
51 Quoted in ibid.
52 Conclusion made after examining *Official Reports of the Debates of the House of Commons of the Dominion of Canada* (Ottawa: Printer to the King's Most Excellent Majesty, 1914-21). Annual approval of the Army Act is stipulated in War Office, *Manual of Military Law*, 14. A review of the *Globe and Mail* (Toronto) from 1914 to 1918 also shows that there was a lack of debate in the Canadian media on this issue.
53 War Office, *Manual of Military Law*, 24.
54 LAC, RG 24, Series C-1-b, Reel C-5053.
55 War Office, *Manual of Military Law*, 444-45.
56 Today courts martial are still made up of five members randomly chosen from a list of Canadian officers. One of these members is chosen to act as president. "Backgrounder: Composition of General Courts Martial," *National Defence and the Canadian Forces*, http://www.dnd.ca/.
57 General Staff, War Office, *Field Service Regulations, Part II, Organization and Administration, 1909*, 135.
58 Jean-Pierre Gagnon, *Le 22ᵉ Battaillon (canadien-français), 1914-1919* (Ottawa: Les Presses de l'Université Laval et le Ministère de la Défense Nationale, 1986), 300. The 175,000 members of the Chinese Labour Corps who served primarily on the western front were excluded from the Suspension of Sentences Act. Oram, *Worthless Men*, 108.
59 Death sentences for cowardice were also passed on James Finlay Pringle of the 10th Battalion in February 1916, Metro Marchuk of the 47th Battalion in September 1917, and J. Ogorodnick of the 47th Battalion in September 1917.

Chapter 3: The Crimes

1 Tim Cook, *At the Sharp End: Canadians Fighting in the Great War, 1914-1916*, vol. 1 (Toronto: Viking Canada, 2007), 381.
2 Library and Archives Canada (hereafter LAC), RG 150, Series 8, File 649-D-10631, Reel T-8657.

3. LAC, RG 9, Series III-D-3, Vol. 4913, Reel T-10705, File 354, Part 2, War Diary of 2nd Canadian Infantry Battalion.
4. Doyle received an uncharacteristic four letters of recommendation. They came from commanders at the corps, division, brigade, and battalion levels. LAC, RG 150, Series 8, File 649-D-10631, Reel T-8657; RG 150, Acc. 1992-93/166, Box 2653.
5. LAC, RG 150, Series 8, File 649-D-19314, Reel T-8657; RG 150, Acc. 1992-93/166, Box 2690.
6. CWM, Diary of John Patrick Teahan, Call No. 58A 1 113.2, Part I, 15 November 1914-31 March 1915 (entry undated), p. 7. Also published as John Patrick Teahan, *Diary Kid*, ed. Grace Keenan Price (Ottawa: Oberon Press, 1999), 16-17. Teahan originally enlisted in 1914 and served as a member of the Royal Canadian Dragoons in the CEF before transferring to the British Expeditionary Force (BEF) in 1915. He was reported missing in action at Thiepval in October 1916.
7. LAC, RG 150, Series 8, File 649-A-3297, Reel T-8651.
8. Anderson was slightly wounded at Passchendaele before he rejoined the 46th Battalion on 23 November 1917. He served a short time before being granted leave to England on 30 November. LAC, RG 9, Series III-D-3, Vol. 4939, Reel T-10745-10746, File 437, Part 1, War Diary of the 46th Canadian Infantry Battalion; RG 150, Series 8, File 649-A-3297, Reel T-8651; RG 150, Acc. 1992-93/166, Box 142.
9. LAC, RG 150, Series 8, File 649-C-20041, Reel T-8656.
10. Ibid.; RG 150, Acc. 1992-93/166, Box 1629.
11. LAC, RG 150, Series 8, File 649-D-20642, Reel T-8660.
12. Daley received one recommendation for commutation of his death sentence and two recommendations for execution, including McFarland's. Ibid.
13. LAC, RG 150, Acc. 1992-93/166, Box 2274.
14. LAC, RG 9, Series III-D-3, Vol. 4939, Reel T-10745, File 435, Part 1, War Diary of the 44th Canadian Infantry Battalion; RG 150, Series 8, File 649-H-18217, Reel T-8666; RG 150, Acc. 1992-93/166, Box 4464.
15. LAC, RG 150, Series 8, File 649-H-18217, Reel T-8666.
16. Ibid.
17. Ibid.
18. Ibid.; RG 150, Acc. 1992-93/166, Box 4464. Private Stephen Fowles, who deserted with Holmes in October 1917, deserted again while under suspended sentence in April 1918. Following a court martial in May, Fowles was executed for the crime of desertion on 19 June. LAC, RG 150, Series 8, File 649-F-4236, Reel T-8663; RG 150, Acc. 1992-93/166, Box 3249.
19. CWM, Diary of John Patrick Teahan, Call No. 58A 1 113.2, Part I, 15 November 1914-31 March 1915 (entry undated), p. 8; Teahan, *Diary Kid*, 17.
20. Jonathan Vance, "Understanding the Motivation to Fight," paper presented at the Cultures of War and Peace, Annual Symposium of the Academies of Arts, Humanities, and Sciences of Canada, Canadian Museum of Civilization, Ottawa, 14 November 2008.
21. Information derived from attestation papers. LAC, RG 150, Acc. 1992-93/166, various boxes.
22. A. Fortescue Duguid, Letter from Adjutant General to Officers Commanding Divisions and Districts, 6 August 1914, Appendix 44 in *Official History of the Canadian Forces in the Great War 1914-1919, General Series Vol. 1, From the Outbreak of War to the Formation of the Canadian Corps, August 1914-September 1915, Chronology, Appendices, and Maps* (Ottawa: J.O. Patenaude, 1938), 37.
23. Estimate by Richard Holt, who completed a dissertation on recruitment, training, and reinforcements in the CEF from 1914 to 1918. Statistic quoted in email correspondence to the author, 27 July 2009.

24 LAC, RG 150, Acc. 1992-93/166, Box 7488.
25 After being found guilty of desertion, Orr was sentenced to ten years of penal servitude. His sentence was commuted, and he continued to serve until being demobilized on 29 October 1919. LAC, RG 150, Series 8, File 649-O-4611, Reel T-8682; RG 150, Acc. 1992-93/166, Box 7488.
26 LAC, RG 150, Series 8, File 649-T-6635.
27 LAC, RG 9, Series III-D-3, Vol. 4925, Reel T-10720-10721, File 397, Part 2, War Diary of the 16th Canadian Infantry Battalion; RG 150, Series 8, File 649-T-6635, Reel T-8683; RG 150, Acc. 1992-93/166, Box 9671.
28 Lord Moran, *The Anatomy of Courage*, 2nd ed. (London: Constable, 1966), x.
29 LAC, RG 9, Series III-D-3, Vol. 4936, Reel T-10740-10741, File 427, War Diary of the 29th Canadian Infantry Battalion, 6-7 May 1917.
30 LAC, RG 150, Series 8, File 649-F-6037, Reel T-8663.
31 Ibid.
32 Ibid.
33 Fletcher's medical records indicate no diagnosis of shell shock or exhaustion. Ibid.; LAC, RG 150, Acc. 1992-93/166, Box 3150.
34 Sir Andrew MacPhail, *Official History of the Canadian Forces in the Great War, 1914-1919: The Medical Services* (Ottawa: Authority of the Minister of National Defence, under Direction of the General Staff, 1925), 279. The three cases of self-inflicted wounds among men whom I studied include Francis Button, who shot himself in the forearm on 1 April 1918 and was awarded twenty-eight days of field punishment number 1; Robert Masterson, who shot himself in the left index finger on 28 July 1917 and was awarded seven days of the same punishment; and William George Porter, who shot himself in his left arm on 7 December 1916 and was awarded forty-two days of field punishment number 1. LAC, RG 150, Acc. 1992-93/166, Boxes 1354 (Button), 6025 (Masterson), and 7915 (Porter).
35 Cathryn Corns and John Hughes-Wilson, *Blindfold and Alone: British Military Executions in the Great War* (London: Cassell, 2001), 104; Gerard Oram, *Death Sentences Passed by Military Courts of the British Army, 1914-1924*, ed. Julian Putkowski (London: Francis Boutle Publishers, 1998), 15.
36 The medical records of Delisle indicate treatment for convulsions in September 1917. Records also indicate that a mental examination with undetermined results was conducted on 13 May 1918, only eight days prior to his execution. The medical records of Fowles show a diagnosis of mutism in October 1917. LAC, RG 150, Acc. 1992-93/166, Boxes 243 (Arnold), 2421 (Delisle), and 3249 (Fowles).
37 Tom Brown, "Shell Shock in the Canadian Expeditionary Force, 1914-1918: Canadian Psychiatry in the Great War," in *Health, Disease, and Medicine: Essays in Canadian History*, ed. Charles G. Roland (Hamilton: Hannah Institute for the History of Medicine, McMaster University, 1984), 309.
38 Charles S. Myers, "A Contribution to the Study of Shell Shock: Being an Account of Three Cases of Loss of Memory, Vision, Smell, and Taste, Admitted into the Duchess of Westminster's War Hospital, Le Touquet," *The Lancet* 185, 4772 (1915): 320.
39 Brown, "Shell Shock in the Canadian Expeditionary Force, 1914-1918," 314.
40 Ibid., 318-22.
41 LAC, RG 9, Series III-D-3, Vol. 4912, Reel T-10704, File 350, Part 2, War Diary of the 1st Canadian Infantry Battalion; RG 150, Series 8, File 649-B-18119, Reel T-8654.
42 LAC, RG 150, Series 8, File 649-B-18119, Reel T-8654.
43 LAC, RG 9, Series III-D-3, Vol. 4913, Reel T-10704-10705, File 351, War Diary of the 1st Canadian Infantry Battalion; RG 150, Acc. 1992-93/166, Box 843.
44 LAC, RG 150, Acc. 1992-93/166, Box 1452.

45 LAC, RG 150, Series 8, File 240-C-16, Reel T-8691; RG 150, Acc. 1992-93/166, Box 1452.
46 *The King's Regulations and Orders for the Army* (London: His Majesty's Stationery Office, 1914), 130.
47 LAC, Series 8, various files, various reel numbers.
48 William Boyd, *With a Field Ambulance at Ypres: Being Letters Written March 7-August 15, 1915* (Toronto: Musson Book Company, 1916), 24-25. Boyd went on to become a professor of pathology at the Universities of Manitoba, Toronto, and British Columbia. He was made a companion of the Order of Canada in 1968. See H.J. Barrie, "Boyd, William," in *The Canadian Encyclopedia*, http://www.thecanadianencyclopedia.com/.
49 A.E. Snell, *The C.A.M.C. with the Canadian Corps during the Last Hundred Days of the Great War* (Ottawa: F.A. Acland, 1924), 75.
50 Ibid., 78.
51 Carolyn Strange, "The Politics of Punishment: The Death Penalty in Canada, 1867-1976," Canadian Legal History Project Working Paper Series 92-10 (Winnipeg: University of Manitoba, 1992), 14.
52 Ibid.
53 B.J. Murdoch, *The Red Vineyard* (1929; reprinted, Glasgow: Robert Maclehose, University Press, 1959), 72.
54 Selig's personnel record is incomplete, and it fails to record whether Selig ultimately survived the war. LAC, RG 150, Series 8, File 649-S-7115, Reel T-8682; RG 150, Acc. 1992-93/166, Box 8771.
55 LAC, RG 150, Series 8, File 649-C-4074, Reel T-8653.
56 Ibid.
57 Ibid.; RG 150, Acc. 1992-93/166, Box 2019.
58 MacPhail, *Official History of the Canadian Forces in the Great War, 1914-1919*, 277.
59 LAC, RG 150, Series 8, File 649-E-6333, Reel T-8660; RG 150, Acc. 1992-93/166, Box 2890.
60 LAC, RG 150, Series 8, File 649-D-20642, Reel T-8660.
61 Ibid.
62 LAC, RG 150, Acc. 1992-93/166, Box 2274. While a large portion of Daley's life remains unknown, personnel records reveal that in his later years Daley relocated to Quebec, and his last residence is listed as Queen Mary Veterans' Hospital in Montreal.
63 LAC, RG 150, Series 8, File 649-O-4818, Reel T-8682.
64 LAC, RG 9, Series III-D-3, Vol. 4915, Reel T-10707, File 360, Part 1, War Diary of the 4th Canadian Infantry Battalion; RG 150, Series 8, File 649-O-4818, Reel T-8682; RG 150, Acc. 1992-93/166, Box 7403.
65 LAC, RG 150, Series 8, File 649-H-21539, Reel T-8666.
66 LAC, RG 9, Series III-D-3, Vol. 4922, Reel T-10716, File 385, Part 1, War Diary of the 13th Canadian Infantry Battalion; RG 150, Series 8, File 649-H-21539, Reel T-8666; RG 150, Acc. 1992-93/166, Box 4022.
67 LAC, RG 9, Series III-C-3, Vol. 4121, Folder 2, File 6, Unaddressed Letter of 1 June 1916, from R.J. Kentish, Brigadier General Commanding 76th Infantry Brigade, 3rd Division.
68 LAC, MG 30, Series E50, Elmer Jones Papers, Folder 3, Canadian Corps Officers' School, Lecture, "The Duties and Responsibilities of an Officer," by Brigadier General, General Staff, Canadian Corps, 21 July 1916, p. 2.
69 LAC, MG 30, Series E50, Elmer Jones Papers, Vol. 1, File 3, Canadian Corps Officers' School of Instruction, Notes of Leadership for Company Officers, p. 3.
70 Leonard V. Smith, *Between Mutiny and Obedience: The Case of the French Fifth Infantry Division during World War I* (Princeton: Princeton University Press, 1994).

71 LAC, RG 41, CBC, *In Flanders' Fields,* Vol. 11, File 22nd Battalion, W.R. Lindsay, Tape 1, pp. 9-10. Also see Thomas-Louis Tremblay, *Journal de guerre (1915-1918),* ed. Marcelle Cinq-Mars (Outremont, QC: Athéna, 2006).
72 Maxime Dagenais, "Une permission! ... C'est bon pour une recrue: Discipline and Illegal Absences in the 22nd (French-Canadian) Battalion, 1915-1919" (MA thesis, University of Ottawa, 2006), 72-81.
73 Desmond Morton, *When Your Number's Up: The Canadian Soldier in the First World War* (Toronto: Random House, 1993), 107.
74 Desmond Morton and J.L. Granatstein, *Marching to Armageddon: Canadians and the Great War, 1914-1919* (Toronto: Lester and Orpen Dennys Publishers, 1989), Appendix B, 279.
75 LAC, RG 150, Series 8, File 649-F-3335, Reel T-8663.
76 Fetterley was convicted of two charges of desertion. His first charge came after absenting the trenches on 4 April 1917. He was arrested on 22 April but seized an opportunity to desert again when he was wrongfully released from close arrest while awaiting trial. LAC, RG 150, Series 8, File 649-F-3355; RG 150, Acc. 1992-93/166, Box 3066.
77 LAC, RG 150, Series 8, File 649-S-34602, Reel T-8688.
78 Ibid.; RG 150, Acc. 1992-93/166, Box 9146.
79 The provost marshal was the commander of the military police. Before the First World War, Jarvis was a decorated member of the Royal North West Mounted Police and a decorated soldier of the Boer War.
80 The Lemay referred to here was the same Arthur Lemay who was later sentenced to death on 24 March 1917 and subsequently had his sentence commuted. LAC, RG 9, Series III-D-3, Vol. 5050, Reel T-10942, File 931, War Diary of the Second Canadian Division, Assistant Provost Marshal.
81 LAC, RG 24, Series C-1-b, Reel C-5053; RG 150, Series 8, various files and reels.
82 Colonel G.W.L. Nicholson, *Canadian Expeditionary Force, 1914-1919* (Ottawa: Queen's Printer and Controller of Stationery, 1962), 297.
83 LAC, RG 150, Series C-1-b, Reel C-5053; RG 150, Acc. 1992-93/166, Box 83.
84 Tim Cook, *Shock Troops: Canadians Fighting in the Great War, 1917-1918,* vol. 2 (Toronto: Viking Canada, 2008), 367.
85 LAC, RG 41-B-III-1, Vol. 6, CBC, *In Flanders Fields,* "Episode 10: The Battle for Passchendaele," 28.
86 The 1911 census, the last census conducted before the outbreak of the First World War, indicated that there were 3,999,081 persons of British origin in the Canadian population. "Estimated Population of Canada, 1605 to Present," http://www.statcan.gc.ca/; "Origins of the Population" (1911), in *Historical Statistics of Canada,* ed. F.H. Leacy (Ottawa: Statistics Canada and Social Science Federation of Canada, 1983), Series A 125-163.
87 The latest estimate is that between 7,000 and 8,000 men with Russian passports served in the CEF. Individuals described as "Russian" could have been from a wide range of ethnicities given the number of ethnicities that made up the Russian Empire at the time. This number includes conscripts, men who did not go overseas, as well as Finns and ethnic Germans. This number was arrived at after contacting Peter Broznitsky who is attempting to gather data regarding the number of Russians and Ukrainians who served in the CEF during the First World War. Peter Broznitsky, letter to the author, 8 April 2009. See http://www.russiansinthecef.com.
88 "Origins of the Population" (1911), *Historical Statistics of Canada,* Series A 125-163.
89 Vadim Kukushkin, *From Peasants to Labourers: Ukrainian and Belarusan Immigration from the Russian Empire to Canada* (Montreal: McGill-Queen's University Press, 2007), 132-33.

90 Four other men had signed their attestation papers, but three of them had signed on forms filled in with typed text, making it impossible to hypothesize about the recruits' knowledge of the English language. The attestation paper of Dimitro Sinizki could not be found. RG 150, Acc. 1992-93/166, Boxes 843 (Bodnarchuk); 846 (Bogdanov); 5258 (Krivetsky); 5261 (Kudatski); 5667 (Lipowich); 5916 (Marchuk); 7447 (Oleinik); 8769 (Sekum); 9146 (Sokol); 9867 (Ukovitch); and 10683 (Zuk).Aboriginal Canadians also experienced significant language barriers in the CEF. One Aboriginal Canadian is included among the studied cases; John Sewell's attestation paper was also signed with an X. RG 150, Acc. 1992-93/166, Box 8785.
91 LAC, RG 150, Series 8, File 649-O-5048, Reel T-8682.
92 Ibid.
93 Ibid.
94 Ibid.; RG 150, Acc. 1992-93/166, Box 7447.
95 LAC, RG 150, Series 8, File 649-U-561, Reel T-8686.
96 Ibid.
97 Ibid.
98 Ibid.; RG 150, Acc. 1992-93/166, Box 9867.
99 LAC, RG 150, Series 8, File 649-L-21864, Reel T-8674.
100 Ibid.; RG 150, Acc. 1992-93/166, Box 5667.

Chapter 4: The Court Martial Process

1 My efforts to identify the soldier in this letter were unsuccessful. No documents relating to an attempted suicide while in prison appear in the cases that I researched. Letter from Charles Douglas Richardson to Edna, 9 April 1916, in *The Canadian Letters and Images Project*, http://www.canadianletters.ca/.
2 Cathryn Corns and John Hughes-Wilson, *Blindfold and Alone: British Military Executions in the Great War* (London: Cassell, 2001), 92.
3 Library and Archives Canada (hereafter LAC), RG 150, Series 8, File 639-O-2589, Reel T-8673.
4 LAC, RG 150, Acc. 1992-93/166, Box 6965.
5 LAC, RG 150, Series 8, File 649-O-2589, Reel T-8673.
6 LAC, RG 150, Acc. 1992-93/166, Box 7520.
7 LAC, RG 9, Series III-D-3, Vol. 4947, Reel T-10756, File 467, War Diary of the 4th Battalion, Canadian Mounted Rifles; RG 150, Series 8, File 649-S-34711, Reel T-8688; RG 150, Acc. 1992-93/166, Box 8769.
8 LAC, RG 150, Series 8, File 649-C-2025, Reel T-8653.
9 Ibid.
10 LAC, RG 9, Series III-D-3, Vol. 4938, Reel T-10743, File 433, Part 2, War Diary of the 42nd Canadian Infantry Battalion; RG 150, Series 8, File 649-C-2025, Reel T-8653; RG 150, Acc. 1992-93/166, Box 1617.
11 Tim Cook, *Shock Troops: Canadians Fighting in the Great War, 1917-1918*, vol. 2 (Toronto: Viking Canada, 2008), 249.
12 LAC, RG 9, Series III-C-3, Vol. 4121, Folder 2, File 6, Unaddressed Letter of 1 June 1916, from R.J. Kentish, Brigadier General Commanding the 76th Infantry Brigade, 3rd Division.
13 Gerard Oram, *Worthless Men: Race, Eugenics, and the Death Penalty in the British Army during the First World War* (London: Francis Boutle Publishers, 1998), 91.
14 LAC, RG 150, Series 8, File 649-T-3533, Reel T-8683; RG 150, Acc. 1992-93/166, Box 9781.
15 LAC, RG 150, Series 8, File 649-H-24911, Reel T-8668.
16 Ibid.; RG 150, Acc. 1992-93/166, Box 4257.
17 Guy Chapman, *A Passionate Prodigality* (London: MacGibbon and Kee, 1933), 73-74.

18 Anthony Babington, *For the Sake of Example: Capital Courts-Martial, 1914-1920* (New York: St. Martin's Press, 1983), 15.
19 Gerard Oram, *Military Executions during World War I* (New York: Palgrave Macmillan, 2003), 9.
20 Tim Cook, *At the Sharp End: Canadians Fighting in the Great War, 1914-1916*, vol. 1 (Toronto: Viking Canada, 2007), 90.
21 Gerard Oram, *Death Sentences Passed by Military Courts of the British Army, 1914-1924*, ed. Julian Putkowski (London: Francis Boutle Publishers, 1998), 13. The Canadian statistic was derived by averaging the time between the date of a trial and the final recommendation for punishment in ten commuted cases. These cases were randomly chosen.
22 LAC, RG 150, Series 8, File 649-D-3990, Reel T-8655; RG 150, Acc. 1992-93/166, Box 2722.
23 Evidence of summary executions by firing squads or at the hands of French officers, in some cases authorized by French military command, was cited on the *Shot at Dawn* website.
24 I conducted a review of Haig's published personal papers to determine his views on courts martial and the confirmation process but found no references to the topic. Douglas Haig, *The Private Papers of Douglas Haig, 1914-1919*, ed. Robert Blake (London: Eyre and Spottiswoode, 1952); Douglas Haig, *Douglas Haig: War Diaries and Letters, 1914-1918*, ed. Gary Sheffield and John Bourne (London: Weidenfeld and Nicolson, 2005); John Charteris, *Field-Marshal Earl Haig* (Toronto: Cassell and Company, 1929).
25 Townsend was apprehended by military police at Calais, France, on 1 October 1916. LAC, RG 150, Series 8, File 649-T-14196, Reel T-8686.
26 At his trial, Townsend claimed to have suffered from prolonged memory loss and could not remember how he had come to be in Calais. Townsend also testified that he had written his suicide note while in a dugout. Ibid.
27 Ibid.; RG 150, Acc. 1992-93, Box 9752.
28 LAC, RG 9, Series III-D-3, Vol. 5050, Reel T-10942, File 931, War Diary of the 2nd Canadian Division, Assistant Provost Marshal; RG 24, Series C-1-b, Reel C-5053.
29 Details derived from documents found in court martial files of executed soldiers, LAC, RG 24, Series C-1-b, Reel C-5053; RG 24, Vol. 2538, File HQS 1822-2, "Points to Which Attention Should Be Paid by Officers Charged with the Carrying Out of a Death Sentence."
30 Michael F. Snape, "British Army Chaplains and Capital Courts-Martial in the First World War," *Royal Army Chaplain's Department Journal* 44 (2005): 10.
31 As evidence of this belief, Snape cites a 1900 survey of ecclesiastical opinion conducted by the Society for the Abolition of Capital Punishment in which all episcopal respondents expressed their support for the death penalty. Ibid., 6.
32 Ibid., 10.
33 Corns and Hughes-Wilson, *Blindfold and Alone*, 403-8.
34 I made a thorough review of *Official Reports of the Debates of the House of Commons of the Dominion of Canada* (Ottawa: Printer to the King's Most Excellent Majesty, 1914-21) and the *Globe and Mail* [Toronto] from 1914 to 1918.
35 These statistics were derived from a random sample of fifty persons who sat on court martial cases that I studied. I compared individuals named as panelists in these trials with their attestation papers, which required individuals to state their civilian professions. LAC, RG 150, Series 8, 649-T File Series; RG 150, Acc. 1992-93/166, various files.
36 Corns and Hughes-Wilson, *Blindfold and Alone*, 96. The original memorandum is held by the Public Records Office of Great Britain, WO 374/1612.
37 Corns and Hughes-Wilson, *Blindfold and Alone*, 94; Oram, *Death Sentences Passed by Military Courts of the British Army, 1914-1924*, 13.
38 LAC, RG 150, Series 8, File 649-T-13605, Reel T-8686.

39 LAC, RG 150, Acc. 1992-93/166, Box 9838.
40 LAC, RG 150, Series 8, File 649-T-13605, Reel T-8686.
41 Ibid.; RG 150, Acc. 1992-93/166, Box 9838.
42 Corns and Hughes-Wilson, *Blindfold and Alone*, 99.
43 LAC, RG 150, Series 8, File 649-F-4108, Reel T-8663.
44 Ibid.
45 Ibid.; RG 150, Acc. 1992-93/166, Box 3284.
46 LAC, RG 150, Series 8, File 649-M-30429, Reel T-8677.
47 Ibid.
48 Ibid.; RG 150, Acc. 1992-93/166, Box 5922.
49 LAC, RG 9, Series III-D-3, Vol. 4931, Reel T-10732-10733, File 413, War Diary of the 22nd Infantry Battalion; RG 150, Series 8, File 649-C-15241, Reel T-8656.
50 LAC, RG 150, Series 8, File 649-C-15241, Reel T-8656.
51 LAC, RG 9, Series III-D-3, Vol. 4931, Reel T-10733, File 413, War Diary of the 22nd Canadian Infantry Battalion; RG 150, Series 8, File 649-C-15241, Reel T-8656; RG 150, Acc. 1992-93/166, Box 1574.
52 LAC, RG 150, Series 8, File 649-B-36307, Reel T-8658.
53 LAC, RG 9, Series III-D-3, Vol. 4915, Reel T-10708, File 361, War Diary of the 4th Canadian Infantry Battalion; RG 150, Acc. 1992-93/166, Box 459.
54 LAC, RG 150, Series 8, File 649-G-865, Reel T-8662; RG 150, Acc. 1992-93/166, Box 3374.

Chapter 5: The Confirmation Process

1 Library and Archives Canada (hereafter LAC), RG 9, Series III-D-3, Vol. 4946, Reel T-10754-10755, File 464, War Diary of the 1st Canadian Mounted Rifles; RG 150, Series 8, File 649-R-10396, Reel T-8680; RG 150, Acc. 1992-93/166, Box 8162.
2 LAC, RG 150, Series 8, File 649-R-10396, Reel T-8680.
3 Ibid.; RG 150, Acc. 1992-93/166, Box 8162.
4 It is generally assumed that these files were lost during the bombing of the Public Records Office in 1940.
5 Information derived from S.S. 412, "Circular Memorandum on Courts-Martial for Use on Active Service," Issued by the Adjutant General's Branch of the Staff, General Headquarters, cited in Christopher Pugsley, *On the Fringe of Hell: New Zealanders and Military Discipline in the First World War* (Toronto: Hodder and Stoughton, 1991), 107.
6 *The King's Regulations and Orders for the Army* (London: His Majesty's Stationery Office, 1914), 130.
7 LAC, RG 150, Series 8, File 649-D-717, Reel T-8655; RG 150, Acc. 1992-93/166, Box 2527.
8 Macdonell commanded the 7th Infantry Brigade before being promoted to command of the First Canadian Division in June 1917. He survived the war, though his only son, Ian Macdonell, a member of the Royal Flying Corps, was shot down and killed during the Battle of the Somme in 1916. A.C. Macdonell retired from the military in 1925 and died in 1942. Ian McCulloch, "'Batty Mac': Portrait of a Brigade Commander of the Great War, 1915-1917," *Canadian Military History* 7, 4 (1998): 11.
9 LAC, RG 150, Series 8, File 649-D-717, Reel T-8655; RG 150, Acc. 1992-93/166, Box 2527.
10 LAC, RG 150, Series 8, File 649-S-3158, Reel T-8682.
11 Ibid.
12 Ibid.; RG 150, Acc. 1992-93/166, Box 10590.
13 LAC, RG 150, Series 8, File 649-S-3158, Reel T-8682.
14 Ibid.; RG 150, Acc. 1992-93/166, Box 8629.
15 LAC, RG 150, Series 8, File 649-J-976, Reel T-8667.
16 Ibid.

17 Desmond Morton, "Lipsett, Louis James," in *Dictionary of Canadian Biography Online, 1911-1920*, vol. XIV, http://www.biographi.ca/.
18 LAC, RG 41, CBC, *In Flanders' Fields*, Vol. 17, 116th Battalion, General Pearkes, Tape 3, p. 11.
19 LAC, RG 150, Series 8, File 649-J-976, Reel T-8667; RG 150, Acc. 1992-93/166, Box 4823.
20 LAC, RG 150, Series 8, File 649-C-20820, Reel T-8656. The war diaries of the 38th Battalion show that they experienced heavy bombardments throughout the month of November and were engaged in an attack on 18 November 1916. LAC, RG 9, Series III-D-3, Vol. 4938, Reel T-10743, File 432, Part 1, War Diary of the 38th Canadian Infantry Battalion.
21 LAC, RG 150, Series 8, File 649-C-20820, Reel T-8656; RG 150, Acc. 1992-93/166, Box 1490.
22 LAC, RG 150, Series 8, File 649-C-33393, Reel T-8659.
23 Ibid.; RG 150, Acc. 1992-93/166, Box 2042.
24 Richard A. Yates and Ruth Whidden Yates, *Canada's Legal Environment: Its History, Institutions, and Principles* (Scarborough, ON: Prentice Hall, 1993), 200.
25 LAC, RG 24, Series C-1-b, Reel C-5053; RG 150, Series 8, File 649-A-799, Reel T-8651; RG 150, Acc. 1992-93/166, Box 304.
26 LAC, RG 150, Acc. 1992-93/166, Box 10454.
27 LAC, RG 24, Series C-1-b, Reel C-5053.
28 Daniel G. Dancocks, *Sir Arthur Currie: A Biography* (Toronto: Methuen, 1985), 66-67.
29 LAC, RG 150, Acc. 1992-93/166, Boxes 10226 (Welsh); 5660 (Ling); and 3249 (Fowles).
30 Michael F. Snape, "British Army Chaplains and Capital Courts-Martial in the First World War," *Royal Army Chaplain's Department Journal* 44 (2005): 8.
31 LAC, RG 150, Acc. 1992-93/166, Box 83. For more on William Alexander's case, see Chapter 3. The three other men include Frederick Arnold (Box 243), Edward Fairburn (Box 2978), and Edward Reynolds (Box 8206).
32 LAC, RG 150, Acc. 1992-93/166, Box 5427.
33 LAC, RG 150, Series 8, File 649-L-9560, Reel T-8671.
34 Ibid.; RG 150, Acc. 1992-93/166, Box 5427.
35 LAC, RG 24, Series C-1-b, Reel C-5053.
36 The date of his demobilization is unspecified in the records. LAC, RG 150, Series 8, File 649-E-2194, Reel T-8660; RG 150, Acc. 1992-93/166, Box 2893.
37 For a full summary of Sekum's case, see Chapter 4. LAC, RG 150, Series 8, File 649-S-34711, Reel T-8688.
38 Major General J.H. MacBrien, Chief of the General Staff, "Some Notes Regarding the Award and Confirmation of Sentences of Death on Canadian Soldiers in the Great War, 1915-1918," 16 February 1922, LAC, RG 24, Vol. 2538, File HQ 1822-2.
39 LAC, RG 150, Series 8, various files and reels.
40 LAC, RG 150, Series 8, File 649-B-5663, Reel T-8652.
41 Ibid.
42 Ibid.; RG 150, Acc. 1992-93/166, Box 760.
43 LAC, RG 150, Series 8, File 649-T-6957, Reel T-8683.
44 Ibid.
45 Ibid.
46 Ibid.
47 Ibid.
48 LAC, RG 9, Series III-D-3, Vol. 4941, Reel T-10748, File 442-443, War Diary of the 52nd Canadian Infantry Battalion; RG 150, Series 8, File 649-T-6957, Reel T-8683; RG 150, Acc. 1992-93/166, Box 9710.
49 Desmond Morton, *When Your Number's Up: The Canadian Soldier in the First World War* (Toronto: Random House, 1993), 279.
50 LAC, RG 150, Series 8, File 649-T-6957, Reel T-8683.

51 Desmond Morton, "The Supreme Penalty: Canadian Deaths by Firing Squad in the First World War," *Queen's Quarterly* 79, 3 (1972): 346.
52 LAC, RG 9, Series III-D-3, Vol. 4931, Reel T-10732-10733, File 413, War Diary of the 22nd Canadian Infantry Battalion; RG 150, Series 8, File 649-D-3990, Reel T-8655.
53 The three men who were executed and referenced in Dubuc's letter were Eugene Perry, executed on 11 April 1917; Gustave Comte, executed on 3 July 1917; and Joseph LaLancette, executed on 3 July 1917. LAC, RG 150, Series 8, File 649-D-3990, Reel T-8655.
54 Ibid.; RG 150, Acc. 1992-93/166, Box 2722.
55 LAC, RG 150, Series 8, File 240-B-43, Reel T-8691.
56 Horne survived the war and retired from the military in 1926. He died of unknown causes in 1929. See Simon Robbins, "Henry Horne: First Army, 1916-1918," in *Haig's Generals*, ed. Ian F.W. Beckett and Steven J. Corvi (Barnsley, UK: Pen and Sword, 2006), 97-121.
57 LAC, RG 150, Series 8, File 240-B-43, Reel T-8691.
58 Ibid.; RG 150, Acc. 1992-93/166, Box 1354.
59 LAC, RG 150, Acc. 1992-93/166, Box 5116.
60 Andrew Godefroy, *For Freedom and Honour? The Story of 25 Canadian Volunteers Executed in the First World War* (Nepean, ON: CEF Books, 1998), 38-39.
61 LAC, RG 24, Series C-1-b, Reel C-5053.
62 LAC, RG 9, Series III-D-3, Vol. 4985, Reel T-10816-10817, File 620, Part 1, War Diary of the 1st Canadian Machine Gun Battalion; RG 150, Series 8, File 649-M-12799, Reel T-8675.
63 LAC, RG 150, Series 8, File 649-M-12799, Reel T-8675.
64 Ibid.
65 Ibid. For a full reading of Millar's case, see Chapter 2.
66 LAC, RG 150, Series 8, File 649-T-3533, Reel T-8683.
67 Historian J.L. Granatstein shows this evolution of opinion in his work. See J.L. Granatstein and J.M. Hitsman, *Broken Promises: A History of Conscription in Canada* (Toronto: Oxford University Press, 1977); and J.L. Granatstein, "Conscription and My Politics," *Canadian Military History* 10, 4 (2001): 37.
68 F.P. Crozier, *A Brass Hat in No Man's Land* (London: Cape, 1930), 47.
69 Reviewing several biographies, I could not find specific comments regarding Haig's attitude toward general use of the death penalty. From his comments on Australian discipline, one can assume that Haig believed in the deterrent effect of executions. See General Sir James Marshall-Cornwall, *Haig as Military Commander* (London: B.T. Batsford, 1973); J.P. Harris, *Douglas Haig and the First World War* (New York: Cambridge University Press, 2008); Gary Mead, *The Good Soldier: The Biography of Douglas Haig* (London: Atlantic Books, 2007); and John Peaty, "Haig and Military Discipline," in *Haig: A Reappraisal 70 Years On*, ed. Brian Bond and Nigel Cave (South Yorkshire, UK: Leo Cooper, 1999), 200-1.
70 Chris Madsen, *Another Kind of Justice: Canadian Military Law from Confederation to Somalia* (Vancouver: UBC Press, 1999), 33-34.
71 Pugsley, *On the Fringe of Hell*, 133.
72 Anthony Babington, *For the Sake of Example: Capital Courts-Martial, 1914-1920* (New York: St. Martin's Press, 1983), 191.
73 Douglas Haig, *The Private Papers of Douglas Haig, 1914-1919*, ed. Robert Blake (London: Eyre and Spottiswoode, 1952), 290. Field Marshal William Birdwood was the commander of the Australian Imperial Force. Contrary to Haig's complaints, Birdwood was in favour of the death penalty and unsuccessfully lobbied the Australian government for its use until the end of 1917. Pugsley, *On the Fringe of Hell*, 133.
74 Haig, *The Private Papers of Douglas Haig, 1914-1919*, 291.
75 Pugsley, *On the Fringe of Hell*, 134.

76 John Peaty, "Capital Courts-Martial during the Great War," in *Look to Your Front: Studies in the First World War by the British Commission for Military History*, ed. Brian Bond et al. (Staplehurst, UK: Spellmount Publishers, 1999), 98.
77 Quoted in Leonard Sellers, *For God's Sake Shoot Straight! The Story of the Court-Martial and Execution of Sub. Lt. Edwin Dyett* (London: Leo Cooper, 1995), 125-33.
78 Peaty, "Capital Courts-Martial during the Great War," 97; Gerard Oram, *Worthless Men: Race, Eugenics, and the Death Penalty in the British Army during the First World War* (London: Francis Boutle Publishers, 1998), 56.
79 LAC, RG 150, Series 8, File 649-Y-398, Reel T-8690.
80 Ibid.; RG 150, Acc. 1992-93/166, Box 10661.
81 LAC, RG 9, Series III-D-3, Vol. 4913, Reel T-10705, File 354, Part 1, War Diary of the 2nd Canadian Battalion; RG 150, Series 8, File 649-S-864, Reel T-8682.
82 LAC, RG 150, Series 8, File 649-S-864, Reel T-8682.
83 Patrick Brennan, "Byng's and Currie's Commanders: A Still Untold Story of the Canadian Corps," *Canadian Military History* 11, 2 (2002): 8; LAC, RG 150, Series 8, File 649-S-864, Reel T-8682.
84 Given his behaviour, a medical examination was administered; however, a medical board found no signs of insanity or shell shock. LAC, RG 150, Series 8, File 649-S-864, Reel T-8682; RG 150, Acc. 1992-93/166, Box 9094.
85 LAC, RG 9, Series III-D-3, Vol. 4944, Reel T-10752, File 455, Part 1, War Diary of the 87th Canadian Infantry Battalion; RG 150, Series 8, File 649-P-1663, Reel T-8676.
86 LAC, RG 150, Series 8, File 649-P-1663, Reel T-8676.
87 Ibid.; RG 150, Acc. 1992-93/166, Box 7672.
88 Although attestation papers do not indicate levels of education obtained by soldiers, we can make some assumptions based on professional backgrounds, but no firm conclusions can be reached. The usefulness and significance of standardized tests were debated even among some of the creators of such tests.
89 LAC, RG 9, Series III-D-3, Vol. 4943, Reel T-10751, File 453, War Diary of the 78th Canadian Infantry Battalion; RG 150, Series 8, File 649-P-11436, Reel T-8678.
90 LAC, RG 150, Series 8, File 649-P-11436, Reel T-8678.
91 Ibid.; RG 150, Acc. 1992-93/166, Box 7736.
92 LAC, RG 9, Series III-D-3, Vol. 4944, Reel T-10752, File 455, Part 1, War Diary of the 87th Canadian Infantry Battalion; RG 150, Series 8, File 649-S-11591, Reel T-8685.
93 LAC, RG 150, Series 8, File 649-S-11591, Reel T-8685.
94 Ibid.
95 Ibid.; RG 150, Acc. 1992-93/166, Box 8785.
96 Timothy C. Winegard, *For King and Kanata: Canadian Indians and the First World War* (Winnipeg: University of Manitoba Press, 2012), 114-17.
97 David B. Chandler, *Capital Punishment in Canada: A Sociological Study of Repressive Law* (Toronto: McClelland and Stewart, 1976), 215-19.
98 Carolyn Strange, "The Politics of Punishment: The Death Penalty in Canada, 1867-1976," Canadian Legal History Project Working Paper Series 92-10 (Winnipeg: University of Manitoba, 1992), 20.
99 *Official Report of the Debates of the House of Commons of the Dominion of Canada*, 3rd Session, 12th Parliament, 5 February 1914 (Ottawa: Printer to the King's Most Excellent Majesty, 1914), 492-93.
100 Ibid., 498.
101 *Official Report of the Debates of the House of Commons of the Dominion of Canada*, 5th Session, 12th Parliament, 18 February 1915 (Ottawa: Printer to the King's Most Excellent Majesty, 1915), 270.

102 LAC, RG 24, Vol. 2538, HQS 1822-2, Letter from Sir Arthur Currie to Major General J.H. MacBrien, 3 February 1922. Currie mistakenly referred to the shooting of one French Canadian in the 42nd Battalion, when the original should have read the 14th Battalion.
103 Jean-Pierre Gagnon, *Le 22ᵉ Battaillon (canadien-français), 1914-1919* (Ottawa: Les Presses de l'Université Laval et le Ministère de la Défense Nationale, 1986), 308. The quotation was derived from an unofficial translation provided by Roger Sarty of Wilfrid Laurier University.
104 Bozan was apprehended five days later. He was found guilty of desertion and sentenced to ten years of penal servitude. It is unknown what became of Bozan since his personnel file does not contain any papers. LAC, RG 9, Series III-D-3, Vol. 4944, Reel T-10751-10752, File 454, Part 1, War Diary of the 85th Canadian Infantry Battalion; RG 150, Series 8, File 649-B-15985, Reel T-8654; RG 150, Acc. 1992-93/166, Box 1356.
105 Gerard Oram, *Death Sentences Passed by Military Courts of the British Army, 1914-1924*, ed. Julian Putkowski (London: Francis Boutle Publishers, 1998), 14.
106 LAC, RG 24, Series C-1-b, Reel C-5053.
107 Tim Cook, *Shock Troops: Canadians Fighting in the Great War, 1917-1918*, vol. 2 (Toronto: Viking Canada, 2008), 73-91.
108 Cathryn Corns and John Hughes-Wilson, *Blindfold and Alone: British Military Executions in the Great War* (London: Cassell, 2001), 188.
109 LAC, RG 24, Series C-1-b, Reel C-5053; RG 150, Acc. 1992-93/166, Box 2978.
110 Kenneth L. Avio examines clemency decisions made by the Canadian cabinet in murder cases from 1926 to 1957. See Kenneth L. Avio, "The Quality of Mercy: Exercise of the Royal Prerogative in Canada," *Canadian Public Policy* 13, 3 (1987): 370.
111 Statistics Canada, *Historical Statistics of Canada*, "Section Z: Justice," http://www.statcan.gc.ca/.
112 Strange, "The Politics of Punishment," 19.
113 The name of the assistant adjutant was illegible and could not be determined. LAC, RG 150, Series 8, File 652-D-44, Reel T-8693.
114 LAC, RG 9, Series III-D-3, Vol. 4939, Reel T-10745, File 435, Part 1, War Diary of the 44th Canadian Infantry Battalion; RG 150, Acc. 1992-93/166, Box 2650.
115 LAC, RG 150, Series 8, File 652-D-44, Reel T-8693.
116 Ibid.

Chapter 6: Pardon Campaigns

1 Douglas C. Peifer, "The Past in the Present: Passion, Politics, and the Historical Profession in the German and British Pardon Campaigns," *Journal of Military History* 71, 4 (2007): 1118-19.
2 Cathryn Corns and John Hughes-Wilson, *Blindfold and Alone: British Military Executions in the Great War* (London: Cassell, 2001), 104-5; Gerard Oram, *Death Sentences Passed by Military Courts of the British Army, 1914-1924*, ed. Julian Putkowski (London: Francis Boutle Publishers, 1998), 15.
3 Julian Putkowski and Julian Sykes, *Shot at Dawn: Executions in World War One by Authority of the British Army Act* (1989; rev. ed., London: Leo Cooper, 1992).
4 Anthony Babington, *For the Sake of Example: Capital Courts-Martial, 1914-1920* (New York: St. Martin's Press, 1983).
5 Putkowski and Sykes, *Shot at Dawn*, n.p.
6 "Campaign to Pardon Troops Hits Setback," *The Independent* [London], 16 August 1993, 6.
7 Ibid.
8 Pardon for Soldiers of the Great War, Private Member's Bill Presented on 18 October 1994, Parliament of the United Kingdom, http://www.publications.parliament.uk/.

9 Corns and Hughes-Wilson, *Blindfold and Alone,* 444.
10 Ibid., 467.
11 Ibid., 466.
12 Bess Twiston-Davies, "Public Pays Its Respects to the First World War Deserters," *Daily Telegraph* [London], 5 January 2001.
13 Maxine Firth, "Court Offers Hope to Family of Soldier Shot for Cowardice," *The Independent* [London], 25 October 2005; "'Cowardice' Was Likely Shell-Shock, Family of Executed U.K. Soldier Says," *National Post* [Don Mills, ON], 25 October 2005, Section A, 18.
14 "Speaking Notes for the Honourable Ronald J. Duhamel, Minister of Veterans Affairs, Regarding First World War Military Executions," *Veterans Affairs Canada,* http://www.veterans.gc.ca/.
15 Tim Cook, *Clio's Warriors: Canadian Historians and the Writing of the World Wars* (Vancouver: UBC Press, 2006), 245.
16 Kim Honey, "Decision on Soldiers Decried," *Globe and Mail,* 13 December 2001, Section A, 19.
17 *Official Reports of the Debates of the House of Commons of Canada* (Ottawa: Printer to the Queen's Most Excellent Majesty, 1990-2001).
18 *Official Report of the Debates of the House of Commons of Canada,* 1st Session, 37th Parliament, 11 December 2001 (Ottawa: Printer to the Queen's Most Excellent Majesty, 2001), 8088.
19 For more on this topic, see J.L. Granatstein and J.M. Hitsman, *Broken Promises: A History of Conscription in Canada* (Toronto: Oxford University Press, 1977). Mennonites were exempted from the Military Service Act, but there was confusion in practice. Although many Mennonites in Manitoba and Saskatchewan were exempted from all service and not required to register, Mennonites in Ontario were often exempted from combat service only. The confusion was caused by unclear rules and local tribunals that were unaware of exemption policies. Eventually, the policy was clarified so that all Mennonites were subject to the same policy of full exemption. For more on the Mennonite experience, see Adolf Ens, *Subjects or Citizens? The Mennonite Experience in Canada, 1870-1925* (Ottawa: University of Ottawa Press, 1994); and Amy Shaw, *Crisis of Conscience: Conscientious Objection in Canada during the First World War* (Vancouver: UBC Press, 2009).
20 Although definitive statements cannot be made without evidence, my hypothesis is that, if more non-professionals were involved in the debate, there would have been a greater number of people in favour of pardons, representing the common view that military justice in the First World War was particularly brutal. *H-Net Canada,* 9-11 January 2007, http://www.h-net.org/~canada/.
21 For a full reading of the Pardon for Soldiers of the Great War Act (2000), see http://www.legislation.govt.nz/.
22 "Pardon Dead Soldiers, Says Select Committee," *Evening Post* [Wellington], 28 June 2000, 8.
23 Peter Leese, *Shell-Shock: Traumatic Neurosis and the British Soldiers of the First World War* (New York: Palgrave Macmillan, 2002), 176.
24 George L. Mosse, *Fallen Soldiers: Reshaping the Memory of the World Wars* (New York: Oxford University Press, 1990), 4.
25 Two sample studies on home front support include Gary Sheffield, *Forgotten Victory: The First World War: Myths and Realities* (London: Review, 2002), which discusses British support, and Ian Hugh Maclean Miller, *Our Glory and Our Grief: Torontonians and the Great War* (Toronto: University of Toronto Press, 2002), which provides a regional history of Canadian support.

26 Erich Maria Remarque, *All Quiet on the Western Front,* trans. A.W. Wheen (New York: Fawcett Crest, 1928); Wilfred Owen, *The Poems of Wilfred Owen,* ed. Edmund Blunden (London: Chatto and Windus, 1931). Although a collection of Owen's poetry was published in 1920, the 1931 edition was more influential. It did not have the commercial success of Remarque's *All Quiet on the Western Front,* but it did establish Owen's reputation among British war poets and helped to shape the modern view of the war. Samuel Hynes, *A War Imagined: The First World War and English Culture* (New York: Atheneum, Maxwell Macmillan International, 1991), 436-37. For a full reading of postwar literature and modernism, see Paul Fussell, *The Great War and Modern Memory* (New York: Oxford University Press, 1975); and Hynes, *A War Imagined.*
27 Hynes, *A War Imagined,* 425.
28 Janet S.K. Watson, *Fighting Different Wars: Experience, Memory, and the First World War in Britain* (New York: Cambridge University Press, 2004), 195.
29 Jonathan F. Vance, *Death So Noble: Memory, Meaning, and the First World War* (Vancouver: UBC Press, 1997).
30 For a full account of Haig's 1925 visit, see John Scott, "Three Cheers for Earl Haig: Canadian Veterans and the Visit of Field Marshal Sir Douglas Haig to Canada in the Summer of 1925," *Canadian Military History* 5, 1 (1996): 35-40.
31 Leon Wolff, *In Flanders Fields: The 1917 Campaign* (New York: Viking, 1958).
32 Alan Clark, *The Donkeys: A History of the British Expeditionary Force in 1915* (London: Pimlico, 1991); A.J.P. Taylor, *The First World War: An Illustrated History* (London: Hamish Hamilton, 1963). *The Donkeys* later served as an inspiration for the stage play and subsequent film *Oh! What a Lovely War.*
33 Modris Eksteins, "Memory and the Great War," in *The Oxford Illustrated History of the First World War,* ed. Hew Strachan (New York: Oxford University Press, 1998), 316.
34 *The Great War,* British Broadcasting Corporation (BBC), 1964, 26 episodes.
35 Sheffield, *Forgotten Victory,* 18-24.
36 "The Gallipoli Campaign," Australian Government, Department of Veterans Affairs, http://www.dva.gov.au/.
37 "The Truth about the Young Men Who Died at Dawn," *Daily Mail* [London], 21 July 2001.
38 "Daughter's Plea for Great War Pardon," *BBC News,* 7 November 2003, http://news.bbc.co.uk/.
39 Corns and Hughes-Wilson, *Blindfold and Alone,* 441.
40 Alan Hamilton, "Remembrance at Last for Executed Soldiers," *The Times* [London], 13 November 2000, 5L.
41 British statistic derived from John Peaty, "Capital Courts-Martial during the Great War," in *Look to Your Front: Studies in the First World War by the British Commission for Military History,* ed. Brian Bond et al. (Staplehurst, UK: Spellmount Publishers, 1999), 92. Canadian statistic derived from Teresa Iacobelli, "Arbitrary Justice? A Comparative Analysis of Canadian Death Sentences Passed and Death Sentences Commuted during the First World War" (MA Research Paper, Wilfrid Laurier University, 2004), 21.
42 Peter Taylor-Whiffen, "Shot at Dawn: Cowards, Traitors, or Victims?," *BBC News,* 1 March 2002, http://www.bbc.co.uk/.
43 Library and Archives Canada (hereafter LAC), RG 24, Vol. 2538, File HQ 1822-2, "Some Notes Regarding the Award and Confirmation of Sentences of Death on Canadian Soldiers in the Great War, 1915-1918," Major General G.H. MacBrien, Chief of the General Staff, 16 February 1922.
44 Putkowski and Sykes, *Shot at Dawn,* 16.

45 G.D. Sheffield, *Leadership in the Trenches: Officer-Man Relations, Morale, and Discipline in the British Army in the Era of the First World War* (New York: Palgrave Macmillan, 2000), 178-79.
46 Randy Boswell, "Executed WWI Soldiers Get 'Dignity': Ottawa Expresses Sorrow to the Families of 23 Canadians Killed for Cowardice or Desertion: 'Rubbish,' Historian Says," *National Post* [Don Mills, ON], 12 December 2001, Section A, 4.
47 Ibid.
48 Shawn McCarthy, "More than 80 Years Ago, They Were Shot for Desertion. Today, They'd Be Sent Home with Battle Fatigue. Now, Canada Makes Amends," *Globe and Mail*, 12 December 2001, Section A, 3; Shawn McCarthy, "Casualties of Shame," *Globe and Mail*, 22 December 2001, Section F, 4.
49 Paul Samyn, "Executed Soldier's Honour Restored," *Winnipeg Free Press*, 12 December 2001, Section A, 6.
50 LAC, RG 150, Series 8, File 649-F-4236, Reel T-8663; RG 150, Acc. 1992-93/166, Box 3249.
51 This story has been quoted in several news articles, including Allison Bray, "When Being Late on Leave Meant the Firing Squad," *Winnipeg Free Press*, 10 April 1995, Section B, 4; Lindor Reynolds, "Minister Vows to Seek Pardon for Executed Soldiers," *Winnipeg Free Press*, 5 November 2000, Section A, 1; Paul Samyn, "No Pardon for Soldiers Shot at Dawn: Duhamel Offers Statement of Sorrow to Canadians Executed by British," *Winnipeg Free Press*, 11 December 2001, Section A, 3; McCarthy, "More than 80 Years Ago, They Were Shot for Desertion"; Samyn, "Executed Soldier's Honour Restored."
52 LAC, RG 150, Series 8, File 649-F-4236, Reel T-8663; RG 150, Acc. 1992-93/166, Box 3249.
53 Quoted in McCarthy, "Casualties of Shame."
54 This issue was raised by Member of Parliament Edward Garnier. Corns and Hughes-Wilson, *Blindfold and Alone*, 481.
55 "UK Battle to Clear the 'Cowards,'" *BBC News*, 11 November 1999, http://news.bbc.co.uk/.
56 "Pardon Bill under Fire from RSA," *Evening Post* [Wellington], 11 April 2000, 2.
57 Taylor-Whiffen, "Shot at Dawn," http://www.bbc.co.uk/.
58 "... And in the Morning, We Will Remember Them," *Evening Post* [Wellington], 24 April 2000, 4.
59 Quoted in McCarthy, "Casualties of Shame."

Conclusion

1 The recipient was listed only as "minister," but I have assumed that the letter was sent to the minister of militia and defence. Note that Colonel Dennistoun was the deputy judge advocate general at this time. Library and Archives Canada (hereafter LAC), RG 24, Vol. 6643, Folder 5, JAG Opinions, Rulings, Discharge – Discipline, Letter from JAG to the Honourable Minister, 15 September 1919.
2 Ibid.
3 R.C. Fetherstonhaugh, *The Royal Montreal Regiment 14th Battalion CEF, 1914-1925* (Montreal: Montreal Gazette Printing Company, 1927); Colonel W.W. Murray, *The History of the 2nd Canadian Battalion (East Ontario Regiment) Canadian Expeditionary Force in the Great War, 1914-1919* (Ottawa: Mortimer, 1947), 350. More recently, all of the executed soldiers are listed, with their true cause of death, in Edward H. Wigney, *The CEF Roll of Honour: Members and Former Members of the Canadian Expeditionary Force Who Died as a Result of Service in the Great War, 1914-1919* (Ottawa: Eugene Ursual, 1996).
4 LAC, RG 24, Vol. 2538, File HQS 1822-2, "Memorandum re Method of Notifying Next of Kin of Men Who Have Suffered Death by Sentence of Field General Courts-Martial."

5 LAC, RG 24, Series C-1-b, Reel C-5053; RG 150, Acc. 1992-93/166, Box 5660.
6 LAC, RG 24, Series C-1-b, Reel C-5053.
7 Ibid. The author's signature is illegible.
8 Ibid. The author's signature is illegible.
9 Ibid.
10 Ibid.
11 Bruce Crane, *It Made You Think of Home: The Haunting Journal of Deward Barnes, Canadian Expeditionary Force: 1916-1919* (Toronto: Dundurn Group, 2004), 172.
12 Deborah Cowley, ed., *Georges Vanier, Soldier: The Wartime Letters and Diaries, 1915-1919* (Toronto: Dundurn Press, 2000), 216.
13 LAC, CBC, *In Flanders' Fields*, 8th Battalion, C.E. Barnes, Tape 2, p. 1.
14 George Coppard, *With a Machine Gun to Cambrai: The Tale of a Young Tommy in Kitchener's Army, 1914-1918* (London: Her Majesty's Stationery Office, 1969), 48.
15 LAC, RG 24, Series C-1-b, Reel C-5053.
16 Ibid.
17 O'Brien was shot in the arm in June 1916 and rejoined his unit in November. He was later wounded at the Battle of Vimy Ridge in April 1917, and he never returned to service. O'Brien has no entry on his record between rejoining his unit and being wounded at Vimy Ridge. LAC, RG 150, Acc. 1992-93/166, Box 7405.
18 Desmond Morton, *When Your Number's Up: The Canadian Soldier in the First World War* (Toronto: Random House, 1993), 251-52.
19 Anthony Babington, *For the Sake of Example: Capital Courts-Martial, 1914-1920* (New York: St. Martin's Press, 1983), 194.
20 *Report of the Committee Constituted by the Army Council to Enquire into the Law and Rules of Procedure Regulating Military Courts-Martial, 1919*, quoted in ibid.
21 Ibid., 194-95.
22 Ibid., 195.
23 David French, "Discipline and the Death Penalty in the British Army in the War against Germany during the Second World War," *Journal of Contemporary History* 33, 4 (1998): 538.
24 Ibid., 540-43.
25 The case of Pringle has been the subject of much speculation. Although he was a known deserter, many believe that he was innocent of the murder that he was convicted of and that there was far too much reasonable doubt to convict and subsequently execute him. For a full reading of the case, see Andrew Clark, *A Keen Soldier: The Execution of Second World War Private Harold Pringle* (Toronto: Alfred A. Knopf, 2002).
26 Andrew Godefroy, *For Freedom and Honour? The Story of 25 Canadian Volunteers Executed in the First World War* (Nepean, ON: CEF Books, 1998), 74.
27 Charles R. Epp, *The Rights Revolution: Lawyers, Activists, and Supreme Courts in Comparative Perspective* (Chicago: University of Chicago Press, 1998), 163; "History of the Court Martial Appeal Court of Canada," *Court Martial Appeal Court of Canada*, http://www.cmac-cacm.ca/.
28 "History of the Court Martial Appeal Court of Canada," *Court Martial Appeal Court of Canada*, http://www.cmac-cacm.ca/.
29 Kenneth L. Avio, "The Quality of Mercy: Exercise of the Royal Prerogative in Canada," *Canadian Public Policy* 13, 3 (1987): 370.
30 While the death penalty was abolished in Canada in 1976, the last executions took place in 1962 with the hanging of two men in Toronto, both convicted of murder in separate incidents.

Bibliography

Archival Sources

Canadian War Museum, Ottawa
Canadian Broadcasting Corporation. *Flanders' Fields: A Story of the Canadian Corps.* Transcripts, seventeen episodes, 1964.
Shaw, William Antliff. Letters Home.
Teahan, John Patrick. Diary.

Library and Archives Canada (LAC), Ottawa
MG 30, Series E50, Elmer Jones Papers
RG 9, Militia and Defence, Series III-C-3 and Series III-D-3
RG 24, National Defence, Series C-1-b
RG 24, Vol. 2538, File HQS 1822-2
RG 24, Vol. 6643, Folder 5, JAG Opinions, Rulings
RG 41, Canadian Broadcasting Corporation, Series B-III-1
RG 150, Ministry of Overseas Military Forces of Canada, Courts Martial of the First World War, Personnel Files of the First World War

Other Sources

Audoin-Rouzeau, Stéphane. *Men at War, 1914-1918: National Sentiment and Trench Journalism in France during the First World War.* Translated by Helen McPhail. Oxford: Berg, 1995.
Avio, Kenneth L. "The Quality of Mercy: Exercise of the Royal Prerogative in Canada." *Canadian Public Policy* 13, 3 (1987): 366-79.
Babington, Anthony. *For the Sake of Example: Capital Courts-Martial, 1914-1920.* New York: St. Martin's Press, 1983.
Banning, Lieutenant Colonel S.T. *Military Law Made Easy.* 11th ed. London: Gale and Polden, 1917.
Barkan, Elazar. "Restitution and Amending Historical Injustices in International Morality." In *Politics and the Past: On Repairing Historical Injustices,* edited by John Torpery, 91-102. New York: Rowman and Littlefield, 2003.
Barris, Ted. *Victory at Vimy: Canada Comes of Age, April 9-12, 1917.* Toronto: Thomas Allen Publishers, 2007.
Baynes, John. *Morale: A Study of Men and Courage: The Second Scottish Rifles at the Battle of Neuve Chapelle.* New York: Frederick A. Praeger, 1967.
Beckett, Ian F.W., and Keith Simpson, eds. *A Nation in Arms: A Social Study of the British Army in the First World War.* Manchester: Manchester University Press, 1985.
Berton, Pierre. *Vimy.* Markham, ON: Penguin Books Canada, 1986.
Blackadder Goes Forth. Produced by John Lloyd. BBC One, 1989. Six episodes.
Blair, Dale James. "Beyond the Metaphor: Football and War, 1914-1918." *Journal of the Australian War Memorial* 28 (1996): n.p. (online).

Bourke, Joanna. *Dismembering the Male: Men's Bodies, Britain, and the Great War.* Chicago: University of Chicago Press, 1996.
Bouvier, Patrick. *Déserteurs et insoumis: Les Canadiens français et la justice militaire (1914-1918).* Outremont, QC: Athéna, 2003.
Boyd, William. *With a Field Ambulance at Ypres: Being Letters Written March 7-August 15, 1915.* Toronto: Musson Book Company, 1916.
Brennan, Patrick. "Byng's and Currie's Commanders: A Still Untold Story of the Canadian Corps." *Canadian Military History* 11, 2 (2002): 5-16.
Brown, Tom. "Shell Shock in the Canadian Expeditionary Force, 1914-1918: Canadian Psychiatry in the Great War." In *Health, Disease, and Medicine: Essays in Canadian History,* edited by Charles G. Roland, 308-32. Hamilton: Hannah Institute for the History of Medicine, McMaster University, 1984.
Cassel, Jay. *The Secret Plague: Venereal Disease in Canada, 1838-1839.* Toronto: University of Toronto Press, 1987.
Chandler, David B. *Capital Punishment in Canada: A Sociological Study of Repressive Law.* Toronto: McClelland and Stewart, 1976.
Chapman, Guy. *A Passionate Prodigality.* London: MacGibbon and Kee, 1933.
Charteris, John. *Field-Marshal Earl Haig.* Toronto: Cassell and Company, 1929.
Clark, Alan. *The Donkeys: A History of the British Expeditionary Force in 1915.* London: Pimlico, 1991.
Clark, Andrew. *A Keen Soldier: The Execution of Second World War Private Harold Pringle.* Toronto: Alfred A. Knopf, 2002.
Clayton, Anthony. *Paths of Glory: The French Army, 1914-1918.* London: Cassell, 2003.
Cobb, Humphrey. *Paths of Glory.* New York: Viking Press, 1935.
Cook, Tim. *At the Sharp End: Canadians Fighting in the Great War, 1914-1916.* Vol. 1. Toronto: Viking Canada, 2007.
–. *Clio's Warriors: Canadian Historians and the Writing of the World Wars.* Vancouver: UBC Press, 2006.
–. "'More a Medicine than a Beverage': 'Demon Rum' and the Canadian Trench Soldier of the First World War." *Canadian Military History* 9, 1 (2000): 7-22.
–. *Shock Troops: Canadians Fighting in the Great War, 1917-1918.* Vol. 2. Toronto: Viking Canada, 2008.
Coppard, George. *With a Machine Gun to Cambrai: The Tale of a Young Tommy in Kitchener's Army, 1914-1918.* London: Her Majesty's Stationery Office, 1969.
Corns, Cathryn, and John Hughes-Wilson. *Blindfold and Alone: British Military Executions in the Great War.* London: Cassell, 2001.
Cornwall, Mark. "Morale and Patriotism in the Austro-Hungarian Army, 1914-1918." In *State, Society, and Mobilization in Europe during the First World War,* edited by John Horne, 173-91. Cambridge, UK: Cambridge University Press, 1997.
Corrigan, Gordon. *Mud, Blood, and Poppycock: Britain and the First World War.* New York: Cassell, 2003.
Cowley, Deborah, ed. *George Vanier, Soldier: The Wartime Letters and Diaries, 1915-1919.* Toronto: Dundurn Press, 2000.
Crane, Bruce. *It Made You Think of Home: The Haunting Journal of Deward Barnes, Canadian Expeditionary Force, 1916-1919.* Toronto: Dundurn Group, 2004.
Crozier, F.P. *A Brass Hat in No Man's Land.* London: Cape, 1930.
Dagenais, Maxime. "Une permission! ... C'est bon pour une recrue: Discipline and Illegal Absences in the 22nd (French-Canadian) Battalion, 1915-1919." MA thesis, University of Ottawa, 2006.
Dancocks, Daniel G. *Sir Arthur Currie: A Biography.* Toronto: Methuen, 1985.

Eksteins, Modris. "Memory and the Great War." In *The Oxford Illustrated History of the First World War,* edited by Hew Strachan, 305-18. New York: Oxford University Press, 1998.

–. *Rites of Spring: The Great War and the Birth of the Modern Age.* Toronto: Lester and Orpen Dennys, 1989.

England, Robert. *Discharged: A Commentary on Civil Re-Establishment of Veterans in Canada.* Toronto: Macmillan, 1943.

Englander, David. "Discipline and Morale in the British Army." In *State, Society, and Mobilization in Europe during the First World War,* edited by John Horne, 125-43. New York: Cambridge University Press, 1997.

–. "Mutinies and Military Morale." In *The Oxford Illustrated History of the First World War,* edited by Hew Strachan, 191-202. New York: Oxford University Press, 1998.

Ens, Adolf. *Subjects or Citizens? The Mennonite Experience in Canada, 1870-1925.* Ottawa: University of Ottawa Press, 1994.

Epp, Charles R. *The Rights Revolution: Lawyers, Activists, and Supreme Courts in Comparative Perspective.* Chicago: University of Chicago Press, 1998.

Evans, Richard J. *Rituals of Retribution: Capital Punishment in Germany, 1600-1987.* Oxford: Oxford University Press, 1996.

Fetherstonhaugh, R.C. *The Royal Montreal Regiment 14th Battalion CEF, 1914-1925.* Montreal: Montreal Gazette Publishing Company, 1927.

Fortescue, Duguid A. *Official History of the Canadian Forces in the Great War 1914-1919, General Series Vol. 1, From the Outbreak of War to the Formation of the Canadian Corps, August 1914-September 1915, Chronology, Appendices, and Maps.* Ottawa: J.A. Patenaude, 1938.

French, David. "Discipline and the Death Penalty in the British Army in the War against Germany during the Second World War." *Journal of Contemporary History* 33, 4 (1998): 531-45.

Fuller, J.G. *Troop Morale and Popular Culture in the British and Dominion Armies, 1914-1918.* Toronto: Oxford University Press, 1990.

Fussell, Paul. *The Great War and Modern Memory.* New York: Oxford University Press, 1975.

Gagnon, Jean-Pierre. *Le 22e Bataillon (canadien-français), 1914-1919.* Ottawa: Les Presses de l'Université Laval et le Ministère de la Défense Nationale, 1986.

Gammage, Bill. *The Broken Years: Australian Soldiers in the Great War.* Canberra: Australian National University Press, 1974.

General Staff. War Office. *Field Service Regulations.* London: His Majesty's Stationery Office, 1914.

Gibson, Craig. "'My Chief Source of Worry': An Assistant Provost Marshal's View of Relations between 2nd Canadian Division and Local Inhabitants on the Western Front, 1915-1917." *War in History* 7, 4 (2000): 413-41.

Gill, D., and G. Dallas. "Mutiny at Étaples Base in 1917." *Past and Present* 69, 1 (1975): 88-112.

Godefroy, Andrew. *For Freedom and Honour? The Story of 25 Canadian Volunteers Executed in the First World War.* Nepean, ON: CEF Books, 1998.

Gooch, John. "Morale and Discipline in the Italian Army, 1915-1918." In *Facing Armageddon: The First World War Experienced,* edited by Hugh Cecil and Peter Liddle, 434-47. London: Leo Cooper, 1996.

Graham, Stephen. *A Private in the Guards.* London: Macmillan, 1919.

Granatstein, J.L. "Conscription and My Politics." *Canadian Military History* 10, 4 (2001): 35-38.

Granatstein, J.L., and J.M. Hitsman. *Broken Promises: A History of Conscription in Canada.* Toronto: Oxford University Press, 1977.

Graves, Robert. *Goodbye to All That.* London: Penguin Books, 1960.

The Great War. BBC, 1964. Twenty-six episodes.

Haig, Douglas. *Douglas Haig: War Diaries and Letters, 1914-1918.* Edited by Gary Sheffield and John Bourne. London: Weidenfeld and Nicolson, 2005.

–. *The Private Papers of Douglas Haig, 1914-1919.* Edited by Robert Blake. London: Eyre and Spottiswoode, 1952.

Harris, J.P. *Douglas Haig and the First World War.* New York: Cambridge University Press, 2008.

Harrison, Charles Yale. *Generals Die in Bed.* New York: William Morrow, 1930.

Hay, Douglas. "Property, Authority, and the Criminal Law." In *Albion's Fatal Tree: Crime and Society in Eighteenth-Century England,* edited by Douglas Hay et al., 17-49. New York: Pantheon Books, 1975.

Hayes, Geoffrey, et al., eds. *Vimy Ridge: A Canadian Reassessment.* Waterloo, ON: Wilfrid Laurier University Press, 2007.

Hindle, Karen, Philip Rosen, and Law and Government Division. *Legal Aid in Canada.* Ottawa: Library of Parliament, 2004.

Holmes, Richard. *Firing Line.* London: J. Cape, 1985.

House of Commons of Canada. *Official Reports of the Debates of the House of Commons of Canada, 1990-2001.* Ottawa: Printer to the Queen's Most Excellent Majesty, 1990-2001.

House of Commons of the Dominion of Canada. *Official Reports of the Debates of the House of Commons of the Dominion of Canada, 1914-1921.* Ottawa: Printer to the King's Most Excellent Majesty, 1914-21.

Hunter, T.M. *Some Aspects of Disciplinary Policy in the Canadian Services, 1914-1946.* Canadian Army Historical Section Report 91. Ottawa: Army Headquarters Historical Section, 1960.

Hynes, Samuel. *A War Imagined: The First World War and English Culture.* New York: Atheneum, 1991.

Iacobelli, Teresa. "Arbitrary Justice? A Comparative Analysis of Canadian Death Sentences Passed and Death Sentences Commuted during the First World War." MA research paper, Wilfrid Laurier University, 2004.

Iacovetta, Franca, and Wendy Mitchinson, eds. *On the Case: Explorations in Social History.* Toronto: University of Toronto Press, 1998.

Japrisot, Sebastien. *A Very Long Engagement.* Translated by Linda Coverdale. New York: Picador, 1991.

Keegan, John. "Towards a Theory of Combat Motivation." In *Time to Kill: The Soldier's Experience of War in the West, 1939-1945,* edited by Paul Addison and Angus Calder, 3-11. London: Pimlico, 1997.

Kellett, Anthony. *Combat Motivation: The Behaviour of Soldiers in Battle.* Boston: Kluwer, 1982.

King, Peter. *Crime, Justice, and Discretion in England, 1740-1820.* Oxford: Oxford University Press, 2000.

The King's Regulations and Orders for the Army. London: His Majesty's Stationery Office, 1914.

Kukushkin, Vadim. *From Peasants to Labourers: Ukrainian and Belarusan Immigration from the Russian Empire to Canada.* Montreal: McGill-Queen's University Press, 2007.

Leacy, F.H., ed. *Historical Statistics of Canada.* Ottawa: Statistics Canada and Social Science Federation of Canada, 1983.

Leed, Eric J. *No Man's Land: Combat and Identity in World War I.* New York: Cambridge University Press, 1979.
Leese, Peter. *Shell-Shock: Traumatic Neurosis and the British Soldiers of the First World War.* New York: Palgrave Macmillan, 2002.
Leyton-Brown, Ken. *The Practice of Execution in Canada.* Vancouver: UBC Press, 2010.
Maclean Miller, Ian Hugh. *Our Glory and Our Grief: Torontonians and the Great War.* Toronto: University of Toronto Press, 2002.
Macphail, Sir Andrew. *Official History of the Canadian Forces in the Great War, 1914-1919: The Medical Services.* Ottawa: Authority of the Minister of National Defence, under Direction of the General Staff, 1925.
Madsen, Chris. *Another Kind of Justice: Canadian Military Law from Confederation to Somalia.* Vancouver: UBC Press, 1999.
–. "Military Law, the Canadian Militia, and the North-West Rebellion of 1885." *Journal of Military and Strategic Studies* 1, 1 (1998): n.p. (online).
Manning, Frederic. *Her Privates We.* New York: G.P. Putnam's Sons, 1930.
Mantle, Craig Leslie. "Loyal Mutineers: An Examination of the Connection between Leadership and Disobedience in the Canadian Army since 1885." In *The Unwilling and the Reluctant: Theoretical Perspectives on Disobedience in the Military,* edited by Craig Leslie Mantle, 43-85. Kingston: Canadian Defence Academy Press, 2006.
–, ed. *The Apathetic and the Defiant: Case Studies of Canadian Mutiny and Disobedience, 1812-1919.* Kingston: Canadian Defence Academy Press, 2007.
Marshall-Cornwall, General Sir James. *Haig as Military Commander.* London: B.T. Batsford, 1973.
McCulloch, Ian. "'Batty Mac': Portrait of a Brigade Commander of the Great War, 1915-1917." *Canadian Military History* 7, 4 (1998): 11-28.
McDougall, Colin. *Execution.* Toronto: Macmillan, 1958.
Mead, Gary. *The Good Soldier: The Biography of Douglas Haig.* London: Atlantic Books, 2007.
Moore, Christopher. *The Law Society of Upper Canada and Ontario's Lawyers, 1797-1997.* Toronto: University of Toronto Press, 1997.
Moore, William. *The Thin Yellow Line.* New York: St. Martin's Press, 1975.
Moran, Lord. *The Anatomy of Courage.* 2nd ed. London: Constable, 1966.
Morton, Desmond. "'Kicking and Complaining': Demobilization Riots in the Canadian Expeditionary Force, 1918-1919." *Canadian Historical Review* 61, 3 (1980): 334-60.
–. "The Supreme Penalty: Canadian Deaths by Firing Squad in the First World War." *Queen's Quarterly* 79, 3 (1972): 345-52.
–. *When Your Number's Up: The Canadian Soldier in the First World War.* Toronto: Random House, 1993.
Morton, Desmond, and Jack Granatstein. *Marching to Armageddon: Canadians and the Great War, 1914-19.* Toronto: Lester and Orpen Dennys, 1989.
Mosse, George L. *Fallen Soldiers: Reshaping the Memory of the World Wars.* New York: Oxford University Press, 1990.
Murdoch, Reverend B.J. *The Red Vineyard.* Glasgow: University Press, 1959.
Murray, Colonel W.W. *The History of the 2nd Canadian Battalion (East Ontario Regiment) Canadian Expeditionary Force in the Great War, 1914-1919.* Ottawa: Mortimer, 1947.
Myers, Charles S. "A Contribution to the Study of Shell Shock: Being an Account of Three Cases of Loss of Memory, Vision, Smell, and Taste, Admitted into the Duchess of Westminster's War Hospital, Le Touquet." *The Lancet* 185, 4772 (1915): 316-20.
Nicholson, Colonel G.W.L. *Canadian Expeditionary Force, 1914-1919.* Ottawa: Queen's Printer and Controller of Stationery, 1962.

Offenstadt, Nicolas. *Les fusillés de la Grande Guerre et la mémoire collective: 1914-1999.* Paris: O. Jacob, 1999.
Oh! What a Lovely War. Produced by Brian Duffy and Richard Attenborough. Paramount Pictures, 1969.
Oram, Gerard. *Death Sentences Passed by Military Courts of the British Army, 1914-1924.* Edited by Julian Putkowski. London: Francis Boutle Publishers, 1998.
–. "The Greatest Efficiency: British and American Military Law, 1866-1918." In *Comparative Histories of Crime,* edited by Barry Godfrey et al., 159-77. Portland: Willan Publishing, 2003.
–. *Military Executions during World War I.* New York: Palgrave Macmillan, 2003.
–. *Worthless Men: Race, Eugenics, and the Death Penalty in the British Army during the First World War.* London: Francis Boutle Publishers, 1998.
Owen, Wilfred. *The Poems of Wilfred Owen.* London: Chatto and Windus, 1930.
Parliament of Canada. *An Act to Amend the National Defence Act and to Make Consequential Amendments to Other Acts.* C. 35, Div. 2, 10 December 1998, 1st Session, 36th Parliament. Ottawa: Queen's Printer for Canada, 1999.
Parliament of the United Kingdom of Great Britain. *An Act to Provide, during Twelve Months, for the Discipline and Regulation of the Army and Air Force.* C. 22, Part 2, 29 April 1930, 1st Session, 35th Parliament. London: Eyre and Spottiswoode, 1930.
Parsons, Andrew. "Morale and Cohesion in the Royal Newfoundland Regiment." MA thesis, Memorial University of Newfoundland, 1995.
Passchendaele. Produced by Paul Gross et al. Alliance Films, 2008.
Paths of Glory. Produced by James B. Harris. United Artists, 1957.
Peaty, John. "Capital Courts-Martial during the Great War." In *Look to Your Front: Studies in the First World War by the British Commission for Military History,* edited by Brian Bond et al., 89-104. Staplehurst, UK: Spellmount Publishers, 1999.
–. "Haig and Military Discipline." In *Haig: A Reappraisal 70 Years On,* edited by Brian Bond and Nigel Cave, 196-221. South Yorkshire, UK: Leo Cooper, 1999.
Pedroncini, Guy. *Les mutineries de 1917.* Paris: Presses Universitaires de France, 1967.
Peifer, Douglas C. "The Past in the Present: Passion, Politics, and the Historical Profession in the German and British Pardon Campaigns." *Journal of Military History* 71, 4 (2007): 1107-32.
Pugsley, Christopher. *On the Fringe of Hell: New Zealanders and Military Discipline in the First World War.* Toronto: Hodder and Stoughton, 1991.
Putkowski, Julian, and Julian Sykes. *Shot at Dawn: Executions in World War One by Authority of the British Army Act.* London: Leo Cooper, 1989.
Remarque, Erich Maria. *All Quiet on the Western Front.* Translated by A.W. Wheen. New York: Fawcett Crest, 1928.
Robbins, Simon. "Henry Horne: First Army, 1916-1918." In *Haig's Generals,* edited by Ian F.W. Beckett and Steven J. Corvi, 97-121. Barnsley, UK: Pen and Sword, 2006.
Scott, John. "Three Cheers for Earl Haig: Canadian Veterans and the Visit of Field Marshal Sir Douglas Haig to Canada in the Summer of 1925." *Canadian Military History* 5, 1 (1996): 35-40.
Sellers, Leonard. *For God's Sake Shoot Straight! The Story of the Court-Martial and Execution of Sub. Lt. Edwin Dyett.* London: Leo Cooper, 1995.
Shaw, Amy. *Crisis of Conscience: Conscientious Objection in Canada during the First World War.* Vancouver: UBC Press, 2009.
Sheffield, Gary. *Forgotten Victory, the First World War: Myths and Realities.* London: Review, 2002.

–. *Leadership in the Trenches: Officer-Man Relations, Morale, and Discipline in the British Army in the Era of the First World War.* New York: St. Martin's Press, 2000.
Shephard, Ben. *A War of Nerves: Soldiers and Psychiatrists, 1914-1994.* London: Pimlico, 2002.
Shils, Edward A., and Morris Janowitz. "Cohesion and Disintegration in the Wehrmacht in World War II." In *Military Conflict: Essays in the Institutional Analyses of War and Peace,* edited by Morris Janowitz, 170-220. Beverly Hills: Sage Publications, 1975.
Smith, Leonard V. *Between Mutiny and Obedience: The Case of the French Fifth Infantry Division during World War I.* Princeton, NJ: Princeton University Press, 1994.
–. "The French High Command and the Mutinies of Spring 1917." In *Facing Armageddon: The First World War Experienced,* edited by Hugh Cecil and Peter Liddle, 79-92. London: Leo Cooper, 1996.
Snape, Michael F. "British Army Chaplains and Capital Courts-Martial in the First World War." *Royal Army Chaplain's Department Journal* 44 (2005): 6-11.
Snell, A.E. *The C.A.M.C. with the Canadian Corps during the Last Hundred Days of the Great War.* Ottawa: F.A. Acland, 1924.
Strachan, Hew. "The Soldier's Experience in Two World Wars: Some Historiographical Comparisons." In *Time to Kill: The Soldier's Experience of War in the West, 1939-1945,* edited by Paul Addison and Angus Calder, 369-78. London: Pimlico, 1997.
Strange, Carolyn. "The Politics of Punishment: The Death Penalty in Canada, 1867-1976." Canadian Legal History Project Working Paper Series 92-10. Winnipeg: University of Manitoba, 1992.
Tanenbaum, Jan Karl. Review of *Between Mutiny and Obedience,* by Leonard V. Smith. *American Historical Review* 100, 2 (1995): 534.
Taylor, A.J.P. *The First World War: An Illustrated History.* London: Hamish Hamilton, 1963.
Teahan, John Patrick. *Diary Kid.* Edited by Grace Keenan Price. Ottawa: Oberon Press, 1999.
Thurtle, Ernest. *Shootings at Dawn: The Army Death Penalty at Work.* London: Victoria House Printing, n.d.
Tremblay, Thomas-Louis. *Journal de guerre (1915-1918).* Edited by Marcelle Cinq-Mars. Outremont, QC: Athéna, 2006.
Vance, Jonathan F. *Death So Noble: Memory, Meaning, and the First World War.* Vancouver: UBC Press, 1997.
–. "Understanding the Motivation to Fight." Address given at Cultures of War and Peace, Annual Symposium of the Academies of Arts, Humanities, and Sciences of Canada, Canadian Museum of Civilization, Ottawa, 14 November 2008.
Vanier, Georges. *Georges Vanier, Soldier: The Wartime Letters and Diaries, 1915-1919.* Edited by Deborah Cowley. Toronto: Dundurn Press, 2000.
A Very Long Engagement. Produced by Francis Boespflug et al. Warner Independent Pictures, 2004.
War Office. *Manual of Military Law.* London: His Majesty's Stationery Office, 1914.
Watson, Janet S.K. *Fighting Different Wars: Experience, Memory, and the First World War in Britain.* New York: Cambridge University Press, 2004.
Wigney, Edward H., ed. *The C.E.F. Roll of Honour: Members and Former Members of the Canadian Expeditionary Force Who Died as a Result of Service in the Great War, 1914-1919.* Ottawa: Eugene Ursual, 1996.
Wilkins, James L. *Legal Aid in the Criminal Courts.* Toronto: University of Toronto Press, 1975.

Wilson, James Brent. "The Morale and Discipline in the British Expeditionary Force, 1914-1918." MA thesis, University of New Brunswick, 1978.
Wilson, John. *And in the Morning*. Toronto: Kids Can Press, 2003.
Winegard, Timothy C. *For King and Kanata: Canadian Indians and the First World War*. Winnipeg: University of Manitoba Press, 2012.
Wolff, Leon. *In Flanders Fields: The 1917 Campaign*. New York: Viking, 1958.
Yates, Richard A., and Ruth Whidden Yates. *Canada's Legal Environment: Its History, Institutions, and Principles*. Scarborough, ON: Prentice Hall, 1993.

Index

14th Battalion, 105
22nd Battalion, 1, 21-22, 55, 57, 105-06

A Very Long Engagement, 8, 19-20
abolition of death penalty: in British military, 135; in Canada, 33, 105; in Germany, 32
Aboriginal Canadians, 61, 103-4
adjutant general, 72, 76-79, 108-9, 126
All Quiet on the Western Front, 2, 117
Amiens, Battle of, 49, 101
Anderson, Captain N., 72-73, 76-77
appeals, 33, 134, 136
Army Act. *See* British Army Act
Australia: decision not to execute, 17, 99-100; and social memory of war, 119
Austro-Hungarian Army, 18

Babington, Anthony, 15, 71, 112
battle exhaustion. *See* shell shock
Bickerdike, Robert, 33-34, 105
Birdwood, William, 99
Blackadder Goes Forth, 8, 19
Blair, Tony, 113
Boer War, 99
Borden, Robert, 98
Bottomley, Horatio, 74
Breaker Morant, 99
British Army Act (Army Act), 24, 39, 111; annual review of, 34, 100, 125
British Expeditionary Force (BEF), 45, 58, 68, 84, 141; treatment of Irish in, 104-5
British High Court, 111, 114
British Royal Legion, 111-12
Browne, Des, 111
Butler, Alexander, 24, 114
Byers, Joseph, 29

Canadian Army Medical Corps (CAMC), 49
chaplain, 74

civilian law, 23, 29-30, 66, 75, 88, 136-37; and executions, 8-9 32-33, 104, 108; and mental competence, 50
Clark, Helen, 124
collective memory, 19, 22, 127
combat motivation, 8, 12-13
combat stress. *See* shell shock
commander-in-chief, 32-33, 71-73, 81, 84, 88, 92-93, 134, 138
Comte, Gustave, 107, 131
Concannon, Don, 120
conscientious objectors, 98
conscription: 6, 98-99, 115, 119
Cook, Tim, 8, 12
Courcelette, Battle of, 54-55
court martial officer, 75-76, 135
court of inquiry, 24
cowardice: definition, 25-26, 36
Currie, Gen. Sir Arthur, 89-90, 105-6

Darling Committee, 134
death penalty, 14, 16, 24, 136-37; Canadians acceptance of in military, 3, 21, 34, 74, 132; in civilian society, 9, 16, 32-33, 105, 108, 136; military personnel views on, 97, 99-100, 133-35
De Fehr, Benjamin, 24, 114
Department of Militia and Defence, 130-31
Directorate of History, 6, 114
district court martial, 28
drunkenness (as defence), 39, 80-81
Dubuc, Arthur-Édouard, 54-55, 95
Duhamel, Ronald J., 114-15, 123

enlistment, 42-44, 59
ethnicity, 7, 16, 62, 104, 106
executions, 32-33, 39, 73-74, 95-97, 106-8, 124-25, 130-34, 140; in Australian army, 99-100; in civilian society, 32-33, 108; in German army, 18; in historical writings,

3, 5, 11, 14-17, 20-21; statistics on, 4-5, 11, 23, 32, 45, 55, 71, 107, 111

Farr, Harry, 111, 114, 120, 123
field general court martial (FGCM), 1, 28, 30, 32, 76-77
field punishment number 1, 24, 27-28
firing squad, 74, 132-33
forestry units, 41-42
Fowles, Stephen, 40, 45, 89, 123
France, 32; social memory of war, 19
French army, 13, 72; mutinies in, 12, 17, 54, 58, 139
French Canadians: and conscription, 98, 115; and military discipline, 21-22, 55, 61, 104-6
French, John, 32, 72

Gallipoli, Battle of, 119
general court martial, 28, 77
German army, 12, 18
Germany: death penalty in, 32

H-Net Canada, 116
Hill 70, 57-58
Hipkin, John, 112, 114, 120
Horne, Gen. Henry, 84, 95-96

imprisonment, 35-36
intention, 24, 78-81, 85, 101-2, 106
Italian army, 57; discipline in, 18

judge advocate general, 84

Kemp, Sir Edward, 33-34
Kentish, Brigadier Gen. Reginald John, 53, 68-69, 134

Labour Party (Britain), 14, 112-13
leadership, 13, 42, 54-55, 68, 118-19, 140
leave, 13, 38-39, 53, 121, 139-40
legal aid, 30, 137
Lens (France), 57-58
Ling, Wilson Norman, 89, 130-31
"Lions led by donkeys," 13, 118
Lipsett, Major Gen. Louis, 87
Ludendorff, Gen. Erich, 18-19

MacBrien, Major Gen. J.H., 56, 91, 97-99, 105-6; and Dimitro Sinizki case, 26

Macdonell, Gen. Archibald Cameron, 85
Mackinlay, Andrew, 112-13
Major, John, 112-13
malingering, 14, 46, 135
Manual of Military Law, 9, 24, 28, 30, 34-36, 66, 70, 75, 77
medical board, 20, 85
medical exams, 48-49, 135
medical officers, 45, 48, 49, 51, 85
Memorial Cross, 131
Mewburn, Sydney Chilton, 129
military law, 3-4, 6, 9-10, 23-24, 28, 94, 122, 136-37, 141; and pardons campaigns, 126; and precedent, 35, 110
Military Service Act, 98, 115
Military Voters Act, 98
Moles, Thomas, 59, 132
Moore, William, 5, 15
morale, 18-19, 23, 53-57, 59, 95, 99, 122, 135, 139-40; in historical writings, 7-8, 11-13, 15
Moran, Lord, 7-8, 11-12, 43
Morton, Desmond, 3, 7-8, 21; and official expression of sorrow, 123
murder, 4, 14, 18, 21, 24, 112, 114, 129, 135; in civilian law, 30, 32-33, 104-5, 108, 136
mutiny, 4, 14, 24, 112, 129, 135; at Fort Sam Houston, 18
Myers, Charles S., 45

National Defence Act, 136-37
New Zealand: and military death sentences, 17, 100; and pardons campaigns, 9, 19, 116, 119, 121, 124-25
Neurasthenia. *See* shell shock

officers: on court martials, 29, 31-32, 35, 49, 66, 68, 70-71, 75; discipline of, 28; letters of recommendations from, 7, 32, 73, 81, 84-85, 90-93, 109, 138; officer-men relations, 12, 26, 53-56, 107, 122, 139
Official Book of Remembrance, 114
official expression of sorrow (Canada), 114-15, 123, 126
Oh! What a Lovely War, 8, 19, 119
Oram, Gerard, 7, 15-16, 71, 76, 100, 107; and race and ethnicity, 7, 16, 104-5

Pardon for Soldiers of the Great War Bill (New Zealand), 116

pardons, 4-5, 15-16, 19, 75, 111-17, 120-26, 140; Pardons Bill, 114
Passchendaele (movie), 8, 20
Passchendaele, Battle of, 58, 101, 108, 118
Paths of Glory, 8, 19-20
Peck, Mark, 116
Pegahmagabow, Francis, 104
penal servitude, 35-36, 74, 100, 129, 139
Plamodon, Louis, 115
Poems of Wilfrid Owen, 117
Poincaré, Raymond, 72
Poor Prisoner's Defence Act, 30
Pringle, Harold, 21, 135
prisoner's friend, 30-31, 66, 137
provost, 41, 56, 74
psychiatry, 45-47, 50
Putkowski, Julian, 5, 15, 112, 122

race: and executions, 7, 16, 103-4
recruitment, 14, 42-43, 97
redress campaigns, 116, 125
regimental court martial, 28
Reid, John, 113
Royal Canadian Air Force, 4
Royal Canadian Navy, 4
Royal Newfoundland Regiment, 4
royal prerogative of mercy, 33
Russian army, 57-58
Russian immigrants in CEF, 59-62, 97, 104

Second World War, 13-14, 18, 21, 125, 135
self-inflicted wounds, 44, 95
self-mutilation. *See* self-inflicted wounds
separation allowance, 59-61

shell shock, 3, 13-14, 45-49, 74, 85-86, 136, 139-40; in historical writings, 7, 11, 13, 15, 19; and pardons, 112-14, 116, 119, 121, 126
shirkers, 42, 56
Shot at Dawn (book), 5, 15, 112, 120
Shot at Dawn (website), 8, 121-22, 124, 126
shot at dawn campaigns, 112-13, 121
Shot at Dawn Memorial, 114
Sinizki, Dimitro, 25-26, 36, 59
Smith, Leonard, 17, 54
Somme, Battle of, 54, 107-8, 139
statement in mitigation of punishment, 31, 77, 94
summary executions, 18, 121
Suspension of Sentences Act, 35
Sykes, Julian, 5, 15, 112

Thurtle, Ernest, 14, 100
treason, 14, 24, 32, 112, 135
Tremblay, Lieutenant-Colonel Thomas Louis, 1, 54-55, 106

Ukrainian immigrants: in the CEF, 59, 61, 97

Vance, Jonathan, 8, 41, 118
Vimy Ridge, Battle of, 100, 107-8, 119, 139

war neurosis. *See* shell shock
witnesses, 29-30, 66-68, 77, 126, 136

youth: at court martial, 31, 69-70; and pardons campaigns, 15, 120-21

STUDIES IN CANADIAN MILITARY HISTORY

John Griffith Armstrong, *The Halifax Explosion and the Royal Canadian Navy: Inquiry and Intrigue*

Andrew Richter, *Avoiding Armageddon: Canadian Military Strategy and Nuclear Weapons, 1950-63*

William Johnston, *A War of Patrols: Canadian Army Operations in Korea*

Julian Gwyn, *Frigates and Foremasts: The North American Squadron in Nova Scotia Waters, 1745-1815*

Jeffrey A. Keshen, *Saints, Sinners, and Soldiers: Canada's Second World War*

Desmond Morton, *Fight or Pay: Soldiers' Families in the Great War*

Douglas E. Delaney, *The Soldiers' General: Bert Hoffmeister at War*

Michael Whitby, ed., *Commanding Canadians: The Second World War Diaries of A.F.C. Layard*

Martin Auger, *Prisoners of the Home Front: German POWs and "Enemy Aliens" in Southern Quebec, 1940-46*

Tim Cook, *Clio's Warriors: Canadian Historians and the Writing of the World Wars*

Serge Marc Durflinger, *Fighting from Home: The Second World War in Verdun, Quebec*

Richard O. Mayne, *Betrayed: Scandal, Politics, and Canadian Naval Leadership*

P. Whitney Lackenbauer, *Battle Grounds: The Canadian Military and Aboriginal Lands*

Cynthia Toman, *An Officer and a Lady: Canadian Military Nursing and the Second World War*

Michael Petrou, *Renegades: Canadians in the Spanish Civil War*

Amy J. Shaw, *Crisis of Conscience: Conscientious Objection in Canada during the First World War*

Serge Marc Durflinger, *Veterans with a Vision: Canada's War Blinded in Peace and War*

James G. Fergusson, *Canada and Ballistic Missile Defence, 1954-2009: Déjà Vu All Over Again*

Benjamin Isitt, *From Victoria to Vladivostok: Canada's Siberian Expedition, 1917-19*

James Wood, *Militia Myths: Ideas of the Canadian Citizen Soldier, 1896-1921*

Timothy Balzer, *The Information Front: The Canadian Army and News Management during the Second World War*

Andrew Godefroy, *Defence and Discovery: Canada's Military Space Program, 1945-74*

Douglas E. Delaney, *Corps Commanders: Five British and Canadian Generals at War, 1939-45*

Timothy Wilford, *Canada's Road to the Pacific War: Intelligence, Strategy, and the Far East Crisis*

Randall Wakelam, *Cold War Fighters: Canadian Aircraft Procurement, 1945-54*

Andrew Burtch, *Give Me Shelter: The Failure of Canada's Cold War Civil Defence*

Wendy Cuthbertson, *Labour Goes to War: The CIO and the Construction of a New Social Order, 1939-45*

P. Whitney Lackenbauer, *The Canadian Rangers: A Living History*

Graham Broad, *A Small Price to Pay: Consumer Culture on the Canadian Home Front, 1939-45*

Peter Kasurak, *A National Force: The Evolution of Canada's Army, 1950-2000*

Isabel Campbell, *Unlikely Diplomats: The Canadian Brigade in Germany, 1951-64*

Printed and bound in Canada by Friesens
Set in Helvetica Condensed and Minion
   by Artegraphica Design Co. Ltd.
Copy editor: Dallas Harrison
Proofreader: Lana Okerlund